EAT *what you* LOVE
RESTAURANT FAVORITES

Running Press
Hachette Book Group
1290 Avenue of the Americas, New York, NY 10104
www.runningpress.com
@Running_Press

Printed in China.

First Edition: April 2019

Published by Running Press, an imprint of Perseus Books, LLC, a subsidiary of Hachette Book Group, Inc. The Running Press name and logo is a trademark of the Hachette Book Group.

The Hachette Speakers Bureau provides a wide range of authors for speaking events. To find out more, go to www.hachettespeakersbureau.com or call (866) 376-6591.

The publisher is not responsible for websites (or their content) that are not owned by the publisher.

Print book cover and interior design by Frances J. Soo Ping Chow
Food and prop stylist: Erin McDowell
Assistant food stylist: Theresa A Katan

Library of Congress Control Number: 2018960752

ISBNs: 978-0-7624-6620-7 (hardcover), 978-0-7624-6621-4 (ebook)

RRD-S

10 9 8 7 6 5 4 3 2 1

EAT *what you* LOVE
RESTAURANT FAVORITES

MARLENE KOCH

food photography by
STEVE LEGATO

RUNNING PRESS
PHILADELPHIA

To Home and Family

CONTENTS

Introduction

There's no place like home . . . to eat! As much as I love dining out, I must confess that I love dining in even more. Yes, I have those pesky dishes to do, but I find the advantages of cooking at home far outweigh washing them. At home, you can have exactly what you want, when you want it, all without a wait or reservation. Dining at home is also less expensive and far better for your health. But what about taste? Please keep reading because I too love sweet, creamy, cheesy, decadent restaurant fare, and when it comes to great taste, rest assured, I've got you covered!

In many ways, this book has been ten years in the making. As both a food lover and a registered dietitian, I passionately believe that everyone deserves to eat the foods they love—no matter what their diet. This belief led me to the creation of my first *Eat What You Love* cookbook, which I am humbled and proud to say is the first of my four *Eat What You Love* bestsellers. The response to it was nothing short of phenomenal, and it quickly became apparent that the decadent-tasting restaurant-inspired recipes—and their equally amazing sugar, fat, calorie, and sodium savings—were a huge hit! Not only did they earn me the moniker of "magician in the kitchen" but a greater bonus came with countless readers sharing how being able to make their favorite restaurant-style recipes at home also happily helped them lose weight, control their blood sugar, and feed their families better.

As such, I am beyond thrilled to share this new book, devoted entirely to the foods we all love when dining out. From coffee-shop grab-'n'-go faves to five-star steak-house specialties, you will find over 140 easy, delicious, better-for-you recipes organized by restaurant type or cuisine. Looking to cure a fast-food craving? Flip to the Fast-Food Fix chapter and you'll find morning 'til night options ranging from sausage 'n' egg burritos for breakfast to a classic meal of a mouthwatering burger, crispy fries, and creamy milkshake for lunch or dinner. I guarantee you'll be lovin' it (and the over 1,000 calories you save!). In the mood for Mexican fare? Simply mosey over to the Mexican Favorites chapter. From appetizers to desserts—and everything in between—you'll be saying olé when you realize how quick and easy it is to whip up Quick & Easy Queso Dip or 10-Minute Chicken Taquitos with Creamy Avocado Salsa. Over 110 of the recipes, including sure-to be-new-favorites like IHOP-inspired Red Velvet Pancakes with Cream Cheese Drizzle and Sweet & Sour Pork for Two, are new. The remainders are restaurant make-over all-stars selected from the almost 1,000 recipes across my *Eat What You Love* cookbooks that simply could not be left out (there was no way I could not include my "addictive" orange chicken recipe in a chapter dedicated to beloved Asian dishes). That said, look carefully if you have made any of these beloved recipes before, as many have brand-new tweaks and are now even better.

Speaking of making things even better, not only does making restaurant-style dishes at home allow you to slash literally thousands of calories along with excess fat, carbs, sugar, and sodium, I found many of the popular restaurant dishes I taste-tested could actually taste even better—so of course, I made those adjustments too! I'm also excited to share some of the tricks I learned running professional kitchens that make creating restaurant-style recipes and "dining" at home easy to do. Page 30 offers tips on kitchen tools and page 32 easy tips

for creating restaurant-inspired meals at home. As in all of my books, portions sizes are real, not skimpy, and nutrition information is provided with every recipe. A pantry list is provided for the easy-to-find everyday ingredients I use, including multiple choices for sweeteners, with all-natural lower calorie options. The Gluten-Free Guide on page 120 lists the vast number of gluten-free recipes and, even better yet, how virtually *all* of them can become gluten-free with just a simple swap or two!

I can't think of a better cookbook than this one to satisfy my mission of ensuring that *everyone* is indeed able to eat the foods they love—and be healthy too. From fast-food fare and Southern comfort foods to memorable Mexican meals, Italian classics, and steak-house extravaganzas, my husband, boys, family, and friends were thrilled to enjoy the decadent taste of their favorite restaurant drinks and dishes at home (and amazed when they realized they were doing so more healthfully). There's no place better than home!

My best to you and yours,

Marlene

Healthy Eating Tips for Dining Out (or In)

If you have ever tried to eat healthfully when dining out, you also know the challenges it presents. The fact is, foods that are high in sugar, fat, and calories give us pleasure, and restaurants—whose business is to create drinks and dishes that push all the right buttons and have us clamoring for more—know it. The average restaurant entrée—sans a drink, appetizer, or dessert—often provides the calories, fat, salt, and/or sugar we require for an entire day, or more! Sadly, for those of us who love to dine out and also want to feel and look our best, such fare is not our friend. A Boston University study, which analyzed foods from 157 restaurants revealed the average calorie counts of entrées of the most popular ethnic cuisines with the following staggering numbers: Italian entrées averaged a stunning 1,755 calories; American-style 1,494 calories; Chinese 1,474 calories; and Mexican meals a hefty 1,324 calories (and that's without a margarita or chips!). Not surprisingly, the meals we love most also lay claim to the highest sugar, fat, and calorie counts.

If you own any of my previous books, you know how much I love to combine my culinary skills with my nutrition knowledge to create amazingly healthy recreations of popular restaurant fare, so such favorites can be happily enjoyed by all. This book continues in that tradition with over 140 crave-worthy recipes inspired by beloved restaurant dishes. What's even better is while health professionals (including myself) usually recommend avoiding foods that are creamy, crispy, cheesy, smothered, fried, or sweet when dining out, when you make them yourself with the recipes in this book, you can enjoy them all worry-free! Throughout the book, I also share a heaping portion of healthy eating and cooking tips, and on page 15 you'll find my easy-to-follow tips for eating more healthfully for when you do dine out. Bon appétit!

CALORIE CHECK

Reality check. No matter what weight-loss marketers say, nothing affects what you weigh more than the total number of calories you consume. To maintain your weight, the number of calories you eat needs to equal the number of calories you burn. If you eat more calories than your body requires, you will gain weight. Conversely, if you eat fewer calories than you require, you will lose weight. Most people require between 1,600 and 2,400 calories a day. A very active person or large man can burn more calories, whereas an inactive older woman, even less. For purposes of food labeling, the USDA uses 2,000 calories as the daily requirement target. What's most important, however, especially when studying a food label or restaurant nutrition guide, is to know how many calories YOU require each day. (For a personalized estimate of your caloric needs go to marlenekoch.com and click on the Personalized Calorie Calculator.)

What's most important, when studying calories on a restaurant nutrition guide is to know how many calories YOU require each day.

Given this information and the fact the average restaurant meal has over 1,300 calories (again, not counting add-on beverages, appetizers, or dessert!), it's easy to see why keeping your daily calorie needs in check when dining out is difficult. In order to help you make this task easier, I've provided my favorite healthy dining-out tips on page 15. Even better, every recipe in this book has been carefully crafted to deliver restaurant deliciousness with fewer calories so you can eat, sip, and enjoy, rather than worrying about keeping calories in check. (For my weight-watcher friends, you may find yourself doing a happy double-check when you see the double-digit point savings the recipes deliver.)

FAT TIPS

Restaurant chefs love fat! Fat adds flavor and aroma and also has the ability to impart creamy or crispy textures to food. Beyond its culinary virtues, fat is also necessary for good health. Fatty acids help the body absorb essential vitamins and antioxidants and are important for optimal nerve, brain, and heart function. Sadly, for chefs and fat lovers everywhere, there are unhealthy consequences related to consuming fatty restaurant fare: First, foods high in fat are usually excessive in calories. Second, much of the fat layered and loaded into restaurant fare is not the type that is good for you.

When dining out, it's best to minimize ordering creamy, cheesy, or crispy foods as it's not uncommon to find as much as two days' *worth of saturated fat, in a single dish or dessert.*

The reason fat-laden fare is so high in calories is that all fats (whether healthy or not) are dense in calories—delivering more than twice the calories per gram of either protein or carbohydrates. When it comes to your health, "good fats" like those found in nuts, seeds, avocados, liquid oils, and fish are richly satisfying and can lower disease risk while protecting your heart. On the other hand, saturated fats like those found in animal products such as butter, cream, and marbled meat, can increase your risk for heart disease, diabetes, and more. Cream, cheeses, butter, and the like, when used liberally (as is common in restaurants) send fat and saturated fat counts soaring. The USDA dietary recommendation is that no more than 65 grams of fat be consumed a day for a 2,000-calorie diet, and that less than 20 grams of those be saturated fat. When dining out, it's best to minimize ordering creamy, cheesy, or crispy foods, as it's not uncommon to find a day-and-a-half's worth of fat—and as much as *two* days' worth of saturated fat—in a single dish or dessert. While you will find plenty of crave-worthy cheesy, crispy, and/or creamy dishes and desserts in this book (including my Longhorn-Style Parmesan-Crusted Chicken, which has all three of these cravable attributes), the great news is that I've found ways to fashion these tantalizing dishes with a fraction of the usual fat—especially unhealthy saturated fat. Moreover, you will find nutritious good-for-you fats from creamy avocados, olive oil, salmon, and nuts featured throughout the book.

CHOOSE YOUR CARBS

Even though "carbs" often get a bad rap, there's still plenty to love about carbohydrates. While it's true that all carbohydrates when eaten, except fiber, break down into sugar (or blood glucose), that's actually a good thing, as glucose is the preferred fuel for our bodies and brain. But, as you are probably aware, all carbohydrates are not alike. Complex carbs, which include whole grains, veggies, fruit, and beans, promote good health as they are chock-full of vitamins, minerals, antioxidants, and phytochemicals. They also come packaged with fiber, which slows down their breakdown—and their impact on blood sugar. On the other hand, simple and refined carbohydrates, as found in sweetened beverages, cakes, and pastries, unenriched white bread, white rice, and all types of sugars, contain few nutrients and, as such, offer little more than calories. Additionally, their rapid breakdown can spike blood sugar and contribute to weight gain and a heightened risk for diabetes, dementia, and heart disease.

Whether dining out or dining in, choosing complex carbs over simple and refined carbs is the healthy thing to do.

Whether dining out or dining in, choosing complex carbs over simple and refined carbs is a healthy thing to do. Concerns with carbohydrates when dining out are twofold. To start with, most of the carbohydrates you find on your plate (or in your glass) are refined. Second, there are usually too many of them. While 45 to 75 grams of carbohydrates per meal is a healthy amount for most people (excluding athletes), a restaurant plate of pancakes or pasta, or a single sinful dessert, can clock in with upwards of 150 grams of carbohydrates—or easily two meals' worth. Splitting such meals (as suggested on page 15) is a dining-out option, but choosing to make crowd-pleasing pancakes, satisfying pasta dishes, and delectable desserts at home is even better still. My "carb-conscious" recipes boost slow-burning complex carbs and curb refined carbs and added sugars. Plus, the total amount of carbs are kept in check so that everyone, including those concerned about controlling carbs or those with diabetes, can enjoy all the restaurant foods they love!

NIX THE EXCESS SUGAR

We're born with a built-in affinity for sugar and its addictive sweet taste, but as evidence continues to mount about the negative health effects that come with consuming *excess* added sugar, there's no sugarcoating the not-so-sweet facts. (Added sugars are those not naturally found in foods, but sugar "added" to foods to make them sweeter.) Added sugars offer us little more than calories. They also enter the bloodstream rapidly, which can spike blood sugar and insulin levels. In addition, consuming too much sugar contributes to heart disease, obesity, type 2 diabetes, some cancers, dementia, and more.

The recommended allowance for added sugar by the American Heart Association is a mere 6 teaspoons a day (or 24 grams) for women and 9 teaspoons (or 36 grams) for men. In contrast, the average American consumes almost three times that amount.

The recommended allowance for added sugar is a mere 6 teaspoons a day (or 24 grams) for women and 9 teaspoons (or 36 grams) for men.

The top contributor of added sugar in the American diet is sweet beverages, followed by candy, and then desserts. A small sweetened coffee drink, like a blended mocha, actually exceeds the healthy limit for an entire day (see page 38 for my guilt-free makeover with less than a teaspoon of added sugar), while a single restaurant dessert can contain up to a stunning 40 teaspoons of sugar! And while desserts scream sugar, there's plenty of sugar hidden in restaurant dressings and sauces. In this book, virtually every recipe contains a single teaspoon or less of added sugar. Best of all, you would never know it; and I find *that*, rather sweet.

HOLD THE SALT

To prove how chefs rely on salt to create crave-worthy foods one need look no further than the sodium content of the offerings on a restaurant menu—where a single dish can dish up over 5,000 mg of sodium! In addition to adding its own flavor, one that many of us love, salt enhances sweet flavors and tones down bitter ones. Unfortunately, however, high intakes of sodium have been linked to high blood pressure, heart attacks, and stroke. Health experts recommend that most of us consume no more than 2,300 milligrams of sodium, or the equivalent of one teaspoon of salt, a day.

The simplest way to "hold the salt," or reduce the sodium in your diet, is to cook at home.

Seventy-five percent of the sodium we eat comes from processed and restaurant foods (where it's not uncommon to find entrées with several thousand milligrams of sodium).

As such, the simplest way to "hold the salt," or reduce the sodium in your diet, is to cook at home. While taste is my first priority when developing recipes, I also work hard to keep sodium at sensible levels. I minimize the use of high-sodium ingredients, use reduced-sodium products, such as reduced-sodium broth, and also lower-sodium preparation techniques, like draining and rinsing canned goods before adding them to recipes. To reduce the sodium even further, if required or desired, choose no-salt products where applicable and further reduce any added table salt. You can rest assured that every recipe is lower in sodium than its traditional sky-high restaurant counterpart (as even "lighter choice" menu selections tend to be high in sodium.)

Healthy Eating When Dining Out

Surveys show that most Americans eat out on average four to five times a week. As such, caving in to the urge to splurge every time you dine away from home can have both costly and unhealthy consequences. While I find cooking at home to be the easiest—and tastiest—way to dine more healthy, here are some additional tips for eating more healthfully when dining out.

✦ **SELECT RESTAURANTS WISELY.** Take advantage of online menus and nutritional information to find selections that fit both your taste and your nutritional budget before you even leave home. You may be surprised at what you find.

✦ **RETHINK YOUR DRINK.** Choose zero- or low-calorie beverages, to save calories for your meal. If desired, enjoy a single glass of wine or unsweetened cocktail *with* your meal.

✦ **DITCH THE BREAD BASKET OR CHIPS.** Mindlessly eating bread and/or chips can sabotage a healthy dining experience before the entrée ever arrives.

✦ **START YOUR MEAL WITH A SIMPLE SALAD OR BROTH-BASED SOUP.** You'll feel satisfied sooner and be less likely to overeat. Ask for reduced-calorie dressing on the side.

✦ **ORDER A (HEALTHY) APPETIZER INSTEAD OF AN ENTRÉE.** An appetizer and a side salad or cup of soup is often enough food. Request that the appetizer be served with entrées.

✦ **SHARE AN ENTRÉE, OR TAKE ONE-HALF HOME.** Box take-home food as soon as it is brought to the table. Once food is placed in front of us, we tend to eat most (or all) of it.

✦ **OPT FOR GRILLED, STEAMED, OR BROILED ENTRÉES.** Avoid selections that are battered, breaded, creamy, crispy, cheesy, or fried (even "lightly"). Ask for sauces on the side.

✦ **BALANCE YOUR MEAL WITH HEALTHY SIDES.** Choose a baked potato, plain, steamed veggies, or a side salad. Steer away from sides that are creamy, cheesy, or fried.

✦ **ENJOY DESSERT AT HOME.** It'll be easier to pass on the dessert tray; you'll save money; and by the time you get home, you may even change your mind!

Dining with Diabetes

....

Having diabetes presents many challenges and, sadly, dining out is one of them. The truth is that it's not easy for anyone to eat out healthfully these days with the highly tempting array of unhealthy selections ripe for the picking on restaurant menus. But trying to stick to a diabetes meal plan while eating out, well, it can be downright daunting. My stepdaughter, Colleen, has diabetes and over the years I have watched her struggle as she pondered which menu items would actually fit into her meal plan and carb budget. At the same time, I saw how she drooled over the creamy, cheesy, fried, carb-loaded fare her taste buds clamored for.

Fortunately, for Colleen and the rest of us, restaurant menu laws have made it easier than ever before to know the nutritional content of restaurant fare to help in making better-informed choices. After comparing the nutritional content of restaurant guides to the recipes in this book—along with meal plans for those with diabetes—I am beyond thrilled to be able to offer this tempting collection of recipes to those who have or are concerned about diabetes. No longer do you need to be troubled with the arduous task of ferreting out the few healthy carb-conscious selections on a menu, as every single restaurant-worthy recipe in this book has been designed with diabetes in mind! If weight loss is a goal, these recipes can help you with that, too. Just ask Miriam, or any other of the innumerable readers who lost weight and lowered their blood sugar with the recipes in my previous books. Do you dream of being able to enjoy pancakes, pasta, or pizza again? Or maybe burritos, biscuits, burgers, or a warm brownie sundae are more suited to your taste. No problem. These favorites are all here, and now they're ALL meal plan–friendly!

WHAT IS DIABETES?

The term *diabetes* refers to a group of conditions that affect the way your body uses and manages blood glucose—or blood sugar—your body's main source of fuel. When glucose enters your bloodstream from the breakdown of the food you eat, insulin, a hormone produced in your pancreas, acts as a key to allow glucose to enter your cells, where it is used for energy. When you have diabetes this process does not work properly, and glucose builds up in the blood to levels higher than normal. In type 1 diabetes, the pancreas produces little or no insulin. In type 2 diabetes, the pancreas produces insulin, but either not enough and/or the cells become resistant to it. No matter the cause, high blood sugar can result in both short-term and long-term negative health consequences.

PREVALENCE

If you or someone you love has diabetes, you are not alone. An estimated 30 million people in the United States have diabetes and that number is rapidly rising. Type 2 diabetes accounts for 90 to 95% of cases. Among those 20 and older, a new case of diabetes is diagnosed every 19 seconds; and of those over 65, the American Diabetes Association estimates 25% already have diabetes (whether they know it or not). Another 85 million Americans (and an additional 25% of those over 65) are estimated to have pre-diabetes, a condition where your blood sugar is higher than normal, but not quite high enough to be classified as diabetes—yet. Without lifestyle changes, people with pre-diabetes have a very high risk for developing type 2 diabetes.

PREVENTION AND REVERSAL

While one has no control over the onset of type 1 diabetes (an autoimmune disease), there are many lifestyle factors within one's control that contribute to pre- and type 2 diabetes. The great news is that as many as 8 out of 10 cases of type 2 diabetes can actually be prevented with weight loss, physical activity, and by eating a healthy diet. Even after diagnosis, as has been the case for some of my wonderful "Kochbook" fans, type 2 diabetes can be reversed to the point where medications are no longer required. If you have pre-diabetes, the combination of even modest weight loss (as little as 5–7% of your body weight) and exercise (walking 30 minutes a day five days a week) can delay or even prevent the onset of diabetes altogether.

EATING WHAT YOU LOVE WITH DIABETES

Whether you have diabetes, or want to reduce your risk of getting it, it delights me to tell you that this book can help. The truth is there is no such thing as a one-size-fits-all diabetes diet. Persons with, or concerned about, diabetes are advised to follow the same healthy eating guidelines we all should follow. If you are overweight, eating fewer calories is key, as excess weight is the biggest single risk factor for type 2 diabetes (see Prevention and Reversal, page 17). Minimizing saturated fat intake is important for the health of your heart, while keeping total carbs in check (including sugars) helps control blood sugar. You'll find my favorite methods for doing this when dining out on page 15, but the best method, and the most delicious, is to cook! With a fraction of the calories, saturated fat, and carbs of the beloved fare that inspired them, the classic and crave-worthy recipes in this book are a perfect fit for anyone concerned about diabetes. Beyond the recipes, you'll find plenty of healthy eating and ingredient tips along with a complete nutritional analysis for every recipe to make meal planning easy. Diabetes can be difficult; it's my mission to make eating with diabetes deliciously easy!

Meal Planning When Dining Out (or In)

Before I discuss meal planning, rest assured that, as with my previous *Eat What You Love* cookbooks, all you have to do to reap the better-for-you health benefits built into this book is to get cooking! The fact is the majority of my wonderful "Kochbook" fans simply cook from my books for themselves, and their families (and friends), and tell me that knowing that every recipe has already been carefully crafted to deliver good health allows them to enjoy the foods they love without guilt or worry (often for the first time). They are even more delighted when weight loss, lower blood sugar, and/or lower blood pressure ensue.

If you have defined health or weight loss goals, or need to keep your blood sugar in check, meal planning can help you attain your goals. This is especially true when you are away from home, where it is harder to control not only what is offered, but also the ingredients that go into your food. This section will provide you with the basics on meal planning. I'll start by explaining the quickest and easiest way to balance a healthy meal (Hint: All you need is a plate), to how to use calorie, carbohydrate, or food exchange information to help you achieve or maintain your healthiest best. At the end of the section, you'll find the details about how the nutritional information for each recipe was calculated, with extra tidbits about Weight Watcher Smart Point Comparisons, serving sizes, garnishes, and optional ingredients.

MEAL PLANNING WITH YOUR PLATE

When it comes to meal planning, there is no quicker or easier tool than the plate method. All you need to do to eat better is follow the instructions on how to portion your plate and you're on your way to better health. My plate (aka "Marlene's Plate") differs just slightly from the government's USDA "MyPlate," as I find that a slightly higher portion of protein, a little less starch, and more nonstarchy vegetables are even better for satiety, weight control, and blood sugar management.

To create a healthy meal that is moderate in both carbs and calories, use a 9-inch dinner plate (no larger) as your guide. Fill half the plate with nonstarchy vegetables and salad, and then fill one-quarter of the plate with a starchy side or whole-grain bread. The remaining quarter

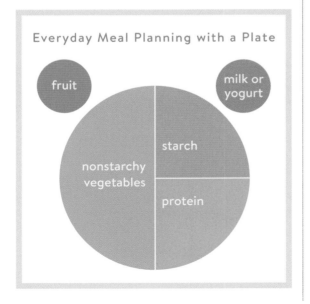

Everyday Meal Planning with a Plate

fruit

milk or yogurt

starch

nonstarchy vegetables

protein

should be comprised of a lean source of protein. If you're dining on pasta, pizza, or another dish that combines a starch and a protein (like my Smothered Chicken Burrito on page 131), dish up one serving and fill the rest of the plate with salad and more nonstarchy veggies. To complete your meal, add one 8-ounce glass of skim or low-fat milk or yogurt and for dessert, add a single serving of whole fruit. (If you need to keep tighter control of your carbs or prefer to finish your meal with one of my sweet treats, then save your dairy and/or fruit servings for snacks.)

MEAL PLANNING WITH CALORIES

As explained in Calorie Check on page 11, a guaranteed way to keep your weight in check is to balance the number of calories you eat each day with what you expend. To plan your meals around calories you first need to know how many calories you require. To assist you in determining your needs, you will find a Personalized Calorie Calculator on the tools page at marlenekoch.com. Calorie budgets for weight loss average between 1,200 and 1,800 calories. Once you know how many calories you require, you can set a calorie budget based on your goals (whether you want to lose, maintain, or gain weight). Evenly dividing your calories throughout the day will keep your hunger at bay and your blood sugar on a more even keel. Labels and restaurant nutrition guides can help you with your food selections, and a food log can help to keep you on track. To look and feel your best, and for maximum satiety, remember to spend most of your calorie budget on filling and/or nutrient-dense foods like nonstarchy vegetables, no- or low-fat dairy foods, whole grains, and lean sources of protein.

I am happy to say that the recipes in this book are all super-calorie bargains. Every one of them has been designed to deliver more taste with fewer calories and, even better, the calorie reduction comes not from the sneaky trick of simply reducing the serving size, but by trimming the excess fat and sugar none of us need. You need look not further than my frosty mocha with 140 calories instead of 550, or a restaurant hollandaise-topped omelette that tops out at just 270 calories instead of 1,050, to see how far the recipes in this book will deliciously stretch your calorie budget.

MEAL PLANNING WITH FOOD EXCHANGES

The exchange system—which groups similar foods, such as starches or fruit, into "exchange lists"—is a traditional meal-planning tool for weight loss and diabetes. The foods within each list contain a comparable amount of calories, carbohydrates, protein, and fat, and affect blood sugar similarly. Thus, the foods or beverages in a particular group are considered equal, and can be "exchanged," or traded for one another. By creating a meal plan that designates the number of servings to be selected from each of the various food groups, the exchange system ensures that all your nutrient needs are met and that carbs, fat, and calories are well balanced.

As an example, in the starch group—which designates a starch serving as 80 calories and approximately 15 grams of carbohydrate—a single slice of bread can be exchanged for one-half cup of cooked oatmeal or a quarter of a large bagel. The number of servings you can choose from each group at each meal or snack is based on your individual needs and health goals, and is best determined by a qualified professional, such as a registered dietitian or a certified diabetes educator. Food exchanges are included with every recipe based on those set forth by the Academy of Nutrition and Dietetics and the American Diabetes Association. Individual groups include:

✦ Starch (breads, pasta, rice, beans, potatoes, and corn)

✦ Vegetable (all nonstarchy vegetables)

✦ Fruit (fruits and fruit juices)

✦ Milk (nonfat and low-fat yogurt)

✦ Meat (lean meats, cheese, and eggs)

✦ Fat (oil, butter, margarine, nuts, and other fats)

✦ Carbohydrate (sugar and desserts)

MEAL PLANNING WITH CARB COUNTING

A healthy diet for anyone—including people with diabetes—is one that contains wholesome, good-for-you foods, including carbohydrate-rich fruits and vegetables, whole grains, and no- or low-fat dairy. That said, of all the nutrients you eat, carbohydrates also have the greatest impact on blood glucose and, as such, controlling the amount of carbs you eat can help keep blood sugar in check. Carbohydrate counting, or carb counting, is a meal-planning tool that helps you control the amount of carbohydrates you consume. As with calories, the amount of carbohydrates we each require varies. (To determine your personal carb budget, go to the tools page at marlenekoch.com and click on the Carbohydrate Calculator.) A carb-counting budget for those with diabetes averages 45 grams of carbohydrate per meal for most women and 60 grams for men (with 15 to 22 grams of carb for snacks).

To "count carbs," you simply add up all of the carbohydrates you are eating, whether it is a meal or a snack, while also striving to keep the total amount within your budget. Keep in mind, however, that while all carbs are counted equally—no matter what their source (be it a cup of beans or a brownie)—it's best for your health to fill your plate with healthy nutrient-rich carbs. (For more on carbs, see page 12. Nonstarchy veggies are incredible carb bargains!)

Every recipe in this book has been designed with carb counting in mind. From pancakes and sandwiches to pasta, pizza, and sweet, satisfying desserts, you won't find a single recipe that can't fit into a healthy or blood-sugar-management carbohydrate budget. The savings—and the counting is on me! (For more personalized information on meal planning and/or carb counting with diabetes, consult a registered dietitian or a certified diabetes educator.)

USING THE NUTRITION INFORMATION IN THIS BOOK

A nutritional analysis complements every recipe so you can easily select recipes based on your own needs.

✦ **NUTRITIONAL ANALYSIS** information was calculated using ESHA Nutrition Food Processor software in conjunction with manufacturers' food labels and includes **ALL** ingredients listed in the recipe with the exception of optional ingredients and those "to taste." If a choice is given, the first item listed was used for the analysis.

✦ **FOOD EXCHANGES** follow the guidelines of the American Diabetes Association. Values have been rounded to the nearest one-half for ease of use. For more information, see page 21.

✦ **WEIGHT WATCHERS®** and **SMARTPOINTS®** are registered trademarks of Weight Watchers International, Inc. Weight Watcher Smart Point Comparisons have been calculated for my wonderful weight-watching friends and fans for use with the Freestyle™ program. Please note: Plugging the numbers from the "nutrition information per serving" directly into a Freestyle SmartPoints calculator, app, or other tool will not yield the same, or correct, point value as all of the nutrients (and calories) for what are "zero" point foods are included in the nutritional analysis provided with each recipe.

✦ **PORTION SIZES** have been designed to satisfy. There is nothing worse than getting excited about the nutrition numbers only to find they relate to a mere bite! I also use common sense when it comes to serving measurements. For example, in an entrée with four chicken breasts and a pan sauce (that serves four), each person gets a breast and an equal portion of sauce. I do not detail the exact amount of sauce, as the measuring would be messy and tedious. Just divide such items evenly and you're good to go. For casseroles that are messy and/or easier to divide by simply portioning in the pan, like lasagna, you will find the serving listed as "one-fourth or one-sixth of the dish." I am also aware that appetites and caloric needs vary. Feel free to adjust the serving sizes to a portion that fits your or your family's needs and desires.

Last, I've created these recipes so you and yours can eat what you love without worry or guilt. Use the numbers as they help you best, but remember to sit back, savor, and most of all, enjoy!

"Dining" In—Ingredient and Preparation Tips

Like most people, my family and I enjoy dining out. There's no denying that it's nice to be waited on, gratifying to be served familiar favorite foods, exciting to be exposed to new tastes, and wonderful not to have to think about doing the dishes! But truth be told, we enjoy restaurant-worthy dining at home even more. There's never a wait to be seated, we can eat in comfort in our own kitchen, we can control what's on the menu and, most important, we know exactly what goes into the making of every drink or dish.

When cooking at home, just like at a restaurant, the choice of ingredients can make or break the dish in terms of both taste and health. It's even more the case when creating healthier yet just as cravable versions of dishes that ordinarily rely on copious amounts of fat, sugar, and salt, for texture and flavor. To ensure that each and every one of my easy recipes has the winning combination of good health and great taste, I spend countless hours in grocery stores looking for and choosing the best ingredients and even more hours plugging recipes into my nutrition software to help me achieve these goals. (I happily do this, so you don't have to!) This section provides you with a pantry list for the ingredients most commonly used in this book, with further details on many of the ingredients that I rely on to create crave-worthy, better-for-you recipes. Beyond the ingredients, you'll find a list of 10 chef-inspired must-have tools and my eight preparation and serving tips to help you easily replicate restaurant-style dishes at home so you can enjoy dining in at home as much as dining out.

RESTAURANT FAVORITE INGREDIENTS

A well-stocked pantry takes the stress out of meal planning and streamlines prep. Below is a list of easy-to-find ingredients I like to keep on hand and that you will find in this book. You will find more information about the ingredients marked with an asterisk on the following pages. See page 146 for more information on ingredients commonly used in Asian-inspired dishes.

IN THE CUPBOARD

Baking Basics
- ❑ Applesauce, unsweetened
- ❑ Baking powder and baking soda
- ❑ *Baking spray
- ❑ *Cocoa powder (Dutch-processed or regular)
- ❑ Extracts (almond, coconut, orange, vanilla)
- ❑ *Flour (all-purpose, cake flour, white whole wheat, Wondra instant)
- ❑ Shortening
- ❑ Sugar (brown, granulated, powdered)
- ❑ *Sweeteners (Truvia for Baking Blend, no-calorie granulated, sucralose)

Flavorful Condiments
- ❑ Barbecue sauce
- ❑ Hoisin sauce
- ❑ Hot sauce (Tabasco, Mexican-style)
- ❑ Liquid smoke
- ❑ *Mayonnaise, light
- ❑ Mustard (Dijon, yellow)
- ❑ Oyster sauce
- ❑ Salsa, jarred
- ❑ Sesame Oil
- ❑ Soy sauce, reduced-sodium
- ❑ Worcestershire sauce

Great Grains
- ❑ *Bread (variety)
- ❑ Breadcrumbs (plain and panko)
- ❑ Brown rice, quick-cooking (I use Uncle Ben's)
- ❑ Cornmeal, yellow
- ❑ Grits, plain, quick-cooking
- ❑ *Oats (quick, old-fashioned)
- ❑ *Pasta (whole-grain blend or gluten-free)

Miscellaneous
- ❑ *Bacon bits, real crumbled
- ❑ Beans, canned, reduced-sodium (black, pinto)
- ❑ Broth, reduced-sodium (chicken, beef)
- ❑ *Cooking spray
- ❑ Evaporated milk, low-fat
- ❑ Jam, low-sugar (variety)
- ❑ Maple-flavored syrup (light or sugar-free)
- ❑ Marinara sauce, jarred
- ❑ *Oils (canola, extra-virgin olive oil)
- ❑ Peanut butter (I like Jif)
- ❑ Pumpkin, 100% pure, solid, packed
- ❑ Spices, dried (variety)
- ❑ Tuna, canned
- ❑ Tomatoes (diced, fire-roasted, paste, pureed)
- ❑ Vinegar (apple cider, balsamic, rice wine)

Fridge

- ❏ Bacon, center-cut
- ❏ *Butter
- ❏ Buttermilk
- ❏ *Cheese, reduced-fat (variety)
- ❏ Chocolate fudge topping, sugar-free or light
- ❏ *Cottage cheese, low-fat
- ❏ *Cream cheese, light and nonfat
- ❏ *Eggs, large
- ❏ Garlic, jarred, minced
- ❏ Ginger, jarred, minced
- ❏ Half-and-half, nonfat
- ❏ *Margarine
- ❏ *Milk, low-fat (or alternative)
- ❏ Parmesan cheese
- ❏ *Sour cream, light
- ❏ *Tortillas (high-fiber, corn)
- ❏ *Yogurt, Greek plain (nonfat or low-fat)

Frozen

- ❏ *Beef, ground, 93% lean
- ❏ Chicken breasts (skinless, boneless breasts)
- ❏ Corn kernels
- ❏ Fruit (assortment)
- ❏ *Ice cream, vanilla (various light or no-added sugar)
- ❏ Peas, frozen
- ❏ Shrimp, frozen
- ❏ Spinach, frozen
- ❏ Tilapia (or other white fish)
- ❏ *Whipped topping, light

Bacon and Bacon Bits

Lean, center-cut, regular pork sliced bacon delivers traditional bacon texture and flavor with less fat and fewer calories (including that of many turkey bacon products). For topping and finishing recipes, I use only real bacon bits or pieces (not the fake bits on the salad aisle). I particularly like bold-flavored Hormel Black Label bacon pieces, sold in a plastic pouch.

Bread

"Light" breads generally have half the calories and carbs (about 45 and 9 per piece, respectively), and more fiber and protein per ounce than traditional breads. Sourdough bread raises blood sugar more slowly than regular white. The brand I buy has 60 calories per slice.

Buttermilk

Buttermilk adds great flavor to recipes and lightens and tenderizes baked goods. To make your own, place 1 tablespoon of vinegar or lemon juice in a measuring cup; pour in enough low-fat milk (or soy or almond "milk") to make 1 cup, let it sit for 5 to 10 minutes, and then stir before using. Alternately, mix ½ cup nonfat or low-fat plain yogurt with ½ cup of milk.

Cheese and Sour Cream

I prefer reduced- or low-fat cheese and sour cream over nonfat, which usually lack good texture and taste. (Greek yogurt is an exception.) When a minimal amount of cheese can contribute big flavor, as is the case with Parmesan and blue cheeses, I opt for full fat.

Cocoa Powder

I like Dutch-processed cocoa powder. The Dutch process reduces cocoa's natural acidity and bitterness and mellows the cocoa, imparting a richer, darker color. Hershey's-brand Special Dark cocoa powder can be found in the baking aisle of most stores. Regular unsweetened cocoa powder can be substituted.

Cooking and Baking Sprays

The difference between a cooking and a baking spray is that a baking spray also contains flour making greasing *and* flouring a pan (especially the hard-to-coat spots) a snap. If you don't have baking spray and the recipe calls for it, dust the pan with flour after using cooking spray. Remember, a light spray with either—two to three seconds—is all it takes.

Cottage Cheese

Cottage cheese is one of my favorite sneaky ingredients for cutting calories and fat while adding protein to recipes—especially when it's creamed. To cream it, blend it with an immersion blender or in a food processor until no curds are left (think thick sour cream). Small, curd low-fat, or 2%, cottage cheese is my preferred choice.

Cream Cheese

While there are some good store brands, Philadelphia-brand cream cheeses are reliable go-tos. Neufchâtel cheese can be used in place of light tub-style cream cheese. Nonfat cream cheese has fewer calories, but does not produce good results when used alone. I do not recommend increasing the amount of it used, or swapping it in for reduced-fat, in any recipe.

Eggs and Egg Substitutes

To maintain the great taste and texture provided by real whole eggs in most recipes I prefer to use a higher ratio of egg whites to yolks (or use only egg whites when appropriate), instead of relying on liquid egg substitute. I find this gives the best results, particularly in baking. There are some recipes, though, such as smoothies and sauces, where a liquid egg substitute is perfect.

$$\text{1 large egg} = \text{2 large egg whites} = \text{¼ cup liquid egg substitute}$$

Flours

All-purpose flour is the gold standard; it has the perfect amount of protein for structure and creates a light texture. Cake flour has less protein and, as such, creates a lighter, more tender crumb. To make your own cake flour, use 2 tablespoons of cornstarch and enough all-purpose flour to fill a 1-cup measure for each cup of cake flour needed. For whole-grain goodness, white whole wheat flour is my pick. It has a lighter taste than whole wheat flour but just as much fiber. A common brand is King Arthur. If avoiding gluten, there are many gluten-free "flour" blends available. I particularly like Cup4Cup gluten-free flour blend.

Ice Cream

Traditional light "no-added sugar" ice cream works well for my shakes and "tacos," but so do the newer light ice creams that offer less sugar and more protein than regular ice cream. They can be found in pints, which boast between 240 and 320 calories per container. Quality varies considerably by brand. Halo Top is one good-quality, readily available brand.

Lean Ground Beef, Turkey, and Pork

Lean ground beef, turkey, and pork, make it possible to keep meat on a healthy table. I prefer 93% lean ground beef and turkey, and 95% lean ground pork. I find meat with any less fat can be dry and mealy. (Tip: 93% lean beef is actually 39% fat—not 7% as is easy to assume. The "% lean" you see on the label refers to the percent of fat based on weight.)

Margarine or Butter

Smart Balance Buttery Spread Original (in the tub, 67% fat) has 65% less saturated fat than butter, and no trans fats. Soft and tub margarines with less than 65% fat by weight do not work well in cooking or baking as their water content is too high. I prefer butter when a small amount makes a noticeable taste difference. Use it where and when it suits you best.

Mayonnaise

At 1,440 calories per cup, regular mayonnaise packs a weighty punch. Fortunately, I've found that a 50/50 blend of light mayonnaise and low-fat (or nonfat) plain yogurt makes a great replacement. You may add additional light mayo or light sour cream to the yogurt if you prefer. I do not recommend low-fat mayonnaise; it is not as tasty as the light variety.

Milk and Nondairy Milk Alternatives

I prefer reduced- or low-fat dairy products over nonfat products. One percent milk is my go-to. Another good choice is Fairlife brand, which has more protein and less sugar than regular milk. If you prefer one of the many other "milks" (such as soy, almond, or coconut) these can be used in most recipes with little to no adjustment. Light soy milk will yield the closest taste and texture results. To make up for any loss of body in sauces and soups, stir in ¼ to ½ teaspoon of cornstarch. (Note: Nondairy "milks" cannot thicken instant pudding mix.)

Nonfat Half-and-Half

Nonfat or fat-free half-and-half has the creaminess of regular half-and-half without the fat. Reasonable substitutes are 2% or nonfat evaporated milk or real half-and-half (which adds extra fat and calories). Nonfat regular milk is not a good substitute.

Oats

Old-fashioned oats, rolled oats, and the quick-cooking variety may be interchanged. Instant oatmeal is not a suitable replacement for any of them. (To ensure oats are gluten-free check the package.)

Oils

All liquid oils contain the same amount of fat, so it's the flavor, or lack there of, that determines what I use for a particular recipe. For cooking, canola oil is heart-healthy and works well. The distinctive flavor of more expensive extra-virgin olive oil breaks down under heat and, as such, is best reserved for dressings and drizzling as opposed to cooking. Distinctively flavored sesame oil (made from sesame seeds) can be found in the Asian section of most markets, and has no equal substitute.

Pasta

From traditional pasta and whole-grain "blend" pastas to those higher in fiber and protein and gluten-free, there are plenty of pastas to choose from. For fewer calories and more nutrients, look for a pasta that provides at least 5 grams of fiber per serving. Pasta shape can be varied with what you have on hand.

Sweeteners:

No- and Low-Calorie Granulated Sweeteners

The choice is yours. Every recipe in this book was tested with both a generic no-calorie sucralose-based granulated sweetener and all-natural stevia-based Truvia for Baking. Both are found next to the sugar in most markets. No-calorie granulated sucralose measures 1:1 for sugar, and has the least carbs and calories. (See the comparison chart below.) Truvia for Baking (made with 25% real sugar) measures 1:2. When using Truvia for Baking *use half as much—as it has twice the sweetening effect*—and expect slightly longer baking times. If you prefer packets for beverages, each packet has the sweetness, though not the volume, of 2 teaspoons sugar or sweetener.*

Regular Sugar Substitution

When using regular sugar in baked goods, omit ¼ teaspoon of baking soda per cup of sweetener and expect to increase baking time by as much as 7 to 10 minutes for cakes, 5 minutes for muffins, and 3 to 5 minutes for cookies. Check all baked goods according to the recipe's test for doneness. (Tip: the normal substitution for sugar is 1:1 for measured granulated no-calorie sweetener, however you can cut one-fourth of the sugar called for in most baked goods with the only effect being slightly reduced sweetness.)

	Granulated Sucralose	Stevia/Sugar Baking Blend	Sugar
Equivalent Measure	1 cup	½ cup	1 cup
Calories	96	190	784
Carbohydrates	24	47 (usable)	190
Recipe Adjustments	None	May need a few more minutes' baking time	See "Granulated sugar" above

All sugar substitute packets are equivalent to the sweetness of 2 teaspoons of sugar. Do not measure packets' contents; the contents are far more intense than measurable amount. (Not recommended for baked goods.)

Tortillas

Tasty reduced-carbohydrate, low-calorie, high-fiber tortillas are widely available and found next to the regular tortillas. Mission Carb Balance and La Tortilla Factory Light tortillas are two I like. Mission brand flour tortillas crisp well, La Tortilla Factory only slightly so. When shopping for high-fiber tortillas, look for wraps that offer over 8 grams of fiber each. One hundred percent corn tortillas are gluten-free.

Yogurt

I specify plain Greek yogurt in many of the recipes. Thick and creamy Greek yogurt averages half the carbs and sugar and twice the protein of traditional American-style yogurts. Either nonfat or low-fat (2%) Greek yogurt can be used (I like Fage and Chobani brands). Tip: To ensure that the yogurt is truly "Greek," check the label to make sure the only ingredients are milk and active cultures and it has over 20 grams of protein per cup.

Whipped Topping

Light whipped topping has a fraction of the calories and fat of heavy cream. Cool Whip Lite and truwhip both work well. Be sure to thaw either before using. (Tip: Place it in the fridge when you bring it home.) I prefer light, *not* nonfat, whipped topping. The minimal calorie savings are not worth the difference in taste and texture. For garnishing, light real whipped cream sold in aerosol cans is a calorie bargain (just don't overdo it!). It does not work, however, as a substitute for light whipped topping that is to be mixed into a recipe.

RESTAURANT-INSPIRED RECIPES—FAVORITE TOOLS

It goes without saying that measuring cups and spoons, cutting boards, bowls, and a basic set of pots and pans are required when making recipes. When doing so with restaurant-quality, consistency, and focus in mind, here are some other essentials that come in handy.

✦ **KITCHEN SCALE**. For accuracy in making a dish, nothing is more valuable than a food scale. Once you have one, I guarantee you'll use it more than you ever thought you would.

✦ **SHARP KNIVES.** Sharp knives make food prep faster and easier; they produce cleaner cuts and more uniform pieces, and they're safer. (A knife sharpener is a good investment too.)

✦ **MICROPLANE GRATERS.** Beyond having the attributes of sharp knives, ultra-sharp graters require little skill to produce fine zest and wafer-thin shards of cheese for garnishing and more.

✦ **MISE EN PLACE BOWLS.** Having all your ingredients ready allows you to focus on the steps. I have two sets of small bowls (and also find 2 and 4 cup Pyrex measuring cups handy).

◆ **A SHARP SLICER.** You don't need an expensive mandoline or expert knife skills to make perfectly sliced tomatoes, cucumbers, or onions. An inexpensive V-slicer works wonders.

◆ **MULTIPLE MIXING SPOONS, SPATULAS, AND WHISKS.** Various sizes and shapes mean you always have the perfect tool for the job (like lifting a flaky piece of fish to neatly plate it).

◆ **TONGS.** Several pairs with metal tips and rubber tips. From flipping meat, chicken, and bacon, to serving pasta and sides, tongs are like having an extra hand (that can take the heat!).

◆ **NONSTICK SKILLETS.** 8-, 10-, and 12-inch. These are the workhorse pans in any kitchen. Be sure you have lids from pots that can be used for steaming, or purchase a large universal lid.

◆ **NONSTICK GRILL PAN.** Want to grill or create grill marks in a hurry? Just set one of these no-fuss pans on your stovetop and you're set to go—year-round. I frequently purchase these for gifts.

◆ **INSTANT-READ THERMOMETER.** There's no better way to determine doneness. See page 192 for more information and a cooked-to-perfection temperature chart.

CREATING RESTAURANT-INSPIRED MEALS AT HOME

Here's some great news. You don't have to be a restaurant chef to produce restaurant-worthy dining occasions at home! As important as chopping, searing, and perfect plating are planning, organization, and paying attention to detail—and, of course, using a good recipe. Here are some tips to bring it all together.

EIGHT EASY TIPS FOR DINING IN

1. **KEEP YOUR PANTRY WELL STOCKED (SEE PAGE 25).** Keep tabs on condiments, canned goods, and spices and add "backups" like canned milk and broth packets to your larder. Don't forget to keep fresh citrus like lemons, limes, or oranges, along with green onions, parsley, cilantro, or tomatoes, on hand for last-minute garnishing.

2. **INVEST IN THE RIGHT TOOLS.** Having the right tools (see page 30) will help ensure that you get the best results. Don't skimp on the most valuable tools. Money spent on a good sharp knife, pots, and solid sauté pans will pay back the investment.

3. **MAKE A PLAN.** Read each recipe thoroughly, noting the ingredients, required equipment, and timing. When making more than one dish, pre-determine the best sequence of events ahead of time.

4. **GET ORGANIZED.** With your plan set, it's time to prep! Create a "mise en place" by gathering tools and prepping, measuring, and organizing all ingredients.

5. **EMBRACE THE HEAT.** Chefs know that the power of a good sear adds color and flavor when cooking meats and vegetables; fully preheat skillets and ovens as directed.

6. **TASTE!** Taste as you go, add seasonings to taste, and adjust accordingly; enough said.

7. **CREATE A PRETTY PLATE.** Food always looks great on white dishes. Get creative and lay sauces down first and/or layer protein atop starches like potatoes or rice, clean any splatters from the rim, and *always* add a garnish. Garnishes should complement the dish and be edible.

8. **SET THE SCENE.** It doesn't need to be elaborate. Nice napkins, whether paper or cloth, a set table (flowers and/or candles optional), and soft music make all food taste better.

EAT *what you* LOVE
RESTAURANT FAVORITES

RECIPES

COFFEEHOUSE / DONUT SHOPS

COFFEEHOUSE / DONUT SHOPS

Coffee Coolatte

McCafé-Style Frosty Caramel
& Mocha Frappés

Better-for-You Strawberry Banana Smoothie

DIY Cold-Brew Mocha Iced Coffee

Bacon and Egg Avocado Toast

Egg, Spinach, and Sausage Wake-Up Wrap

Small Batch Apple Fritter Donut Muffins

Fast-Fix Fruit & Cream Cheese Danish

Classic Cinnamon Coffee Cake

Quick 'N' Easy Blueberry Banana Breakfast Loaf

Almond Joy Hot Chocolate

For the Love of
SUGAR

Cooking—and especially baking—with less sugar can be challenging. That's why I'm happy to say that today there are more reduced-calorie sweetening options than ever, including those that are all-natural. While there are many options, I have found the following to be easy-to-find, easy-to-use, economical, safe, and most of all, deliciously sweet for cooking and baking.

Every recipe that calls for a "sweetener" was tested with the sweeteners below. Use the information below to select the sweetening choice, or to assist with another alternative, that suits you and yours best.

SUCRALOSE. Recipes were tested and analyzed with granulated no-calorie sucralose-based sweeteners, which measure 1:1 for sugar. It is the sweetener that delivers the best-tasting results for the fewest calories and carbs. (Packets work well for beverages*.)

ALL-NATURAL STEVIA (BAKING BLEND). There are many types and brands of all-natural stevia-based sweeteners; they differ greatly, however, in sweetness, taste, and safeness. Recipes were tested with Truvia Baking Blend, made with 25% real sugar. It has 75% fewer calories and carbs when compared to sugar and no unpleasant aftertaste (as is common with stevia). The blend is twice as sweet as sugar, so you *simply halve the amount of sweetener called for in any recipe* (see chart below). Baking time may need to be extended slightly. The caloric difference per serving when compared to sucralose for the recipes in this book is less than 10 calories. Packets work well in beverages.*

GRANULATED SUGAR. Even if you choose to use regular sugar, my recipes are healthier than their higher-calorie counterparts. When using regular sugar in baked goods, omit ¼ teaspoon of baking soda per cup of sweetener and expect to increase the baking time by a couple of minutes for cakes, 3 to 5 minutes for cookies, and up to 5 minutes for muffins. Check all baked goods according to the recipe's test for doneness. (Tip: The normal substitution for sugar is 1:1 for measured granulated no-calorie sweetener; however, you can cut one-fourth of the sugar called for in most baked goods with the only effect being slightly reduced sweetness.)

	Granulated Sucralose	Stevia/Sugar Baking Blend	Sugar
Equivalent Measure	1 cup	½ cup	1 cup
Calories	96	190	784
Carbohydrates	24	47 (usable)	190
Recipe Adjustments	None	May need a few more minutes' baking time	See "Granulated sugar" above

All sugar substitute packets are equivalent to the sweetness of 2 teaspoons of sugar. Do not measure packets' contents; the contents are far more intense than measurable amount. (Not recommended for baked goods.)

Coffee Coolatte

IF YOU'RE A DUNKIN' FAN, you're probably familiar with their extremely popular "Coffee Coolatta." This cool, creamy, light, coffee-flavored drink debuted in 1994, but was pulled from the menu in 2017 in favor of a more "coffee forward" beverage. Many Coolatta fans were displeased, including one dear reader who asked if I could help. Joanne, this one's for you and, as requested, it's not only just as sip-worthy, it's a whole lot healthier too!

MAKES 1 SERVING

⅔ cup strong coffee
(or 1 teaspoon instant coffee dissolved in ⅔ cup water)

⅓ cup low-fat milk

2 tablespoons nonfat
half-and-half

2 tablespoons granulated
sweetener*

¾ teaspoon vanilla extract

¼ teaspoon almond extract

2 teaspoons cocoa powder

1 teaspoon sugar (optional)

1 ¼ cups crushed ice

See page 36 for sweetener options.

1. Place all the ingredients except the ice in a blender. Blend to mix.

2. Add crushed ice and blend on high until the ice is completely incorporated. Serve immediately.

DARE TO COMPARE: A medium Coffee Coolatta with whipped cream clocked in with 630 calories with an entire day's worth of saturated fat—and a not-so-cool 92 grams of sugar. Want whip? A 2-tablespoon squirt of aerosol whipped cream adds just 15 calories.

NUTRITION INFORMATION PER SERVING: Calories 75 | Carbohydrate 10 g (Sugars 4 g) | Total Fat 1.5 g (Sat Fat 1 g) | Protein 4 g | Fiber 1 g | Sodium 45 mg | Food Exchanges: ⅓ Low-Fat Milk, ¼ Carbohydrate | Weight Watcher Smart Point Comparison: 3

McCafé-Style Frosty Caramel & Mocha Frappés

I JUST HAD TO INCLUDE THIS FROSTY DRINK as it helped a reader lose 100 pounds! Miriam, one of my incredible "Kochbook" fans, realized just how quickly the calories add up with frozen coffee beverages when the first thing she did on her "get healthy" journey was to trade her daily McDonald's McCafé Caramel Frappé for mine (slashing a stunning 425 calories and 16 teaspoons of sugar per drink without sacrificing any of the beloved taste). Love chocolate? See Marlene Says for my Frosty Mocha Frappé!

MAKES 1 SERVING

½ cup low-fat milk

¼ teaspoon instant coffee powder

¼ cup light low-or no-sugar-added butter pecan ice cream

1 tablespoon sugar-free caramel syrup (like Smuckers)

2 teaspoons granulated sweetener (or 1 packet)*

½ cup crushed ice

Light whipped cream and sugar-free caramel syrup (optional)

*See page 36 for sweetener options.

1. Place all the ingredients except the ice in a blender. Blend to mix.

2. Add crushed ice and blend on high until the ice is completely incorporated. Top with a squirt of light whipped cream and/or a drizzle of syrup, if desired. (A 2-tablespoon squirt of aerosol whipped cream and a drizzle of syrup add 30 calories.)

Marlene Says: *For a* **FROSTY MOCHA FRAPPÉ**, *place ¼ cup warm water, 1 teaspoon cocoa powder, and ¾ teaspoon coffee powder in a blender. Blend briefly; add ¼ cup milk, ¼ cup no-sugar-added vanilla ice cream, and 2 tablespoons granulated sweetener (or 3 packets). Blend to mix, then add ¾ cup ice, and blend until creamy. (100 calories, 4 points)*

NUTRITION INFORMATION PER SERVING: Calories 125 | Carbohydrate 20 g (Sugars 7 g) | Total Fat 3 g (Sat Fat 1.5 g) | Protein 5 g | Fiber 0 g | Sodium 140 mg | Food Exchanges: 1 Carbohydrate, ½ Low-Fat Milk | Weight Watcher Smart Point Comparison: 5

Better-for-You Strawberry Banana Smoothie

IT'S HARD TO BEAT THE SWEET, FRUITY TASTE of a cool, creamy, classic strawberry-banana smoothie. Unfortunately, most places that serve them (even those that tout they are made with "real fruit") also add sugar and/or concentrated "fruit" juices to sweeten them up. Instead of extra sugar, this smoothie delivers the same creamy, fruity taste that everyone loves with an extra helping of belly-filling, blood sugar–stabilizing protein. A boiled egg or a handful of nuts served alongside it turns either combo into a good mini meal.

MAKES 1 SERVING

⅔ cup frozen strawberries

½ small banana

⅓ cup plain nonfat Greek yogurt

4 teaspoons granulated sweetener (or 4 packets)

½ cup crushed ice

1. Place all the ingredients in a blender and blend on high until ice is completely incorporated and drink is smooth and creamy.

DARE TO COMPARE: Where calories come from also count. A small, identically-sized, McDonald's McCafé Strawberry Banana Smoothie has 30% more calories. More notable, however, this smoothie has 50% less sugar, no "added" sugar, and four times the protein!

NUTRITION INFORMATION PER SERVING: Calories 130 | Carbohydrate 26 g (Sugars 20 g) | Total Fat 0 g (Sat Fat 0 g) | Protein 9 g | Fiber 4 g | Sodium 30 mg | Food Exchanges: 2 Fruit, ½ nonfat milk | Weight Watcher Smart Point Comparison: 5

DIY Cold Brew Mocha Iced Coffee

IF YOU HAVEN'T NOTICED YET, the hottest new thing in coffee is cold—as in "cold brewed" (See Marlene Says for more on cold-brewed coffee.) I'm a fan of refreshing iced coffee, but not of the unnecessary calories and sugar that often come with it. Fortunately, you can leave most of the calories, and the cost, behind by making it at home. A touch of cornstarch is the secret to creating the mouthfeel found in coffeehouse and bottled iced coffee drinks. Nondairy milk alternatives can also be substituted; for the best result, the creamier the better.

MAKES 1 SERVING

2 tablespoons plus ½ cup strong cold-brewed coffee, divided

1½ tablespoons granulated sweetener* (or 2 packets)

¼ teaspoon Dutch-process cocoa powder (like Hershey's Dark)

¼ teaspoon cornstarch

3 tablespoons nonfat half-and-half or low-fat evaporated milk

½ cup crushed ice

*See page 36 for sweetener options.

1. In a tall microwave-safe glass, whisk together 2 tablespoons coffee, sweetener, cocoa powder, and cornstarch. Place in microwave and microwave on high for 30 seconds or until the mixture rapidly bubbles. Remove and let it cool for a minute or two (to flash-cool it, place the glass in the freezer).

2. Add the remaining ½ cup coffee, stir, and then add milk. Pour over ice to serve.

Marlene Says: *Coffee brewed with cold water is prized for its mellow, yet strong, flavor and reduced bitterness. It also boasts 50% less acid than regular coffee. Look for convenient "cold-brew" coffee packets in the coffee aisle at your local market. They cost a fraction of that already bottled.*

NUTRITION INFORMATION PER SERVING: Calories 35 | Carbohydrate 6 g (Sugars 2 g) | Total Fat 1 g (Sat Fat 0 g) | Protein 1 g | Fiber 0 g | Sodium 65 mg | Food Exchanges: ½ Carbohydrate | Weight Watcher Smart Point Comparison: 1

Bacon and Egg Avocado Toast

THERE'S A GOOD REASON AVOCADO TOAST HAS BECOME POPULAR. Buttery, rich mashed avocado is simply tremendous when slathered on toasted bread; even more so when topped with slices of juicy ripe tomato, a warm freshly cooked egg, and savory bacon. As if the toothsome taste and texture weren't enough, the healthy fat and fiber found in avocados keeps your belly as satisfied as your taste buds. No wonder coffeehouses and cafés from coast to coast are toasting avocado toast!

MAKES 1 SERVING

1 large egg

1 slice sourdough bread

⅓ medium avocado (about ¼ cup mashed)

Pinch of salt

2 slices tomato

2 teaspoons real bacon bits

1 teaspoon minced green onion tops or chives (optional)

1. Spray a small nonstick skillet with cooking spray and place over medium heat. Add the egg and cook until the white is almost cooked, flip, if desired, and cook until the egg is done to your liking.

2. While the egg is cooking, toast the bread. Coarsely mash avocado onto the toast, sprinkle with salt, and top with the tomato slices. Top with the cooked egg, sprinkle with bacon, and garnish with onion, if desired.

Marlene Says: *Creamy avocados, also known as butter fruit, are naturally low in sodium and sugar and high in fiber and healthy monounsaturated fat. The fruit, yes fruit, can also help to keep blood sugar stable. One-quarter cup of mashed avocado has fewer calories than 1 tablespoon of butter!*

NUTRITION INFORMATION PER SERVING: Calories 215 | Carbohydrate 16 g (Sugars 2 g) | Total Fat 14 g (Sat Fat 3 g) | Protein 12 g | Fiber 3 g | Sodium 405 mg | Food Exchanges: 1 Starch, 1 Medium-Fat Meat, 2 Fat | Weight Watcher Smart Point Comparison: 5

Egg, Spinach, and Sausage Wake-Up Wrap

DUNKIN' CLAIMS THEIR POPULAR SAUSAGE WAKE-UP WRAP is "perfectly portioned to help start your day." The reality is the wrap is quite small—prodding you to purchase two. With a larger tortilla, double the protein, and six times the fiber (yet half the fat), this satisfying eye-opening wrap actually delivers on their claim. Once assembled, it keeps well in the fridge for several days, so feel free to make a few at a time. Just warm one up and you're off and running!

MAKES 1 SERVING

1 slice reduced-fat cheddar or American cheese

1 (8-inch) light high-fiber tortilla (like La Tortilla Factory)

⅓ cup fresh spinach leaves

2 ounces lean Breakfast Sausage (page 242) or store-bought

1 large egg

1. Slice the cheese in half and lay both pieces on one half of the tortilla. Top with the spinach and set aside.

2. Pat sausage into a thin oblong patty. Spray a small nonstick skillet with cooking spray and place over medium heat. Add sausage and cook for 1 minute. Flip and cook another minute, or until cooked through. Remove from pan and place on spinach.

3. Wipe out skillet, spray with cooking spray, and return to heat. Add egg and cook until white is almost cooked,. Flip, pierce yolk (if desired), and cook until egg is done to your liking. Place egg on top of sausage and fold empty side of tortilla over egg. (You can let it cool at this point, wrap, and refrigerate for up to 3 days.)

4. To finish, spray skillet with cooking spray, and place wrap cheese-side down in the hot pan. Cook for 1 minute, or until the cheese melts and the tortilla is lightly brown. Flip, and lightly brown the other side.

Marlene Says: *To reheat refrigerated wraps, either heat in a skillet per Step 4, warm in a toaster oven for 5 minutes or until the tortilla is toasted and the filling is hot, or microwave for about 45 seconds on high (the tortilla will remain soft).*

NUTRITION INFORMATION PER SERVING: Calories 260 | Carbohydrate 16 g (Sugars 1 g) | Total Fat 12 g (Sat Fat 4 g) | Protein 27 g | Fiber 7 g | Sodium 550 mg | Food Exchanges: 3½ Lean Meat, 1 Starch | Weight Watcher Smart Point Comparison: 5

Small Batch Apple Fritter Donut Muffins

WHEN I WAS IN HIGH SCHOOL, I wasn't a big donut eater, but there was something about the deep-fried heavenly glazed goodness of an apple fritter that was hard to resist. To this day, I still picture the bits of soft cinnamony apple dotted throughout the dough. Happily, I've found a healthier way to fancy a fritter with this muffin-meets-donut recipe. The secret lies in the sweet cinnamon-laced bits of apple you add to the donut-scented batter. A dusting of sweet powdered sugar seals the deal.

MAKES 6 SERVINGS

¾ cup chopped, peeled apple

1 teaspoon cinnamon, divided

1 tablespoon plus ¼ cup granulated sweetener,* divided

1 cup all-purpose flour

1 teaspoon baking powder

¼ teaspoon baking soda

¼ teaspoon nutmeg

1 large egg

2 tablespoons unsweetened applesauce

2 tablespoons margarine or butter, melted

1 tablespoon powdered sugar

*See page 36 for sweetener options.

1. Preheat oven to 350°F. Line muffin cups with paper or foil liners, and lightly spray inside with nonstick cooking spray.

2. In a small microwave-safe bowl, mix together apple, ½ teaspoon cinnamon, 1 tablespoon sweetener, and 2 tablespoons water. Place in microwave and cook on high for 1½ minutes.

3. In a large bowl, combine flour, baking powder, baking soda, nutmeg, and remaining ½ teaspoon cinnamon and ¼ cup sweetener. Toss cooked apples with flour mixture. In a small bowl or large measuring cup, whisk together egg, applesauce, margarine, and 3 tablespoons water. Make a well in the center of the dry ingredients and pour in the egg mixture. Using a large spoon or spatula, mix just until all the flour is moistened. Do not overmix.

4. Spoon batter into prepared muffin cups. Bake for 13 to 15 minutes or until center springs back when lightly touched. Move muffin tin to a wire rack, and, using a small sifter, dust powdered sugar over tops of muffins.

*Marlene Says: An **APPLE FRITTER DONUT MUFFIN** and a cup of **ALMOND JOY HOT CHOCOLATE** (page 51) are a perfect autumn pairing. Relax and enjoy while saving over 500 calories!*

NUTRITION INFORMATION PER SERVING (1 MUFFIN): Calories 130 | Carbohydrate 21 g (Sugars 4 g) | Total Fat 4 g (Sat Fat 1 g) | Protein 3 g | Fiber 1 g | Sodium 130 mg | Food Exchanges: 1½ Starch | Weight Watcher Smart Point Comparison: 5

Fast-Fix Fruit & Cream Cheese Danish

IMPRESS YOUR GUESTS WITH EASY FAIL-PROOF HOMEMADE PASTRIES! A can of crescent rolls is the secret fast-fix ingredient for these simple-to-make, gorgeous, fruit-filled Danish. I love the look and taste of apricot jam topped with fresh blueberries and the cream cheese drizzle, but just about any combination of jam and berries will do. See Marlene Says for a few suggestions. (Psst . . . There's no need to tell anyone that these have half the fat and calories of the classic baked good!)

MAKES 6 SERVINGS

1 teaspoon all-purpose flour

1 can reduced-fat crescent rolls or 8-ounce crescent roll sheet

4 tablespoons reduced-sugar apricot jam

⅔ cup fresh blueberries

1 large egg white, beaten

2 tablespoons light tub-style cream cheese

2 teaspoons powdered sugar

Scant ⅛ teaspoon almond extract

1. Preheat the oven to 375°F. Sprinkle flour onto a cutting board. Unroll crescent dough and place on the board. Carefully cut the dough in half across the length of the dough. Pinch the perforations together on each half to make 2 long, 3½-inch wide strips.

2. Cut each strip vertically into 3 equal pieces. With your fingers, flatten each piece into a 4 x 5-inch rectangle, pressing outward from the middle to form a flattened pocket in the center. Using a flat knife or your fingers, press edges inward slightly and press them flat to build a raised ¼-inch-wide outer rim. Fill pocket with 2 teaspoons of jam and top with 2 tablespoons berries. Brush the edges with egg white and bake for 14 to 16 minutes or until golden brown.

3. While pastries are baking, in a small bowl, whisk together cream cheese, powdered sugar, almond extract, and 2 teaspoons water (add 1 teaspoon water at a time for easier mixing). Drizzle each pastry with 1 teaspoon of cream cheese glaze.

Marlene Says: I also love these topped with strawberry jam and fresh sliced strawberries, strawberry jam and blueberries (for a red, white, and blue day), or simply with reduced-sugar orange marmalade.

NUTRITION INFORMATION PER SERVING (1 DANISH): Calories 150 | Carbohydrate 23 g (Sugars 7 g) | Total Fat 6 g (Sat Fat 2 g) | Protein 3 g | Fiber 1 g | Sodium 310 mg | Food Exchanges: 1 Starch, ½ Fruit | Weight Watcher Smart Point Comparison: 5

Classic Cinnamon Coffee Cake

OVER THE YEARS, I'VE CREATED MANY DIFFERENT CINNAMON COFFEE CAKES. For this one I've combined all of the best taste elements—tender moist cake, sweet cinnamon-laced middle, and crumbly brown sugar topping—along with my best healthifying techniques (the crushed graham crackers will make you swear there's a lot more sugar than meets the eye). Because half of the ingredients are used more than once, I find it easiest to simply place them all on the counter and measure as I go.

MAKES 9 SERVINGS

2 tablespoons plus 1¾ cups reduced-fat baking mix (like Bisquick Heart Smart), divided

4 tablespoons plus ½ cup granulated sweetener, divided

3 teaspoons cinnamon, divided

2 tablespoons brown sugar, divided

⅓ cup crushed graham crackers

3 tablespoons margarine or butter, melted, divided

¾ cup buttermilk

2 large eggs

1 teaspoon vanilla

2 teaspoons powdered sugar

*See page 36 for sweetener options.

1. Preheat the oven to 350°F. Lightly spray an 8-inch round cake pan with nonstick baking spray.

2. For the crumb topping, in a small bowl combine 2 tablespoons baking mix, 2 tablespoons sweetener, 1 teaspoon cinnamon, 1 tablespoon brown sugar, and graham cracker crumbs. Add 1½ tablespoons margarine and combine until uniformly crumbly. Set aside.

3. For the swirl, in another bowl combine 2 tablespoons sweetener, 2 teaspoons cinnamon and 1 tablespoon brown sugar.

4. In a medium bowl, whisk together buttermilk, eggs, vanilla, and remaining 1½ tablespoons margarine until smooth. Add remaining 1¾ cups baking mix and ½ cup sweetener. Using a large spoon or spatula, stir until smooth. Spoon about 1 cup of batter into prepared pan and spread to cover pan (it will barely cover it). Sprinkle swirl mix on top, then spoon remaining batter over it, and carefully smooth (it's okay if there is an uncovered spot or two). Evenly top batter with crumb topping.

5. Bake for 18 to 20 minutes, or until the center springs back when lightly touched. Dust with powdered sugar before serving.

> **DARE TO COMPARE:** The fat-for-sugar switcheroo! A piece of Starbucks Classic Coffee Cake has 390 calories, 16 grams of fat, and 31 grams of sugar; the reduced-fat has 370 calories, 9 grams of fat, and 41 grams of sugar. This cake is low in fat AND sugar!

NUTRITION INFORMATION PER SERVING (1 PIECE): Calories 170 | Carbohydrate 27 g (Sugars 6 g) | Total Fat 5 g (Sat Fat 1.5 g) | Protein 3 g | Fiber 0 g | Sodium 400 mg | Food Exchanges: 1½ Starch, 1 Fat | Weight Watcher Smart Point Comparison: 6

Quick 'N' Easy Blueberry Banana Breakfast Loaf

I HOPE YOU DON'T MIND that I've taken a bit of license here. Slices of moist banana bread and homey blueberry muffins fill the cases at most coffee shops. Here, I've married the two! Plump blueberries are an added bonus in a super-easy, super-moist, one-bowl banana loaf that I've rounded out with good ol' oats. It's the perfect companion to a hot cup of coffee or tea, or, my husband's favorite, a cold glass of milk.

MAKES 12 SERVINGS

2 cups reduced-fat baking mix (like Bisquick Heart Smart)

½ cup quick oats

½ cup granulated sweetener*

½ teaspoon baking soda

1 cup fresh or frozen blueberries

1⅓ cups mashed banana (about 3 ripe bananas)

¼ cup low-fat milk

2 large eggs, beaten

1 tablespoon canola oil

1 tablespoon molasses

1 teaspoon vanilla extract

*See page 36 for sweetener options.

1. Preheat the oven to 350°F. Lightly coat a 9 x 5-inch loaf pan with nonstick baking spray.

2. In a large bowl, combine the baking mix, oats, sweetener, and baking soda. Whisk to combine. Add blueberries and toss to coat. Add remaining ingredients and using a large spoon or spatula, stir just until all the ingredients are combined. Spoon the batter into the prepared pan and smooth the top.

3. Bake for 55 to 60 minutes (covering loosely with foil after 40 minutes or when the top is brown enough). The loaf is done when a thin paring knife inserted into the center comes out clean. Cool on a wire rack for 15 minutes, then loosen sides and remove from pan.

Marlene Says: *To turn a slice of this bread into a light breakfast, add a boiled egg, ½ cup of yogurt or a small handful of nuts, and a glass of milk.*

NUTRITION INFORMATION PER SERVING (1 SLICE): Calories 140 | Carbohydrate 25 g (Sugars 8 g) | Total Fat 4 g (Sat Fat 0 g) | Protein 4 g | Fiber 2 g | Sodium 210 mg | Food Exchanges: 1 Starch, ½ Fruit | Weight Watcher Smart Point Comparison: 3

Almond Joy Hot Chocolate

IF YOU LOVE THE IRRESISTIBLE COMBINATION of chocolate, almond, and coconut, you're in for a treat. The inspiration for this drink, which is a late-night go-to favorite of mine, was a similar themed hot chocolate offered by Dunkin' for Halloween. My slimmed-down version offers the joy of a "candy bar in a cup" minus a candy bar's calories. I find dark hot chocolate showcases the aromatic almond and coconut flavors better. If you prefer milk chocolate, just swap in a few tablespoons of milk or nonfat half-and-half for some of the water. If you don't feel like a nut, swap vanilla for the almond extract.

MAKES 1 SERVING

1½ tablespoons cocoa powder

2 tablespoons granulated sweetener (or 3 packets)*

½ teaspoon cornstarch

¼ teaspoon coconut extract

⅛ teaspoon almond extract

2 tablespoons light whipped cream

1 teaspoon coconut (optional garnish)

*See page 36 for sweetener options.

1. Whisk together the cocoa powder, sweetener, cornstarch, and ¼ cup water in a microwave-safe mug. Whisk in ¾ cup more water, place mug in microwave, and heat on high for 1½ to 2 minutes, or until the hot chocolate bubbles up to the rim of the cup. Immediately turn off microwave and stir in coconut and almond extracts. Return to microwave for 15 seconds to meld flavors.

2. Top with the light whipped cream and garnish with coconut, if desired.

> **DARE TO COMPARE:** Treat or trick? A Dunkin' Medium Almond Joy Hot Chocolate has 340 calories and 60 grams of carbs. An Almond Joy candy bar has only 220 and 26 grams, respectively. This joy of a drink has a mere 50 calories and 9 grams of carbohydrate.

NUTRITION INFORMATION PER SERVING: Calories 50 | Carbohydrate 9 g (Sugars 2 g) | Total Fat 2 g (Sat Fat 1 g) | Protein 2 g | Fiber 0 g | Sodium 90 mg | Food Exchanges: ½ Carbohydrate | Weight Watcher Smart Point Comparison: 2

FAST-FOOD FIX

FAST-FOOD FIX

3-Minute Egg-White Delight

Sausage 'N' Egg Breakfast Burrito

Chicken, Apple, Pecan Salad with Balsamic Vinaigrette

Stephen's Taco Bell–Style Chicken Quesadilla

Classic Quarter-Pound Burger With Special Sauce

Western Bacon Chicken Sandwich

Filet of Fish Sandwich

Chicken Pepperoni Parm Sandwich

Primo Pico Guacamole Burger

Crispy Chicken Strips with Ranch Dressing

Extra Crispy Onion Rings

Air-Fried Seasoned Fries

Fast, Fresh Apple Pies

Better-Than-Ever Thick and Creamy Milkshakes

For the Love of
CRISPY "FRIED" FOODS
(Air-Fryer Instructions)

Crispy fried foods are some of the most popular items you'll find on any restaurant menu. To healthfully re-create these crave-worthy selections at home, I love my air fryer. It "fries" fabulously with far less fat—evenly and quickly—and cleanup is a breeze! Here are instructions for air-frying the designated recipes in this book.

Filet of Fish Sandwich *(page 63)*
Preheat the air fryer to 360°F. Air-fry coated filets for 8 minutes, or until coating is browned and fish flakes easily when tested with a fork, turning once and lightly coating with cooking spray.

Crispy Chicken Strips with Ranch Dressing *(page 67)*
Preheat the air fryer to 360°F. Spray chicken strips with cooking spray and air-fry for 8 to 9 minutes, or until nicely browned, turning and lightly spraying with cooking spray after 5 minutes.

Extra Crispy Onion Rings *(page 69)*
Preheat the air fryer to 360°F. Add coated onion rings, with only partial overlapping, and air-fry for 10 minutes, or until golden brown and crisp, shaking halfway and lightly coating with cooking spray.

Fast, Fresh Apple Pies *(page 71)*
Preheat the air fryer to 360°F. Carefully add pies and air-fry for 8 to 9 minutes or until golden brown.

Crispy Chicken Avocado Egg Rolls *(page 81)*
Preheat the air fryer to 360°F. Spray egg rolls with cooking spray and air-fry for 15 minutes or until golden brown, turning halfway through. Let cool for 1 minute before cutting.

Warm Chocolate Brownie Sundaes *(page 94)*
Preheat the air fryer to 320°F. Air-fry brownies for 6 minutes. Remove ramekins with tongs (they will be very hot). Let brownie set for 1 to 2 minutes to finish cooking the center.

Chicken 'N' Waffles *(page 98)* and Chicken Fried Chicken *(page 110)*
Preheat the air fryer to 360°F. Spray chicken with cooking spray and air-fry for 9 to 10 minutes, in batches if needed, until browned, turning halfway and lightly coating with cooking spray.

10-Minute Chicken Taquitos with Creamy Avocado Salsa *(page 125)*
Preheat the air fryer to 370°F. Spray taquitos lightly with cooking spray and air-fry, in a single layer, for 5 minutes or until tortilla is crisp. Tortillas will crisp slightly more upon cooking.

3-Minute Egg-White Delight

ONCE A BIT PLAYER ON FAST-FOOD MENUS, egg sandwiches now drive sales, and for good reason. Egg sandwiches are comforting, satisfying, and incredibly versatile. This favorite of mine swaps in lean shaved turkey for sausage or bacon. When warmed and layered with melty cheese, soft puffy egg whites, and silky spinach, it makes for a breakfast sandwich that's truly delightful. The fact it can be made so quickly (total cooking time just three minutes) using only a microwave, is a mere bonus.

MAKES 1 SERVING

1 light English muffin

1½ ounces shaved smoked turkey breast

1 thin slice Swiss cheese

1 cup fresh spinach, baby or regular

2 large egg whites

1. Split and toast the English muffin. While it's toasting, loosely pile the turkey onto a microwave-safe plate, top with the cheese, and set aside. Place the spinach in a small microwave-safe bowl and microwave on high for 30 seconds. Blot excess water from spinach with a paper towel, and set aside.

2. Wipe out bowl, spray with cooking spray, add egg whites, and whisk until frothy. Microwave on high or 1 minute or until fully cooked but still soft. Set aside.

3. Put the plate with the turkey and cheese in the microwave and warm on high for 30 seconds, or until cheese starts to melt. Place it on the toasted muffin half, top evenly with the spinach, add the egg whites, and close with the English muffin top.

Marlene Says: *Protein and fiber are powerful breakfast partners that will help you feel fuller, longer. Aim for at least 20 grams of protein and 5 grams of fiber in your morning meal. To lower the sodium in this sandwich swap in no-salt-added regular turkey breast.*

NUTRITION INFORMATION PER SERVING: Calories 200 | Carbohydrate 23 g (Sugars 2 g) | Total Fat 3.5 g (Sat Fat 1.5 g) | Protein 21 g | Fiber 9 g | Sodium 680 mg | Food Exchanges: 3 Lean Meat, 1½ Starch, 1 Vegetable | Weight Watcher Smart Point Comparison: 4

Sausage 'N' Egg Breakfast Burrito

ON A RECENT ROAD TRIP, I ordered a sausage burrito off McDonald's value menu. Given the other options, it seemed to be a reasonable choice (both calorically and in cost). Regrettably, it was far smaller than expected, leaving me questioning the "value." But there's no question of the value in this burrito, made with my lean Breakfast Sausage (page 242). Packed with plenty of savory sausage and 31 grams of satisfying protein, I'm loving it! (P.S. Breakfast Sausage is also great for Wake-Up Wraps [page 44].)

MAKES 2 SERVINGS

2 large eggs

2 large egg whites

½ cup Breakfast Sausage (page 242), or 4 ounces lean store-bought

2 green onions, chopped

½ cup seeded, diced tomato

2 tablespoons fire-roasted diced green chilies

2 (8-inch) light high-fiber flour tortillas

2 thin slices reduced-fat cheddar cheese

1. In a medium bowl, whisk together the eggs and egg whites. Set aside.

2. Spray a medium nonstick skillet with cooking spray and place over medium heat. Add sausage and cook for 4 minutes or until nearly done. Add green onions and cook for 30 seconds. Add eggs and cook 2 to 3 minutes, stirring and scrambling until just set. Stir in tomato and chilies.

3. Soften the tortillas by heating them in the microwave on high for 30 seconds. Lay a slice of cheese on a tortilla and top with half of the sausage and egg mixture. Fold bottom of tortilla over filling, cover with one of the sides, and roll up burrito-style (leaving the far end open). Repeat with remaining tortilla and ingredients. (A toothpick can be used to close if desired.)

> **DARE TO COMPARE:** A McDonald's sausage burrito is similar in calories, but weighs only half as much. Order two, as you need to do, and you are looking at double the calories and three times the sodium with 25% less belly-filling protein. Make your own and you'll be "lovin' it" at home.

NUTRITION INFORMATION PER SERVING: Calories 295 | Carbohydrate 19 g (Sugars 3 g) | Total Fat 13 g (Sat Fat 5 g) | Protein 31 g | Fiber 8 g | Sodium 510 mg | Food Exchanges: 4 Lean Meat, 1 Starch, ½ Fat | Weight Watcher Smart Point Comparison: 5

Chicken, Apple, Pecan Salad with Balsamic Vinaigrette

THINK YOU'RE EATING HEALTHIER by choosing a salad entrée over a burger at a fast-food joint? Not so fast. For example, there's almost a half a day's worth of sodium and 10 teaspoons of sugar hidden in Wendy's much-loved chicken, fruit, and nut salad, making their Jr. Hamburger a better choice. An even better choice is to make the beloved salad at home. With just a handful of ingredients and an amazing fat-free dressing, this salad couldn't be easier to make, proving "at-home" can be healthy and fast!

MAKES 2 SERVINGS

DRESSING

1 tablespoon honey

1 tablespoon Dijon mustard

3 tablespoons balsamic vinegar

Pinch of salt and pepper

SALAD

4 cups mixed greens

1 small apple, chopped

⅔ cup chopped, cooked skinless chicken breast

¼ cup reduced-fat feta cheese

3 tablespoons chopped toasted pecans

2 tablespoons chopped green onions

1. In a small bowl, whisk together the dressing ingredients with 2 teaspoons of water. Set aside.

2. Place 2 cups of greens on each plate, drizzle with 1 tablespoon dressing and top with half of the apple and chicken and mix slightly.

3. Sprinkle each salad with half of the cheese, drizzle with 2 scant tablespoons dressing, and garnish with the pecans and green onions.

> **DARE TO COMPARE:** Wendy's Apple Pecan Chicken Salad has 590 calories with 40 grams of sugar, and 1,020 milligrams of sodium.

NUTRITION INFORMATION PER SERVING (1 SALAD): Calories 280 | Carbohydrate 27 g (Sugars 21 g) | Total Fat 10 g (Sat Fat 2 g) | Protein 22 g | Fiber 3 g | Sodium 500 mg | Food Exchanges: 3 Lean Meat, 1 Carbohydrate, ½ Fruit | Weight Watcher Smart Point Comparison: 6

Stephen's Taco Bell–Style Chicken Quesadilla

MY SON STEPHEN LOVES TACO BELL and the single item he loves the most, as you've probably guessed, is their creamy-cheesy-chicken quesadilla. While not every recipe in this book winds up being a "clone" (I can't help myself if I can make a dish look or taste better :-)), my goal here was to deliver Stephen his favorite quesadilla. After plenty of tinkering I was thrilled when Stephen declared it essentially identical to his favorite. Mission accomplished (with less than half the calories and 75% less fat to boot)!

MAKES 2 SERVINGS

½ teaspoon cumin

¼ teaspoon paprika

⅛ teaspoon garlic powder

Scant ⅛ teaspoon cayenne pepper

1½ tablespoons light mayonnaise

1½ tablespoons plain nonfat Greek yogurt

1 finely minced jarred jalapeño or 4 drops jalapeño sauce

2 (8-inch) light high-fiber flour tortillas

⅓ cup finely chopped cooked chicken breast

1 green onion, chopped

3 tablespoons reduced-fat cheddar cheese

3 tablespoons reduced-fat mozzarella cheese

1. In a small microwave-safe bowl, combine the first 4 ingredients (cumin through cayenne pepper). Add 1½ tablespoons of water and microwave on high for 15 seconds to meld and soften the spices. Stir in the mayonnaise, yogurt, and jalapeño. Mix well and set aside.

2. Spray a medium nonstick skillet with cooking spray and place over medium-high heat. Spread a generous tablespoon of sauce on half of a tortilla. Top with half of the chicken, green onion, and cheeses. Fold the empty half of the tortilla over the cheese, press, place in the skillet, and cook until the bottom is browned. Spray the top lightly with cooking spray, flip, and cook until the bottom is browned and the cheese is melted. Cut into three triangles and repeat to make the second quesadilla.

NUTRITION INFORMATION PER SERVING (1 QUESADILLA): Calories 220 | Carbohydrate 25 g (Sugars 5 g) | Total Fat 5 g (Sat Fat 1g) | Protein 24 g | Fiber 7 g | Sodium 480 mg | Food Exchanges: 3 Lean Meat, 1½ Starch | Weight Watcher Smart Point Comparison: 5

Classic Quarter-Pound Burger with Special Sauce

SOMETIMES ONLY A GOOD OLD-FASHIONED CLASSIC BURGER WILL DO—a big juicy one with all the fixins—including some special sauce. The sauce for this burger was fashioned after the granddaddy of them all, the special sauce found at the Golden Arches. Adding a touch of breadcrumbs and egg white to the beef locks in the fat and moisture and yields a big quarter-pound cooked burger. Pile on the fresh toppings, melty cheddar, and sauce, and get ready to conquer that big beefy burger craving.

MAKES 4 SERVINGS

2 tablespoons light mayonnaise

2 tablespoons plain nonfat Greek yogurt

1 tablespoon sweet relish

2 teaspoons ketchup

½ teaspoon white vinegar

Salt and pepper, divided

1 pound lean ground beef

3 tablespoons breadcrumbs

1 large egg white

4 slices reduced-fat cheddar cheese

4 light or whole-grain hamburger buns

4 green leaf lettuce leaves

4 thick slices of tomato

4 slices red onion (optional)

1. To make the special sauce, in a small bowl, mix together the first 5 ingredients (mayonnaise through vinegar). Add a pinch of salt and set aside.

2. In a medium bowl, gently combine beef, breadcrumbs, and egg white. Divide mixture into 4 portions and flatten to form flat patties, making a slight depression in the center. Coat a large nonstick skillet with cooking spray and place over medium-high heat. Add patties, season with salt and pepper to taste, and cook for 3 to 4 minutes on each side, or until just cooked through. Top each with a slice of cheese.

3. Warm the buns in the microwave. Top the bottom of each bun with lettuce, tomato, onion, if desired, and a beef patty. Add a generous tablespoon of sauce and top with the top half of the bun.

> **DARE TO COMPARE:** This burger clocks in with one third fewer calories and less than half of the saturated fat, sodium, and points as compared to a Quarter Pounder (burger weight *before* cooking) with cheese. Feel free to add fries (page 70)!

NUTRITION INFORMATION PER SERVING (1 BURGER): Calories 330 | Carbohydrate 27 g (Sugars 5 g) | Total Fat 12 g (Sat Fat 5 g) | Protein 33 g | Fiber 6 g | Sodium 420 mg | Food Exchanges: 4 Lean Meat, 2 Starch | Weight Watcher Smart Point Comparison: 8

Western Bacon Chicken Sandwich

BACON PARTNERED WITH BARBECUE SAUCE is always a hit. Another is this sensational chicken sandwich that comes by way of Carl's Jr., home of the famous Western Bacon Cheeseburger. They actually no longer serve the chicken variation but it really doesn't matter because this at-home version offers the same scintillating sweet and smoky taste combination, only with less than half the calories and a fraction of the fat and carbs. The Extra Crispy Onion Rings on page 69 are a sensational sidekick.

MAKES 4 SERVINGS

4 slices center-cut bacon

4 boneless, skinless chicken breasts (about 1 pound)

Salt and pepper, to taste

4 slices reduced-fat cheddar cheese

4 whole-grain hamburger buns

4 large lettuce leaves

4 thick slices tomato

½ small red onion, sliced

¼ cup barbecue sauce

1. Place the bacon on a paper towel and microwave 4 to 5 minutes or until crisp.

2. Gently pound the chicken breasts to ¼-inch thickness, season with salt and pepper, and set aside. Spray a large nonstick skillet with cooking spray or heat a grill until hot, add chicken, and cook for 3 to 4 minutes on each side or until browned and almost cooked through.

3. Top each breast with a slice of cheese. Add 2 teaspoons water to skillet and quickly cover, or close cover on grill, to finish cooking chicken and melt cheese.

4. Warm the buns. Place 1 lettuce leaf, slice of tomato, and 1 slice of onion on each bun. Top with chicken, barbecue sauce, bacon, and the top half of the bun.

> **DARE TO COMPARE:** Carl's Jr.'s "Famous" Western Bacon Cheeseburger has 720 calories, 34 grams of fat (14 of them saturated), 70 grams of carb, and 1,460 milligrams of sodium.

NUTRITION INFORMATION PER SERVING (1 SANDWICH): Calories 320 | Carbohydrate 25 g (Sugars 5 g) | Total Fat 10 g (Sat Fat 4 g) | Protein 37 g | Fiber 4 g | Sodium 420 mg | Food Exchanges: 5 Lean Meat, 1½ Starch | Weight Watcher Smart Point Comparison: 5

Filet of Fish Sandwich

AIR FRY!
SEE PAGE 54

THE ICONIC SANDWICH KNOWN FAR AND WIDE as the Filet-O-Fish was invented in 1962, by Lou Groen, a McDonald's franchise owner, to make up for lost sales on Fridays when many of his customers didn't eat meat. It sold for 29 cents. After tasting one recently, I was reminded that it's the sauce and soft steamed bun that really makes the sandwich. But I also wanted more . . . more flavor, more freshness—and more actual fish. You get all of that with this sandwich, and air-fryer instructions too.

MAKES 2 SERVINGS

1½ tablespoons plus 2 teaspoons light mayonnaise, divided

1½ tablespoons plain nonfat Greek yogurt

1 tablespoon dill relish

½ teaspoon dried dill

⅛ teaspoon granulated sugar

¼ cup plain breadcrumbs

¼ teaspoon onion powder

⅛ teaspoon garlic salt

2 (4-ounce) white fish fillets, like pollock or cod

2 whole-grain hamburger buns

2 lettuce leaves

2 slices tomato

1. To make the tartar sauce, in a small bowl, mix together 1½ tablespoons mayonnaise with yogurt, relish, dill, and sugar. Set aside.

2. In a flat bowl, combine breadcrumbs, onion powder, and garlic salt. Lightly coat each fish fillet with 1 teaspoon mayonnaise and coat with crumbs. (To air-fry see page 54.)

3. Spray a medium nonstick skillet with cooking spray and place over medium-high heat. When skillet is hot, add fish and cook for 3 to 4 minutes, or until underside is browned. Spray top with cooking spray, flip, and cook until underside is browned and fish is cooked through (it should flake easily when tested with a fork).

4. Warm the buns in the microwave. Top each with lettuce, tomato, fish, 2 tablespoons tartar sauce, and the top half of the bun.

Marlene Says: *Though you barely taste it, the classic sandwich includes cheese. Feel free to add a piece of 2% American cheese if you please.*

NUTRITION INFORMATION PER SERVING (1 SANDWICH): Calories 220 | Carbohydrate 25 g (Sugars 5 g) | Total Fat 5 g (Sat Fat 1g) | Protein 24 g | Fiber 7 g | Sodium 480 mg | Food Exchanges: 3 Lean Meat, 1½ Starch | Weight Watcher Smart Point Comparison: 6

Chicken Pepperoni Parm Sandwich

TAKE CHEESY CHICKEN, SMOTHER IT IN SAVORY MARINARA SAUCE, top it with spicy pepperoni slices, and tuck it into a doughy bun. What's not to love? Arby's saucy Italian-inspired sandwich was clearly conceived to tantalize our taste buds; unfortunately, the sky-high amount of saturated fat and sodium are anything but lovable. After seeing an Arby's ad on television, my chicken parm–loving sons were excited when I told them I was giving this bad boy a go. They were even more delighted with the result!

MAKES 2 SERVINGS

1 boneless, skinless chicken breast (about 7 ounces)

1/4 cup low-fat buttermilk

3 tablespoons panko breadcrumbs

2 tablespoons shredded Parmesan cheese

¼ teaspoon dried oregano

⅛ teaspoon black pepper

1 teaspoon canola oil

⅓ cup Homemade Marinara (page 248) or store-bought

¼ cup shredded reduced-fat mozzarella cheese

8 slices turkey pepperoni

2 whole-grain hamburger buns

1. Cut the chicken breast in half and gently pound each piece to ¼-inch thickness. Pour the buttermilk into a shallow bowl, add the chicken, and let sit for 5 to 10 minutes.

2. In another shallow bowl, combine panko, Parmesan, oregano, and pepper. Remove chicken pieces from buttermilk and coat with crumb mixture.

3. Heat oil in a medium nonstick skillet over medium-high heat. Add chicken and cook on each side for 3 to 4 minutes or until browned and chicken is cooked through. Evenly spoon 2 generous tablespoons marinara, 2 tablespoons mozzarella, and 4 slices of pepperoni on each piece of chicken. Add 2 teaspoons of water to edges of pan, cover, and cook another 1 to 2 minutes or until cheese melts.

4. While the cheese melts, warm the buns. Place the saucy, cheesy chicken into the buns and serve.

> **DARE TO COMPARE:** The "limited-time only" Arby's Chicken Pepperoni Parm sandwich clocked in with 610 calories, a half a day's worth of saturated fat, and a whopping 1,900 milligrams of sodium.

NUTRITION INFORMATION PER SERVING (1 SANDWICH): Calories 280 | Carbohydrate 30 g (Sugars 6 g) | Total Fat 6 g (Sat Fat 2.5 g) | Protein 33 g | Fiber 6 g | Sodium 710 mg | Food Exchanges: 4 Lean Meat, 2 Starch | Weight Watcher Smart Point Comparison: 6

Primo Pico Guacamole Burger

"LAYERED WITH GUACAMOLE, FRESH PICO DE GALLO, creamy ranch sauce, and crisp lettuce"—this description for one of McDonald's newest burgers had me at guacamole—until I lifted the bun and uncovered a tiny smattering of avocado tangled with bits of tomato, onion, and shredded lettuce. Underwhelmed, I set out to make it right. Instead of ranch, I gave my spread some Mexican flair, topped it with a juicy lean burger and a large leaf of lettuce. Then I finished the burger off with a spoonful of "pico" and freshly mashed avocado. I think you will find it "excelente"!

MAKES 4 SERVINGS

2 tablespoons light mayonnaise

2 tablespoons nonfat Greek yogurt

¼ teaspoon Mexican hot sauce

1 pound lean ground beef

3 tablespoons dry breadcrumbs

1 large egg white

Salt and pepper, to taste

4 whole-grain hamburger buns

4 lettuce leaves

½ cup Pico de Gallo (page 243) or store-bought

1 medium ripe avocado

1. In a small bowl, mix together the mayonnaise, yogurt, and hot sauce. Set aside.

2. In a medium bowl, gently combine ground beef, breadcrumbs, and egg white. Divide mixture into 4 portions and flatten to form flat patties, making a slight depression in the middle. Coat a large nonstick skillet with nonstick cooking spray and place over medium-high heat. Add patties, season with salt and pepper to taste, and cook for 3 to 4 minutes on each side, or until just cooked through.

3. Warm the buns in the microwave. On the bottom of each bun, spread 1 tablespoon of mayonnaise mixture, top with a burger, lettuce, and 2 tablespoons pico de gallo. Lightly mash ¼ of the small avocado (about 3 tablespoons) onto the inside of the top half of the bun and close.

NUTRITION INFORMATION PER SERVING (1 BURGER): Calories 325 | Carbohydrate 28 g (Sugars 3 g) | Total Fat 14 g (Sat Fat 4 g) | Protein 29 g | Fiber 8 | Sodium 580 mg | Food Exchanges: 3 ½ Lean Meat | Weight Watcher Smart Point Comparison: 8

Crispy Chicken Strips with Ranch Dressing

AIR FRY!
SEE PAGE 54

FAST FOOD FOUND ITS MATCH in heaven when chicken strips were created. I found my own heavenly match when I first created this recipe for the air fryer. My son James—a chicken strip aficionado—was the judge for the coating. After several tries with various coating mixtures, he declared this mixture of two different breadcrumbs and a few flavorful seasonings as "the best." Buttermilk adds tenderness; the poultry seasoning a bit of Southern flair, and ranch dressing sends them over the top!

MAKES 4 SERVINGS

½ cup buttermilk

1 large egg white

½ teaspoon baking soda

1¼ pounds chicken tenders (about 8)

⅓ cup panko breadcrumbs

⅓ cup dry breadcrumbs

½ teaspoon seasoned salt

½ teaspoon black pepper

¼ teaspoon poultry seasoning

Ranch Dressing (page 247), or store-bought

1. Place a sheet pan in the oven and preheat to 425°F. (To air-fry see page 54)

2. In a large shallow bowl, whisk together buttermilk, egg white, and baking soda. Add chicken to buttermilk mixture and let sit for 5 minutes.

3. In another shallow bowl, combine next 5 ingredients (panko through poultry seasoning). Drizzle 1 tablespoon buttermilk into mixture, and mix well. Coat tenders, one a time, on all sides, with crumb mixture.

4. Spray a sheet pan with cooking spray. Place chicken strips on pan and bake for 8 minutes. Turn the strips, spray lightly with cooking spray, and bake for 5 to 6 more minutes or until nicely browned. Serve with ranch dressing.

> **DARE TO COMPARE:** An order of fast-food chicken tenders with 32 grams of protein like these also has 500 calories, twice as much sodium, and ten times the fat!

NUTRITION INFORMATION PER SERVING (2 STRIPS WITHOUT DRESSING): Calories 185 | Carbohydrate 11 g (Sugars 2 g) | Total Fat 2 g (Sat Fat 1 g) | Protein 32 g | Fiber 3 g | Sodium 435 mg | Food Exchanges: 4 Lean Meat, 1 Starch | Weight Watcher Smart Point Comparison: 4

Extra Crispy Onion Rings

AIR FRY!
SEE PAGE 54

EVERY RECIPE DEVELOPER WILL TELL YOU THAT no recipe is ever truly finished, because there is always the challenge to make it better or tastier. This recipe is an update on the extremely popular Oven-Baked Onion Rings in my first Eat What You Love *book. A change in the breadcrumb mixture renders them extra crisp and an air fryer cooks them faster. No Air Fryer? Rest assured, the oven also produces fabulous results. Crispy Chicken Strips (page 67) pair perfectly!*

MAKES 4 SERVINGS

1 large sweet onion (about ¾ pound), peeled

½ cup panko breadcrumbs

¼ cup finely crushed cornflakes

1 tablespoon cornmeal

½ teaspoon garlic powder

½ teaspoon onion powder

¼ teaspoon salt

Pinch of cayenne pepper (optional)

Pinch of black pepper

2 tablespoons all-purpose flour

½ cup buttermilk

1. Preheat the oven to 400°F. (To air-fry see page 54.)

2. Turn the onion on its side and cut 1-inch-thick slices. Separate slices into rings. In a wide, shallow bowl, mix together next 8 ingredients (panko through black pepper).

3. In a small bowl, whisk flour into buttermilk. Dip each onion ring into buttermilk mixture and then into crumbs using your hands to lift crumbs onto rings (a light misting of cooking spray can be used to help the crumbs stick). Spray breaded rings lightly.

4. Place the onion rings on a wire rack coated with cooking spray that has been placed on top of a baking or sheet pan. Bake the onion rings for 10 minutes, flip, and bake for an additional 10 to 12 minutes, or until crisp and golden brown.

Marlene Says: A combination of crumbs often creates the best coatings when oven "frying." In addition to their varying flavors, large particles create crispness, while fine ones fill the gaps and holes for a more complete coating.

NUTRITION INFORMATION PER SERVING (¼ ONION OR ABOUT 4 TO 5 RINGS): Calories 110 | Carbohydrate 23 g (Sugars 7 g) | Total Fat 1 g (Sat Fat 0 g) | Protein 4 g | Fiber 2 g | Sodium 240 mg | Food Exchanges: 1 Carbohydrate, 1 Vegetable | Weight Watcher Smart Point Comparison: 2

Air-Fried Seasoned Fries

I HESITATED TO INCLUDE A RECIPE FOR FRIES if I could not do them justice, but after cooking a batch of these in my air fryer, they earned their place. To be honest, they are not the crispest "fast-food" fries on the block (if that is prime priority for you), but they more than deliver when it comes to taste. Popping the "fries" into the microwave for a few minutes jump-starts the cooking and replaces the need to blanch or soak the potatoes for them to crisp and brown well.

MAKES 2 SERVINGS

1 large russet potato (about 10 ounces), unpeeled

1 teaspoon olive oil

Sprinkle of turmeric

½ teaspoon seasoned salt

½ teaspoon garlic powder

¼ teaspoon onion powder

⅛ teaspoon black pepper

1. Scrub the potato and cut in half lengthwise. Lay cut side down, and cut each half into ¼-inch slices. Lay slices down flat and cut into ¼-inch-long sticks. Place the fries on a large microwave-safe plate and microwave on high for 3 minutes, or until barely tender when checked with a fork.

2. While potatoes are cooking, preheat air fryer to 400°F.

3. Remove potatoes from the microwave, drizzle with olive oil and very lightly sprinkle with turmeric (just a touch to barely color them), and toss well. Sprinkle with the remaining spices and gently toss to coat. Dump the fries into the air fryer (a single layer browns best) and air-fry for 6 minutes. Shake the basket, and cook 5 to 6 minutes longer or until crisped and golden brown.

Marlene Says: *I do not recommend "oven-frying" the stick-cut fries as they stick too readily to the pan. You can, however, cut the potato into 12 wedges instead. Microwave them for 4 minutes, add an extra teaspoon of oil, and once seasoned cook them in the oven at 450°F for 15 minutes until nicely browned, turning halfway.*

NUTRITION INFORMATION PER SERVING (½ RECIPE): Calories 155 | Carbohydrate 28 g (Sugars 0 g) | Total Fat 3 g (Sat Fat 1 g) | Protein 4 g | Fiber 3 g | Sodium 285 mg | Food Exchanges: 1½ Starch, ½ Fat | Weight Watcher Smart Point Comparison: 4

Fast, Fresh Apple Pies

AIR FRY!
SEE PAGE 54

HANDHELD HOT APPLE PIES ARE AS SYNONYMOUS WITH McDONALD'S as are their signature burgers. In fact, they introduced their fried apple pie in 1968, the same year as the Big Mac. I also hesitated to add this recipe, but as with my Air-Fried Seasoned Fries, my air fryer convinced me otherwise. They're equally tasty when baked, but the fact they take just 10 minutes to cook to perfection in the air fryer is amazing.

MAKES 6 SERVINGS

3 cups peeled diced apple (about 2 apples)

½ teaspoon cornstarch

¾ teaspoon cinnamon

¼ cup granulated sweetener*

½ package refrigerated piecrust

Dusting of flour

1 teaspoon granulated sugar

*See page 36 for sweetener options.

1. Preheat the oven to 400°F (to air-fry, see page 54).

2. Heat a medium saucepan or pot over medium heat. Add the apple and sauté for 2 to 3 minutes or until fragrant. Mix the cornstarch into ½ cup of water. Add it along with the cinnamon and sweetener to the pot, stir, cover, and cook for 5 minutes or until the diced apples are soft.

3. While the apples are cooking, lay piecrust on cutting board and cut out three 5-inch circles. (I use a large oatmeal container lid.) Re-roll scraps and cut three more rounds (using a light dusting of flour if needed). Lightly roll each round to a 6-inch diameter and transfer crusts to a baking sheet.

4. Spoon 2 rounded tablespoons filling onto half of each crust. Carefully fold the empty crust over the filling and press edges to seal. With a sharp knife, make 2 to 3 slits on the top, and, if desired, trim rounded ends and front edge to form a more square shape. Repeat with remaining crusts and apple filling.

5. Lightly sprinkle sugar on top of pies and bake for 18 to 20 minutes or until the crusts are golden brown. Let cool slightly before serving.

> **DARE TO COMPARE:** Fast-food apple pies average double the calories and points, and three times as much sugar, as these.

NUTRITION INFORMATION PER SERVING (1 PIE): Calories 155 | Carbohydrate 23 g (Sugars 6 g) | Total Fat 8 g (Sat Fat 2.5 g) | Protein 1 g | Fiber 1 g | Sodium 160 mg | Food Exchanges: 1 Carbohydrate, 1 Fat, ¼ Fruit | Weight Watcher Smart Point Comparison: 5

Better-Than-Ever Thick and Creamy Milkshakes

WHEN I CREATED MY FIRST AMAZINGLY THICK AND CREAMY MILKSHAKE recipe with a mere one-half cup of ice cream, I was thrilled. Today I'm even more elated as the hottest thing in the freezer case are reduced-calorie pints of ice cream with more protein and less sugar. They allow me, and now you, to enjoy thick, creamy, sweet milkshakes with even more nutritional savings and bonuses than ever before. Use vanilla pudding and vanilla ice cream for a vanilla shake, chocolate pudding with chocolate ice cream for a double chocolate shake, or mix and match flavors to your heart, and waistline's, delight!

MAKES 1 SERVING

⅔ cup low-fat milk

1 tablespoon sugar-free instant pudding mix (vanilla or chocolate)

½ to ⅔ cup crushed ice

½ cup light low, low-sugar ice cream (like Halo Top)

2 teaspoons or 1 packet no-calorie sweetener (optional)

See page 36 for sweetener options.

1. Place the milk and pudding mix into a blender or a large glass (I use an immersion blender, which works perfectly), and blend to mix.

2. Wait about 30 seconds to allow milk to thicken, then add crushed ice (½ cup makes for a very thick shake, ⅔ cup a bit more frosty) and blend on high until the ice is incorporated. Add the ice cream and blend until smooth, thick, and creamy. Taste, add sweetener if desired (for true fast-food sweetness), and blend briefly again.

Marlene Says: *Dairy milk alternatives will not thicken instant pudding, nor the shake.*

DARE TO COMPARE: This shake has 75% fewer calories and 80% less fat, carbs, sugar, and points when compared to a single small Burger King chocolate shake. It also has 2 grams more protein.

NUTRITION INFORMATION PER SERVING: Calories 150 | Carbohydrate 19 g (Sugars 9 g) | Total Fat 2 g (Sat Fat 1 g) | Protein 13 g | Fiber 0 g | Sodium 380 mg | Food Exchanges: ⅔ Low-Fat Milk, ½ Carbohydrate | Weight Watcher Smart Point Comparison: 5

AMERICAN COMFORT

AMERICAN COMFORT

Red Velvet Pancakes with Cream Cheese Drizzle

Spinach & Mushroom Benedict Omelette

Hot Spinach Artichoke Dip

Crispy Chicken Avocado Egg Rolls

Classic Cobb Salad

Cheesecake Factory–Style Cajun Jambalaya Pasta

All-American Meat Loaf With BBQ Gravy

Cheesy Bacon Chicken with Honey-Mustard Drizzle

Pan-Seared Pork Tenderloin with Jack Daniel's Glaze

Herb-Crusted Salmon Fillet with Lemon Butter Sauce

Cheddar Bay snd Rosemary Parmesan Biscuits

Loaded Mashed Potatoes

20-Minute Fresh Strawberry Pie

Warm Chocolate Brownie Sundaes

Red Velvet Pancakes
with Cream Cheese Drizzle

INSPIRED BY IHOP'S FLUFFY RED VELVET PANCAKES, these tasty flapjacks are one heck of a way to start your day. With a delicate chocolate taste, the gorgeous color of red velvet cake, and a drizzle of cream cheese "icing," the only thing I've left out is the excess sodium, sugar, and calories! Add an egg or a glass of milk and fresh raspberries for a lovely (and healthy) way to round out your plate. (P.S. If you love these, you'll love the Small Batch Red Velvet Cupcakes on page 114.)

MAKES 4 SERVINGS

¼ cup light tub-style cream cheese

4 teaspoons powdered sugar, divided

1⅛ teaspoons vanilla extract, divided

3 tablespoons low-fat milk

1 cup all-purpose flour

3 tablespoons cocoa powder, preferably Dutch-process

3 tablespoons granulated sweetener*

1½ teaspoons baking powder

½ teaspoon baking soda

1 cup low-fat buttermilk

2 large eggs, beaten

2½ teaspoons red food coloring

*See page 36 for sweetener options.

1. In a small bowl, whisk together the cream cheese, 1 tablespoon powdered sugar, and ⅛ teaspoon vanilla. Whisk in the low-fat milk, 1 tablespoon at a time, and set aside.

2. In a medium bowl, whisk together next 5 ingredients (flour through baking soda). Make a well in the center, add buttermilk, eggs, food coloring, and remaining teaspoon of vanilla, and whisk just until combined.

3. Spray a nonstick skillet or griddle with cooking spray, and place over medium heat. Pour ¼ cup of batter per pancake into the skillet and spread into a 4-inch circle. Cook pancakes for 3 to 4 minutes, or until bubbles form on top and underside is firm. Flip and cook until done, about 2 to 3 more minutes. Stack on a plate and cover to keep warm.

4. To serve, stack 2 pancakes, drizzle with 1 tablespoon cream cheese topping and dust lightly with remaining 1 teaspoon of powdered sugar.

> **DARE TO COMPARE:** An order of Red Velvet pancakes at IHOP contains 640 calories, a staggering 1,820 milligrams of sodium, 118 grams of carbohydrate—and two days' worth of added sugar.

NUTRITION INFORMATION PER SERVING: Calories 230 | Carbohydrate 32 g (Sugars 6 g) | Total Fat 7 g (Sat Fat 3 g) | Protein 12 g | Fiber 2 g | Sodium 640 mg | Food Exchanges: 2 Starch, 1 Lean Meat | Weight Watcher Smart Point Comparison: 6

Spinach & Mushroom Benedict Omelette

THE INSPIRATION FOR THIS WEEKDAY-EASY yet Sunday-special omelette also comes by way of IHOP. Since omelettes are a favorite of mine, I naturally gravitated to that section of the menu when ordering breakfast at IHOP. What a shock. The omelettes had more calories than some of the dessert-style pancakes! The name of this omelette gives you a clue as to why—yep, the topping is a rich, creamy hollandaise sauce. Yum. The ingredient list may look long, but the recipe is quick & easy.

MAKES 1 SERVING

½ cup sliced mushrooms

2 green onions, chopped (white and green separated)

¾ cup fresh spinach

1 large egg

2 large egg whites (or ¼ cup egg substitute)

1 slice reduced-fat Swiss cheese

1 tablespoon light mayonnaise

1 tablespoon light sour cream

1 tablespoon liquid egg substitute

½ teaspoon lemon juice

½ teaspoon dried tarragon

½ teaspoon butter

¼ cup chopped tomato

1. Spray a medium nonstick skillet with cooking spray and place over medium-high heat. Add the mushrooms to pan and cook for 3 to 4 minutes, or until browned and slightly softened. Add the whites of green onion and cook for 30 seconds. Stir in spinach. As soon as it wilts, remove everything and set aside.

2. In a small bowl, whisk together egg and egg whites. Wipe out skillet, spray with cooking spray, and heat over medium heat. Add eggs, and as they cook, use a spatula to move cooked edges to center and swirl pan to allow uncooked egg to flow to edges. When top is mostly cooked, place cheese and spinach on one half and fold empty half over filling to form omelette. Add 2 teaspoons of water to skillet and cover.

3. While omelette steams (and cheese melts), in a small microwave-safe bowl whisk together next 6 ingredients (mayonnaise through butter). Place in microwave and heat at 50% power for 20 to 30 seconds or until warm (do not use full power as it will curdle). Remove and whisk again.

4. Top the omelette with hollandaise sauce and sprinkle with green onion parts and chopped tomato.

> **DARE TO COMPARE:** IHOP's Spinach & Mushroom Omelette with Swiss cheese and hollandaise has 890 calories—including a full day's worth of both fat and saturated fat. This awesome omelette has 75% fewer calories and 80% less fat—and an astounding 25 fewer "points"!

NUTRITION INFORMATION PER SERVING: Calories 235 | Carbohydrate 6 g (Sugars 2 g) | Total Fat 14 g (Sat Fat 5 g) | Protein 21 g | Fiber 1 g | Sodium 390 mg | Food Exchanges: 3 Lean Meat, 1 Vegetable, 1 Fat | Weight Watcher Smart Point Comparison: 4

Hot Spinach Artichoke Dip

WARM, CREAMY ARTICHOKE DIP appears on more appetizer menus—and at more holiday parties—than I can count. I developed this recipe for my first Eat What You Love *cookbook and can tell you that every time it was made for a television appearance, the production crew attacked it the minute we were off-air. Yes, it's that good. Cheesy, gooey, and packed with spinach, artichokes, and Parmesan cheese, it tastes anything but healthy. Serve it with baked tortilla chips or your favorite veggie dippers.*

MAKES 10 SERVINGS

⅓ cup light tub-style cream cheese

⅓ cup light mayonnaise

⅓ cup light sour cream

1 teaspoon minced garlic

¼ teaspoon black pepper

1 (14-ounce) can or (10-ounce) package frozen artichoke hearts, thawed, and drained

1 (10-ounce) package chopped frozen spinach, thawed and squeezed dry

½ cup white onion, finely diced

½ cup plus 2 tablespoons freshly grated Parmesan cheese, divided

1. Preheat the oven to 350°F.

2. In a medium bowl, mix together the first 5 ingredients (cream cheese through pepper). Chop the artichoke hearts, and add them with remaining ingredients, using ½ cup Parmesan, and stir until well combined.

3. Spread the dip into an 8-inch square or 1-quart baking dish. Sprinkle the remaining 2 tablespoons of Parmesan over the top and bake for 20 to 25 minutes, or until the dip is hot. Serve warm.

Marlene Says: *Feel free to assemble the dip ahead of time and refrigerate. Bring to room temperature and pop it in the oven just before serving.*

NUTRITION INFORMATION PER SERVING (¼ CUP): Calories 100 | Carbohydrate 5 g (Sugars 2 g) | Total Fat 6 g (Sat Fat 2.5g) | Protein 5 g | Fiber 1 g | Sodium 290 mg | Food Exchanges: 1 Vegetable, 1 Lean Meat, 1 Fat | Weight Watcher Smart Point Comparison: 2

Crispy Chicken Avocado Egg Rolls

SEE PAGE 54

"MASH-UPS" OF FAMILIAR FOODS ARE A HALLMARK of casual American comfort food restaurants—as tastefully exhibited in these exceedingly popular East meets West egg rolls. For my slimmed-down version, I use an air fryer. It creates a perfectly crisp, nongreasy wrapper to encase the tender chicken and buttery avocado. If you don't own one, oven instructions are on this page. The wrappers don't cook quite as evenly, but the result is equally tasty. Either way, don't skip the dressing. It brings everything together.

MAKES 8 SERVINGS

8 ounces ground chicken breast

½ teaspoon garlic salt

8 egg roll wrappers

8 teaspoons light tub-style cream cheese

¾ cup seeded, diced tomato

¼ cup minced red onion

1 medium avocado, thinly sliced

½ cup Ranch Dressing (page 247), or store-bought

1. Preheat the oven to 400°F. (To air-fry see page 54.)

2. Spray a medium nonstick skillet with cooking spray and place over medium-high heat. Add chicken, sprinkle with garlic salt, and cook for 3 to 4 minutes, using a fork to finely crumble the meat until cooked through.

3. To form egg rolls, lay an egg-roll wrapper down with a point toward you and spread 1 teaspoon of cream cheese across the center of the wrapper. Top with 2 tablespoons chicken, 1½ tablespoons tomato, 1½ teaspoons onion, and ⅛ of the avocado (about 2 thin slices). Using your finger, apply a dab of water to edges of wrapper. Fold closest point up over filling, fold in sides, and then roll the egg roll toward the far point. Repeat with remaining wrappers and filling.

4. Spray the egg rolls with cooking spray and place on a baking sheet. Bake for 10 minutes, turn, and bake for 5 more minutes or until crispy and brown. To serve, cut the egg rolls in half diagonally and serve each with 1 tablespoon dressing.

> **DARE TO COMPARE:** Kung Phooey. An order comprised of three Avocado Club Egg Rolls at California Pizza Kitchen weighs in with a hefty 1,240 calories and 82 grams of fat.

NUTRITION INFORMATION PER SERVING (1 EGG ROLL WITH DRESSING): Calories 155 | Carbohydrate 15 g (Sugars 1 g) | Total Fat 6 g (Sat Fat 2 g) | Protein 10 g | Fiber 2 g | Sodium 290 mg | Food Exchanges: 1 Starch, 1 Lean Meat, ½ Fat | Weight Watcher Smart Point Comparison: 4

Classic Cobb Salad

LEGEND HAS IT THAT THE NOW-FAMOUS COBB SALAD was created late one evening in 1936, by a food foraging Robert Cobb, owner of the Brown Derby restaurant in Hollywood. The restaurant is long gone, but 80 years later the iconic salad lives on. Gorgeously colorful, the original included chicken, bacon, blue cheese, tomato, chopped egg, and avocado, and so does this one. With its variety of tastes and textures, plenty of protein, and almost a pound of food per salad, it's what a meal salad is all about.

MAKES 2 SERVINGS

¼ cup Blue Cheese Dressing (page 244)

4 cups chopped romaine lettuce

1⅓ cups lightly packed shredded chicken breast

1 cup diced tomato

1 cup diced cucumber

½ cup diced avocado

2 hard-boiled eggs

2 tablespoons real bacon bits

1. Make the dressing and set aside.

2. For each salad, place 2 cups romaine lettuce in a large flat bowl or on a plate and distribute ⅔ cup chicken down the center. Arrange ½ cup tomatoes along one side of chicken, and ½ cup cucumber on the other. Distribute ¼ cup avocado next to tomato. Remove and discard the yolk from one egg, chop the white and remaining whole egg, and arrange half the eggs next to the cucumber on each salad.

3. Drizzle each salad with 2 tablespoons dressing and garnish with bacon bits.

DARE TO COMPARE: The average Cobb salad at a casual sit-down restaurant serves up over 1,000 calories, 70 grams of fat, and 2,000 milligrams of sodium. Homemade is so much better!

NUTRITION INFORMATION PER SERVING: Calories 305 | Carbohydrate 13 g (Sugars 6 g) | Total Fat 15 g (Sat Fat 4 g) | Protein 32 g | Fiber 5 g | Sodium 460 mg | Food Exchanges: 4 Lean Meat, 3 Vegetables, 1 Fat | Weight Watcher Smart Point Comparison: 5

Cheesecake Factory–Style Cajun Jambalaya Pasta

THERE WAS ABSOLUTELY NO WAY I COULD NOT INCLUDE my crave-worthy makeover of the #1 pasta dish at the Cheesecake Factory in a book inspired by restaurant favorites. "Shrimp and chicken sautéed with onion, tomatoes, and peppers in a spicy Cajun sauce served on linguine" is how they describe their preeminent pasta dish, and that's exactly what you'll get here. An excellent source of vitamins from A to E, along with iron, zinc, and potassium, this reader favorite delivers good health and great taste!

MAKES 4 SERVINGS

6 ounces linguine

8 ounces boneless, skinless chicken breast, cut into 1-inch pieces

5 teaspoons Cajun spice blend, divided

2 teaspoons olive oil

2 medium red or yellow bell peppers, sliced into strips

½ medium red onion, sliced into strips

8 ounces large raw shrimp, peeled and deveined

1 garlic clove, minced

¼ teaspoon ground black pepper

1 cup canned diced tomatoes, with juice

¼ cup reduced-sodium chicken broth

2 teaspoons butter

2 tablespoons fresh chopped parsley

1. Cook the pasta according to package directions and set aside.

2. Place chicken in a medium bowl and toss with 3 teaspoons (or 1 tablespoon) Cajun spice. Heat oil in a large nonstick skillet over medium-high heat. Add chicken and sauté for 3 to 4 minutes or until cooked halfway through. Add peppers, onion, and shrimp, and sauté another 1 to 2 minutes or until shrimp are pink.

3. Reduce heat to medium. Add garlic, pepper, remaining 2 teaspoons Cajun spice, tomatoes, and chicken broth to skillet and gently stir. Cook for 5 more minutes, stirring once or twice until chicken is thoroughly cooked and vegetables are tender. Swirl the butter into the sauce.

4. Place the pasta in a large bowl, toss with the sauce, and garnish with chopped parsley.

> **DARE TO COMPARE:** An order of Cajun Jambalaya Pasta at the Cheesecake Factory serves up 1,070 calories, over 50 grams of fat, and 100 grams of carbohydrate.

NUTRITION INFORMATION PER SERVING (1 ¾ CUPS): Calories 325 | Carbohydrate 38 g (Sugars 6 g) | Total Fat 6 g (Sat Fat 1 g) | Protein 30 g | Fiber 6 g | Sodium 790 mg | Food Exchanges: 3 ½ Lean Meat, 2 Starch, 1 Vegetable | Weight Watcher Smart Point Comparison: 6

All-American Meat Loaf With BBQ Gravy

WHEN I LIVED IN DUBLIN, OHIO, there was an American comfort food diner that served the most delicious meaty, yet tender meat loaf, glazed and served with a tangy, sweet spoonful of "BBQ gravy." This is my recreation of that marvelous meat loaf. My family likes it with my Loaded Mashed Potatoes, but it's equally good with a baked russet or sweet potato—which you can bake with the meat loaf. Add another veggie and create your own blue plate special! (A nonstarchy would be best, but we put another starchy one one ht plate in the photo!)

MAKES 5 SERVINGS

2 slices white or wheat bread

1 pound lean ground beef

½ cup diced onion

½ cup finely minced mushrooms

1 large egg, beaten

½ teaspoon garlic salt

¼ teaspoon black pepper

1 tablespoon plus 1 teaspoon Worcestershire sauce

1 (8-ounce) can tomato sauce, divided

2 tablespoons barbecue sauce

1 teaspoon molasses

1. Preheat the oven to 375°F. Line a 9 x 13-inch sheet pan with foil and set aside.

2. Crumble the bread into very small pieces in a large bowl, pour ¼ cup of water over bread, and mash with a fork to combine. Add next 6 ingredients (beef through pepper), 1 tablespoon Worcestershire, and ⅓ cup tomato sauce to bowl. Mix gently to combine (do not overmix to keep meat loaf light). Turn meat mixture onto baking pan and form into an 8 x 5-inch loaf.

3. In a small microwave-safe bowl, combine 1 teaspoon Worcestershire, remaining tomato sauce, barbecue sauce, and molasses. Spoon ¼ cup sauce on top of meat loaf, place in oven, and bake for 50 to 60 minutes until well browned and cooked through, or to an internal temperature between 155°F and 160°F.

4. Just prior to serving, add 1 tablespoon of water to remaining sauce and microwave on high for 1 minute. Serve each slice with 1 tablespoon BBQ gravy.

NUTRITION INFORMATION PER SERVING (1 SLICE WITH GRAVY): Calories 200 | Carbohydrate 12 g (Sugars 6 g) | Total Fat 8 g (Sat Fat 3 g) | Protein 21g | Fiber 2 g | Sodium 590 mg | Food Exchanges: 2 ½ Lean Meat, 1 Carbohydrate | Weight Watcher Smart Point Comparison: 5

Cheesy Bacon Chicken with Honey-Mustard Drizzle

I CAN HONESTLY TELL YOU THAT EVERY PERSON who has ever taken a bite of my version of Outback Steakhouse's most popular entrée, Alice Springs Chicken, immediately responds with "Oh, my goodness, YUM." This quick, easy, and ridiculously tasty take on that dish delivers juicy pan-seared chicken topped with tender cooked mushrooms, melty cheese, and crumbled bacon drizzled with lip-smacking honey-mustard sauce. Yum indeed!

MAKES 4 SERVINGS

4 boneless, skinless chicken breasts (about 1 pound)

1 tablespoon Dijon mustard

1 tablespoon light mayonnaise

1 tablespoon honey

2 teaspoons apple cider vinegar

2 teaspoons butter

1 (8-ounce) package sliced mushrooms

Black pepper, to taste

¾ cup shredded reduced-fat cheddar cheese

8 teaspoons real bacon bits

¼ cup sliced green onions tops

1. Gently pound the chicken breasts to between ½- to ¼-inch thickness. For the honey mustard, in a small bowl, whisk together the next 4 ingredients (mustard through vinegar). Set aside.

2. Melt butter in a large nonstick skillet over medium heat; add mushrooms and cook for 8 minutes, or until browned and tender. Remove from pan and set aside.

3. Coat skillet with cooking spray and turn heat to medium-high. Add chicken and cook for 3 minutes, or until underside is golden brown. Turn, and top each breast with ¼ cup mushrooms. Add pepper to taste, and sprinkle each breast with 3 tablespoons cheese and 2 teaspoons bacon. Add 2 tablespoons water to pan and immediately cover. Cook for 2 minutes, or until cheese is melted and chicken is cooked through.

4. To serve, top each breast with 1 tablespoon green onions and drizzle with a tablespoon of the honey-mustard sauce.

> **DARE TO COMPARE:** An order of Alice Springs Chicken at Outback Steakhouse (without sides) has 750 calories, 44 grams of fat, and 1,550 milligrams of sodium.

NUTRITION INFORMATION PER SERVING (1 TOPPED BREAST): Calories 265 | Carbohydrate 8 g (Sugars 5 g) | Total Fat 10 g (Sat Fat 5 g) | Protein 35 g | Fiber 1 g | Sodium 650 mg | Food Exchanges: 4 ½ Lean Meat | Weight Watcher Smart Point Comparison: 4

Pan-Seared Pork Tenderloin with Jack Daniel's Glaze

STEP INTO A TGI FRIDAYS RESTAURANT and you'll find their best-selling sweet and lightly spicy Jack Daniel's glaze served on everything from chicken and ribs to burgers and steak. It took me more than a few tries to figure out the formula for reducing 75% of the usual sugar (and half of the sodium too), but if you love Friday's JD glaze, I am confident you will love mine, too. This recipe yields ¾ cup of glaze; you will have a few tablespoons left over for another use.

MAKES 4 SERVINGS

¾ cup pineapple juice (or one 6-ounce can)

¼ cup granulated sweetener*

3 tablespoons reduced-sodium soy sauce

2 tablespoons lemon juice

1 tablespoon molasses

1 teaspoon minced garlic

⅛ teaspoon red chili flakes

2 teaspoons cornstarch

2 tablespoons Jack Daniel's whiskey

1¼ pounds trimmed pork tenderloin

Salt and black pepper, to taste

*See page 36 for sweetener options.

1. In a small pot, whisk together the first 7 ingredients (pineapple juice through chili flakes) plus ⅓ cup water. Place over medium heat, bring to a simmer, and simmer on low for 10 to 15 minutes, or until reduced by half. Dissolve the cornstarch in the whiskey and add to the pot. Stir and simmer until sauce thickens and clears, then cover, and turn heat to low.

2. While sauce simmers, slice pork into eight 1¼- to 1½-inch-thick pieces. Turn each piece onto the cut side and gently pound to ¼-inch thickness.

3. Spray a large nonstick skillet with cooking spray and place over high heat. Add the pork and sear for 2 minutes on each side, or until well browned, seasoning lightly with salt and pepper to taste. Place 2 slices of seared pork onto each serving plate and top with 2 tablespoons of the glaze.

Marlene Says: *A tablespoon of this glaze has 25 calories, 4 grams of carbohydrate (including 3 grams of added sugar), no fat, and 115 milligrams of sodium. It keeps in the fridge for at least a week, and can be used on anything from chicken to burgers.*

NUTRITION INFORMATION PER SERVING (¼ RECIPE): Calories 215 | Carbohydrate 11 g (Sugars 7 g) | Total Fat 5 g (Sat Fat 1.5 g) | Protein 30 g | Fiber 0 g | Sodium 310 mg | Food Exchanges: 4½ Lean Meat, ½ Carbohydrate | Weight Watcher Smart Point Comparison: 4

Herb-Crusted Salmon Fillet with Lemon Butter Sauce

DINNER FOR TWO, PLEASE! When you want to indulge in restaurant-quality dining without the hassle of waiting in line or worrying about your waistline, I highly recommend this dish. After enjoying the Herb Crusted Filet of Salmon at the Cheesecake Factory, I was thrilled when my salmon-loving husband declared this equally succulent adaptation, resplendent with a buttery lemon sauce, even better. Plate it with mashed potatoes and fresh asparagus for an easy yet extraordinary meal for you and a very lucky someone.

MAKES 2 SERVINGS

1 medium lemon

2 (5-ounce salmon) fillets

Salt and black pepper, to taste

1 teaspoon dried parsley

½ teaspoon dried tarragon

¼ teaspoon dried thyme

1 teaspoon canola oil

⅓ cup reduced-sodium chicken broth

⅓ cup white wine

1 garlic clove, finely minced

2 teaspoons flour (I like Wondra)

Pinch of seasoned salt

2 teaspoons butter

1. Grate ½ teaspoon of zest from the lemon. Squeeze the lemon juice into a bowl and reserve 1 ½ tablespoons for the sauce. Moisten each fillet with lemon juice and top with zest. Sprinkle with salt and pepper to taste. Blend parsley, tarragon, and thyme, and pat half onto one side of each fillet.

2. Heat oil in a medium nonstick skillet over medium-high heat. Place salmon herb-side down, and cook for 3 to 4 minutes, or until underside is browned. Turn salmon, add 2 tablespoons of water to the pan, cover, and cook for 3 to 4 more minutes, or until it flakes when tested with a fork.

3. While salmon is cooking, add broth, wine, and garlic to a very small pot. Simmer over medium heat until reduced by half (about 5 minutes). Mix flour with 1 tablespoon water and whisk into pot. Continue to whisk, and, when thickened, add the 1 ½ tablespoons reserved lemon juice and seasoned salt. Add butter and whisk until thick enough to lightly coat a spoon.

4. To serve, drape 1 tablespoon sauce over each salmon fillet and pool the remaining sauce around the salmon on the plates.

DARE TO COMPARE: Served with mashed potatoes and asparagus, the Herb Crusted Filet of Salmon at the Cheesecake Factory has 1,300 calories, with 48 grams—or over two days' worth—of saturated fat. Creamy All-Purpose Mashed Potatoes (page 208) and steamed asparagus add just 140 calories.

NUTRITION INFORMATION PER SERVING: Calories 280 | Carbohydrate 2 g (Sugars 0 g) | Total Fat 15 g (Sat Fat 4 g) | Protein 28 g | Fiber 0 g | Sodium 240 mg | Food Exchanges: 4 Lean Meat, 1 Fat | Weight Watcher Smart Point Comparison: 3

Cheddar Bay and Rosemary Parmesan Biscuits

CHEDDAR BAY BISCUITS ARE SYNONYMOUS WITH RED LOBSTER restaurants, and for good reason. Red Lobster serves 1 million of the beloved biscuits every day. And while I can't boast anything close to that, I was still very flattered when a dear colleague shared that she makes these biscuits every week. I think she will be quite excited to see, following Red Lobster's lead, I've also created a Rosemary Parmesan variation. And yes, they too get brushed with flavorful garlic butter.

MAKES 10 SERVINGS

2 cups reduced-fat baking mix (I like Bisquick Heart Smart)

½ teaspoon Old Bay seasoning

⅔ cup shredded reduced-fat sharp cheddar cheese

¾ cup low-fat buttermilk

2 tablespoons butter, melted

½ teaspoon garlic powder

1. Preheat the oven to 425°F. Lightly spray a large cookie sheet with cooking spray.

2. In a large bowl, mix together the baking mix and Old Bay. Add the cheddar and stir with a large spoon until combined. Add the buttermilk and mix until just combined.

3. Remove mixture from bowl and mix slightly with hands, if needed, to finish combining. Divide dough into 10 equal-size drop biscuits (about ¼ cup of dough each) and place on the prepared cookie sheet 2 inches apart. Bake for 13 to 15 minutes or until golden brown.

4. In a small bowl, combine the butter and garlic powder. Brush tops of biscuits with butter and serve warm.

Marlene Says: *To make* **ROSEMARY PARMESAN BISCUITS**, *omit cheddar cheese and add ½ cup finely shredded Parmesan and ½ teaspoon minced fresh rosemary to the baking mix. Before baking, sprinkle each biscuit with ¾ teaspoon Parmesan. Last, add ¼ teaspoon minced fresh rosemary to the garlic butter before brushing it onto the baked biscuits.*

NUTRITION INFORMATION PER SERVING (1 BISCUIT): Calories 130 | Carbohydrate 18 g (Sugars 2 g) | Total Fat 5 g (Sat Fat 2.5 g) | Protein 5 g | Fiber 0 g | Sodium 360 mg | Food Exchanges: 1 Starch, ½ Fat | Weight Watcher Smart Point Comparison: 4

Loaded Mashed Potatoes

IN KEEPING WITH THEIR AFFECTION FOR "MASH-UPS" (pun intended), restaurant chefs are constantly upping the flavor quotient of mashed potatoes by "loading" them up. This recipe was inspired by some I recently had while dining out. The extra flavor knockout punch came from sweet caramelized onions that were added to a garlicky mashed potato mix. Bacon topped them off. With such a flavorful blend, my addition of cauliflower to lighten them up magically disappears.

MAKES 6 SERVINGS

1 pound red potatoes, cubed, or 3 cups

4 cloves peeled garlic

3 cups cauliflower florets or riced cauliflower (fresh or frozen)

1½ cups chopped onion

1 teaspoon butter or oil

½ cup low-fat milk

⅓ cup light sour cream

¼ teaspoon salt, or to taste

¼ teaspoon black pepper

3 tablespoons real bacon bits (optional)

1. Place the potatoes and garlic in a large pot of cold water, bring to a boil, and cook for 5 minutes. Add the cauliflower and reduce the heat to medium low. Cook an additional 10 to 15 minutes, or until the potatoes are tender and the cauliflower soft.

2. While potatoes are cooking, place onions in a microwave-safe bowl and heat on high for 5 minutes. Heat butter in a medium nonstick skillet over medium heat and add onions. Cook, stirring occasionally, until soft and well browned, about 10 to 15 more minutes, adding a tablespoon or two of water as needed to keep onions soft and enhance browning.

3. Drain the potato mixture into a colander and, using a small pot lid or plate, press firmly on the mixture to remove excess water. Transfer mixture back into the pot and add milk, sour cream, and salt and pepper. Using a hand masher or an electric mixer, process just until smooth. Stir in the caramelized onions, adjust salt to taste, and top with bacon, if desired.

Marlene Says: While delicious, I find bacon an optional add-on depending on what I'm serving these with.

NUTRITION INFORMATION PER SERVING (⅔ CUP): Calories 115 | Carbohydrate 19 g (Sugars 6 g) | Total Fat 3 g (Sat Fat 1 g) | Protein 6 g | Fiber 3 g | Sodium 240 mg | Food Exchanges: 1 Starch, 1 Fat | Weight Watcher Smart Point Comparison: 3

20-Minute Fresh Strawberry Pie

WHEN LUSCIOUS STRAWBERRIES ARE IN SEASON, it's fresh strawberry pie time! Commercial kitchens often use strawberry-flavored, sugar-laced gels to bind the berries, but I have a better, tastier alternative. Flavorful frozen strawberries break down easier than fresh to create a glorious glaze economically, and in record time. Just add fresh berries and my crispy fast-fix crust and you've got a restaurant-worthy pie in under 30 minutes! (For a red, white, and blue pie, swap in some blueberries!)

MAKES 8 SERVINGS

½ package refrigerated piecrust (I like Pillsbury)

1 large egg white, beaten until frothy

1¼ cup frozen strawberries, lightly thawed

6 tablespoons granulated sweetener*

2 tablespoons cornstarch

2 tablespoons granulated sugar

1 tablespoon lemon juice

½ teaspoon orange zest

Pinch of salt

5 cups halved (or quartered if large) hulled strawberries

Light whipped topping, thawed (optional)

*See page 36 for sweetener options.

1. Preheat the oven to 425°F. Place the piecrust into a pie plate and crimp the edges. Prick the crust with a fork, line it with foil, and place dried beans or uncooked rice onto the foil to "weight" the crust. Bake for 15 minutes or until crust no longer looks raw when foil is lifted. Remove the weights and foil and brush the crust with egg white. Return to the oven and bake 3 to 4 more minutes or until the bottom of the crust just starts to brown. Set aside.

2. Place ¾ cup water and frozen strawberries in a medium saucepan. Use a fork to partially mash berries. Add sweetener, cornstarch, sugar, lemon juice, zest, and salt. Bring to a low simmer, and cook for 3 to 4 minutes, stirring and mashing the berries until glaze thickens and clears.

3. Place half of the fresh berries in the bottom of the crust, spoon half of the glaze over the berries, and gently move berries to coat. Add remaining berries and repeat. (Tip: For a picture-perfect pie, leave a few tablespoons of warm glaze in the saucepan and individually glaze and place the last few berries on the pie.) Chill for 2 hours before serving. Garnish with whipped topping, if desired.

> **DARE TO COMPARE:** Make it yourself and save. A piece of Fresh Strawberry Pie at Marie Callender's has 470 calories, 24 grams of fat, 60 grams of carb, 33 grams of sugar—and 19 points!

NUTRITION INFORMATION PER SERVING (1 SLICE): Calories 155 | Carbohydrate 25 g (Sugars 9 g) | Total Fat 6 g (Sat Fat 2 g) | Protein 2 g | Fiber 3 g | Sodium 160 mg | Food Exchanges: 1 Starch, 1 Fruit | Weight Watcher Smart Point Comparison: 5

Warm Chocolate Brownie Sundaes

SEE PAGE 54

WHEN I WAS IN HIGH SCHOOL, my friends and I would hit the local Bob's Big Boy to indulge in their Famous Hot Fudge Chocolate Cake layered with ice cream. Today, warm cookie sundaes are all the rage at many restaurants. I portion fudgy brownies for these guilt-free sundaes. You can prep or bake the brownies ahead of time, but be sure to reheat them right before serving for a warm gooey-chocolate-topped-with-cold-creamy-ice cream experience (all for less than 200 calories!). Add a cherry on top if you please. . . .

MAKES 4 SERVINGS

¼ cup semisweet chocolate chips

1 tablespoon butter or margarine

2 ½ tablespoons unsweetened applesauce

1 teaspoon vanilla extract

2 tablespoons brown sugar

¼ cup granulated sweetener*

1 large egg white

2 tablespoons cocoa powder

¼ teaspoon baking soda

⅓ cup all-purpose flour

1 cup light low- or no-sugar-added ice cream

8 teaspoons sugar-free ice cream topping

*See page 36 for sweetener options.

1. Preheat the oven to 350°F. Lightly spray four 6-ounce ramekins with nonstick baking spray and set aside.

2. Place chocolate chips and butter in medium bowl and microwave on high for 45 to 60 seconds (or until chocolate looks shiny and partially melted). Remove bowl from microwave and whisk until smooth. Whisk in applesauce, vanilla, and brown sugar, blending until smooth, and then add sweetener, egg white, cocoa powder, baking soda, and flour, whisking after each addition.

3. Spoon batter into ramekins, using about 3 tablespoons each. Bake for 10 to 12 minutes or until the center just springs back when lightly touched.

4. To serve, top each brownie with ¼ cup ice cream and drizzle with 2 teaspoons topping. (If made in advance, when cool, cover brownies tightly with foil or plastic wrap and warm in the microwave for 15 to 20 seconds before adding ice cream and topping.)

DARE TO COMPARE: Dessert for days! Friendly's restaurant's "Forbidden" Fudge Brownie Sundae has a staggering 1,000 calories, 140 grams of carbohydrates, 1 ½ days' worth of saturated fat, and 3 ½ days' worth of added sugar!

NUTRITION INFORMATION PER SERVING: Calories 195 | Carbohydrate 26 g (Sugars 12 g) | Total Fat 7 g (Sat Fat 3 g) | Protein 4 g | Fiber 3 g | Sodium 145 mg | Food Exchanges: 1½ Carbohydrate | Weight Watcher Smart Point Comparison: 8

SOUTHERN KITCHEN

SOUTHERN KITCHEN

Chicken 'N' Waffles

Crispy Cornmeal Waffles

Easy Southern Slaw

Sweet Potato Casserole

Cracker Barrel-Style Fried Apples

Shrimp and Cheesy Grits

Weeknight Chicken and Dumplings

15-Minute Cajun Catfish with Homemade Tartar Sauce

Simple Smothered Pork Chops for Two

Chicken Fried Chicken with Cream Gravy

Broccoli Bacon Mac and Cheese

Small Batch Red Velvet Cupcakes

Peanut Butter Icebox Pie

Peach and Cherry Cobbler

Chicken 'N' Waffles

SEE PAGE 54

FRIED CHICKEN AND WAFFLES DRIZZLED WITH SYRUP is the perfect blend of breakfast and lunch, so it made perfect sense that my son James requested this dish for his birthday brunch. The best part was making it together. Although neither the waffles (on page 100) nor the chicken are complicated, having one person on waffle duty while the other tends to the chicken is a fun and efficient way to put this brunch time favorite together. (While I LOVE the homemade waffles, frozen store-bought can be substituted.)

MAKES 4 SERVINGS

4 Crispy Cornmeal Waffles (page 100), or store-bought

½ cup low-fat buttermilk

1 large egg white

½ teaspoon baking soda

4 (3-ounce) boneless, skinless chicken breasts

1¼ cup cornflake cereal, crushed

½ teaspoon seasoned salt

½ teaspoon black pepper

¼ teaspoon poultry seasoning

Sugar-free maple syrup (optional)

1. Prepare the waffle batter according to the recipe and set aside. Preheat the oven to 425°F. (To air-fry the chicken see page 54).

2. In a large shallow bowl, whisk together buttermilk, egg white, and baking soda. Pound the chicken to ¼-inch thickness. Add chicken to buttermilk, turn once, and let sit for 5 minutes.

3. In another shallow bowl, combine next 4 ingredients (cornflake crumbs through poultry seasoning). Drizzle 2 teaspoons buttermilk mixture onto crumbs, and mix well. Remove chicken one piece at a time, letting excess buttermilk drip off, and coat with crumb mixture.

4. Cover a sheet pan with foil and spray with cooking spray. Place chicken on pan, spray top with cooking spray, and bake for 18 to 20 minutes, turning halfway through cooking, or until chicken is cooked through and nicely browned.

5. While the chicken is cooking, finish preparing the waffles. Top waffles with chicken and drizzle with syrup, as desired.

> **DARE TO COMPARE:** The Southern-Style Chicken and Waffles at Shari's Café and Pie Shop are served with both syrup and cream gravy. The price? A whopping 1,429 calories! Top each serving of these with a ¼ cup of savory Cream Gravy (page 111) for just 40 more calories!

NUTRITION INFORMATION PER SERVING (1 WAFFLE PLUS CHICKEN): Calories 310 | Carbohydrate 30 g (Sugars 3 g) | Total Fat 8 g (Sat Fat 1 g) | Protein 26 g | Fiber 1 g | Sodium 520 mg | Food Exchanges: 3 Lean Meat, 2 Starch | Weight Watcher Smart Point Comparison: 6

Crispy Cornmeal Waffles

ADDING CORNMEAL ADDS EXTRA TASTE AND TEXTURE to waffles, but can also weigh them down. Cornstarch and beaten egg white are the secrets to keeping these extra light and crispy. Waffle irons vary in the amount of batter required. As such, if you use one-third cup of batter per waffle you will get six waffles; one-half cup of batter will give you four. I use a rounded one-third cup in my waffle iron for five 7-inch round waffles. These freeze beautifully and can be popped into a toaster to reheat.

MAKES 4 TO 6 SERVINGS

½ cup cornmeal

¼ cup all-purpose flour

¼ cup cornstarch

2 tablespoons granulated sweetener*

½ teaspoon baking powder

¼ teaspoon baking soda

¼ teaspoon salt

1 cup buttermilk

2 tablespoons canola oil

1 large egg, separated

*See page 36 for sweetener options.

1. Preheat a waffle iron.

2. In a medium bowl, whisk together the first 7 ingredients (cornmeal through salt). Add the buttermilk, oil, and egg yolk, and whisk until just smooth. In a small bowl, whip the egg white until soft peaks form. Fold the egg white into waffle batter. (You can simply beat the egg white by hand until frothy, but the waffles will not be quite as airy and crisp).

3. Spray the preheated waffle iron with cooking spray. Pour a rounded ⅓ cup batter into the waffle iron, close cover, and cook until steam is no longer escaping from the waffle iron, and waffle is golden brown. Repeat with remaining batter. (See Marlene Says for keeping warm tips.)

Marlene Says: *Waffles are crispest hot off the waffle iron. To keep a batch warm and crispy, place a wire rack on a sheet pan, place cooked waffles on the rack in a single layer, and keep warm in a 200°F oven.*

NUTRITION INFORMATION PER SERVING (1 WAFFLE, YIELD OF 5): Calories 175 | Carbohydrate 24 g (Sugars 2 g) | Total Fat 6 g (Sat Fat 1 g) | Protein 4 g | Fiber 1 g | Sodium 280 mg | Food Exchanges: 1 Carbohydrate, 1 Fat | Weight Watcher Smart Point Comparison: 6

Easy Southern Slaw

CREAMY COOL COLESLAW KISSED WITH a touch of sweetness is a Southern staple. All too often, however, excessive mayonnaise and sugar mask the taste of the fresh ingredients (in addition to adding unnecessary calories). This slaw delivers the comfort of the classic dish with newfound freshness. If you prefer your slaw to have a bit of crunch, let it sit for less time (as little as 15 minutes). This is the ideal side for simple meat or fish entrées like the Cajun Catfish (page 107) or Smothered Pork Chops (page 108).

MAKES 4 SERVINGS

3 tablespoons light mayonnaise

3 tablespoons plain nonfat Greek yogurt

1 ½ tablespoons white vinegar

1 tablespoon granulated sugar

1 tablespoon buttermilk or low-fat milk

1 tablespoon finely minced onion

2 teaspoons lemon juice

¼ teaspoon salt, divided

4 cups cabbage, finely sliced or chopped

1 carrot, peeled and shredded

2 tablespoons fresh cilantro or parsley, chopped

Black pepper, to taste

1. For the dressing, whisk together the first 7 ingredients (mayonnaise through lemon juice) and ⅛ teaspoon salt.

2. For the salad, in a medium bowl, combine the cabbage and carrot. Add the dressing and let sit for 1 hour, or more. Just before serving, toss the slaw with the remaining ⅛ teaspoon salt, cilantro or parsley, and pepper to taste (I like just a pinch).

Marlene Says: *Bags of ready-to-use cabbage mix are a quick convenience and can be used here. Be sure to buy the regular, not the "angel hair" cut, as it is too thin to hold up to the creamy dressing.*

NUTRITION INFORMATION PER SERVING (¾ CUP): Calories 70 | Carbohydrate 10 g (Sugars 6 g) | Total Fat 3 g (Sat Fat 0 g) | Protein 2 g | Fiber 1 g | Sodium 250 mg | Food Exchanges: 1 Vegetable, 1 Fat | Weight Watcher Smart Point Comparison: 1

Sweet Potato Casserole

WHILE MANY THINK OF THIS SIDE DISH PRIMARILY AS A HOLIDAY TABLE TREAT, there are restaurants thoughtful enough to offer it any ol' day. Ruth's Chris Steakhouse is actually one of them, as are a multitude of Southern mom-and-pop diners including Doe's Eat Place in Greenville, Mississippi. Creamy pumpkin is a perfect partner for carbohydrate-rich sweet potatoes, and it stealthily lightens up some of the heft of this rich-tasting, sweet, creamy casserole, now complete with a buttery brown sugar, pecan–studded topping. Guest-worthy? Absolutely!

MAKES 6 SERVINGS

1 pound sweet potatoes or yams

1 cup canned pumpkin

½ cup nonfat half-and-half

1 large egg

1 large egg white

1 teaspoon vanilla extract

½ teaspoon cinnamon

¼ teaspoon salt

½ cup plus 2 tablespoons granulated sweetener, divided*

2 tablespoons brown sugar, divided

2 tablespoons margarine or butter, melted

3 tablespoons toasted chopped pecans

2 tablespoons all-purpose flour

*See page 36 for sweetener options.

1. Preheat the oven to 350°F. Coat a 1½-quart casserole or soufflé dish with nonstick cooking spray.

2. Pierce sweet potatoes with a fork and place in microwave. Cook on high for 10 minutes, or until flesh is soft. Slice sweet potatoes in half and scoop flesh into a large bowl (you should have about 2 cups). Mash in pumpkin and add next 6 ingredients (half-and-half through salt), along with ½ cup sweetener and 1 tablespoon each brown sugar and butter. Beat until smooth.

3. In a small bowl, combine the remaining 2 tablespoons granulated sweetener, 1 tablespoon brown sugar, 1 tablespoon butter, pecans, and flour. Spoon the sweet potato mixture into the casserole dish and smooth the top. Sprinkle the top with the nut mixture and bake for 20 minutes, or until the topping browns and the center puffs.

> **DARE TO COMPARE:** With a not-so-special 580 calories per serving, the Sweet Potato Casserole at Doe's Eat Place clocks in with more carbs than a piece of sugary pecan pie!

NUTRITION INFORMATION PER SERVING (½ CUP): Calories 165 | Carbohydrate 24 g (Sugars 10 g) | Total Fat 5 g (Sat Fat 1 g) | Protein 5 g | Fiber 3 g | Sodium 220 mg | Food Exchanges: 1 Starch, 1 Vegetable, 1 Fat | Weight Watcher Smart Point Comparison: 5

Cracker Barrel–Style Fried Apples

CUSTOMERS CAN'T GET ENOUGH OF THE FRIED APPLES dished up at Cracker Barrel. Served as a side dish at breakfast, lunch, and dinner, the sweet, gooey dessert-style side is a certified crowd-pleaser. I particularly enjoy these apples served with pork, but they are equally good served warm over a stack of pancakes or a scoop of ice cream. The addition of a mere tablespoon of brown sugar and a smidgen of butter at the end of cooking works like magic to create the familiar cravable taste.

MAKES 6 SERVINGS

4 cups sliced apples (about 4 medium apples)

2 tablespoons lemon juice

¼ cup granulated sweetener*

2 tablespoons cornstarch

⅛ teaspoon nutmeg

⅛ teaspoon salt

1½ teaspoons cinnamon

1 tablespoon brown sugar

2 teaspoons butter

See page 36 for sweetener options.

1. In a medium saucepan, toss the apples with the lemon juice. Add 1¾ cups of water, sweetener, cornstarch, nutmeg, and salt. Stir well and place over medium-high heat. Bring to a simmer, reduce heat to medium-low, cover, and cook for 12 to 14 minutes, or until apples are fork-tender.

2. Stir in the cinnamon, brown sugar, and butter, and cook for an additional minute, or until the apples are softened to your liking.

DARE TO COMPARE: Double Trouble: a side of Cracker Barrel Fried Apples has double the calories, carbs, and sugar of these.

NUTRITION INFORMATION PER SERVING (½ CUP): Calories 80 | Carbohydrate 17 g (Sugars 11 g) | Total Fat 1.5 g (Sat Fat 1 g) | Protein 0 g | Fiber 2 g | Sodium 65 mg | Food Exchanges: 1 Fruit | Weight Watcher Smart Point Comparison: 1

Shrimp and Cheesy Grits

THE FIRST TIME I HAD SHRIMP AND GRITS was on the Gold Coast of Florida while vacationing with friends. Soft, creamy, cheesy grits were topped with succulent, perfectly spiced shrimp bathed in diced tomatoes and smoky bacon. It was love at first bite. Unfortunately, the heaviness of the dish lingered far longer than the flavor. That is not a problem here. Brimming with cheesy goodness, plump shrimp, roasted tomatoes and, yes, smoky bacon, this quick-fix recipe is better-for-you-food at its very best. (My spice-loving husband tops his with a bit of hot sauce, and you can too!)

MAKES 4 SERVINGS

½ teaspoon paprika, divided

½ teaspoon garlic salt

¼ teaspoon black pepper

1 pound extra-large or jumbo shrimp, peeled and deveined

1 (15-ounce can) or 1 ¾ cups reduced-sodium chicken broth, divided

¾ cup quick grits (not instant)

⅓ cup reduced-fat shredded sharp cheddar cheese

2 tablespoons nonfat half-and-half

1 medium red bell pepper, diced

6 green onions, sliced (green and white separated)

1 (15-ounce) can fire-roasted diced tomatoes

2 tablespoons lemon juice

2 tablespoons minced fresh parsley

6 teaspoons real bacon bits

1. In a medium bowl, combine ¼ teaspoon paprika, garlic salt, and black pepper. Add the shrimp and toss to coat. Set aside.

2. In a small pot, bring 1 ½ cups broth and ¾ cup water to a boil, add grits, reduce heat to low, and simmer 6 to 8 minutes, stirring once or twice, until thickened and creamy. Stir in cheese and half-and-half. Turn off heat and cover to keep warm.

3. While grits are cooking, spray a large nonstick skillet with cooking spray and place over medium heat. Add red pepper and white parts of green onions and sauté for 7 to 8 minutes, or until peppers are softened. Add shrimp and cook for 30 seconds on each side, then add tomatoes (breaking them up with a fork), remaining ¼ teaspoon of paprika and ¼ cup broth. Stir, and cook for 3 to 4 minutes or until shrimp are cooked through and tomatoes are have broken down. Stir in the lemon juice and 1 tablespoon parsley.

4. For each serving top ¾ cup grits with ¼ of the tomato mixture and shrimp. Garnish with ¼ of the green onion tops, remaining fresh parsley, and bacon bits.

> **DARE TO COMPARE:** An order of Lowcountry Shrimp & Grits at Fatz Cafe in Charleston serves up 744 calories and a whopping 4,040 milligrams of sodium (yes, close to two days' worth, y'all).

NUTRITION INFORMATION PER SERVING (¼ RECIPE): Calories 285 | Carbohydrate 31 g (Sugars 4 g) | Total Fat 5 g (Sat Fat 2 g) | Protein 30 g | Fiber 2 g | Sodium 740 mg | Food Exchanges: 4 Lean Meat, 1 ½ Starch, 1 Vegetable | Weight Watcher Smart Point Comparison: 4

Weeknight Chicken and Dumplings

WHAT'S A SOUTHERN DINER WITHOUT CHICKEN AND DUMPLINGS? A rich-tasting savory base, fresh vegetables, and soft, fluffy, rosemary-scented homemade dumplings make this dish menu-worthy, while precooked chicken and canned broth make it weeknight-friendly. One pot and less than 30 minutes is all it takes to bring it to the table. Leftovers make a wonderful lunch the next day!

MAKES 4 SERVINGS

2 teaspoons olive oil

1 medium onion, chopped

4 medium carrots, peeled and chopped

3 medium celery stalks, chopped

1 ¼ teaspoons poultry seasoning

2 tablespoons all-purpose flour

2 (14-ounce) cans reduced-sodium chicken broth

½ cup plus ⅓ cup low-fat milk, divided

2 cups shredded cooked chicken breast

¼ teaspoon salt

⅔ cup reduced-fat baking mix

2 tablespoons cornmeal

½ teaspoon chopped fresh rosemary

1. In a large soup pot, heat the oil over medium heat. Add the onion and sauté for 3 minutes. Add the carrots, celery, and poultry seasoning, and sauté for 3 to 4 minutes, or until vegetables start to soften. Stir in flour and cook for 1 minute. Stir in broth, ½ cup milk, chicken, and salt, and bring to a boil. Reduce the heat to medium-low, and simmer for 5 minutes.

2. While soup simmers, in a medium bowl, stir together baking mix, cornmeal, rosemary, and remaining ⅓ cup milk, until a stiff batter forms. Drop by 1½ tablespoon portions onto the soup, spacing evenly for 8 dumplings. Cover pot and steam dumplings for 7 to 9 minutes, ensuring that soup stays at a low simmer.

3. Turn off the heat, uncover pot, and let sit for 2 minutes. Stir the soup carefully, without disturbing the dumplings, and serve.

NUTRITION INFORMATION PER SERVING (1½ CUPS): Calories 240 | Carbohydrate 20 g (Sugars 8 g) | Total Fat 8 g (Sat Fat 1 g) | Protein 21 g | Fiber 3 g | Sodium 690 mg | Food Exchanges: 2 Lean Meat, 1½ Starch, 1 Vegetable | Weight Watcher Smart Point Comparison: 3

15-Minute Cajun Catfish with Homemade Tartar Sauce

SKINNY AND SOUTHERN EATS DON'T TYPICALLY GO HAND IN HAND, but with this Cajun-style catfish dinner—clocking in with fewer than 200 calories—you can let the good times roll! In a mere 15 minutes, you'll be serving up perfectly seasoned fish topped with cool, creamy homemade tartar sauce. Balance out the spicy Cajun kick with my Easy Southern Slaw on page 101 (prep it ahead of time if you please) and round out the meal in record time with microwaved ears of corn or sweet potatoes.

MAKES 2 SERVINGS

2 (5-ounce) catfish fillets

1 teaspoon Cajun seasoning

2 tablespoons plain nonfat Greek yogurt

1 tablespoon light mayonnaise

½ teaspoon sweet pickle relish

2 teaspoons minced green onion

½ teaspoon granulated sugar

1. Pat the catfish dry. Sprinkle one side of each fillet with half the seasoning, and lightly mist the seasoned side of the fish with cooking spray.

2. Spray a large nonstick skillet with cooking spray and place over medium-high heat. When skillet is hot, add catfish, seasoned side down, and cook for 2 minutes. Flip and cook for 3 to 4 more minutes, or until fish is cooked through.

3. While the fish is cooking, combine remaining ingredients in a small bowl. Divide the tartar sauce in half and serve over the fish.

Marlene Says: *Feel free to vary your fish. Tilapia, cod, or even salmon would work well here.*

NUTRITION INFORMATION PER SERVING: Calories 185 | Carbohydrate 4 g (Sugars 2 g) | Total Fat 8 g (Sat Fat 1 g) | Protein 25 g | Fiber 0 g | Sodium 390 mg | Food Exchanges: 4 Lean Meat, 1 Fat | Weight Watcher Smart Point Comparison: 1

Simple Smothered Pork Chops for Two

HERE'S ANOTHER LICKETY-SPLIT RECIPE that's scaled for two (though doubling it is absolutely permitted). Simple, yet highly satisfying, the chops and the tangy knock-your-socks-off-slightly spicy buttermilk gravy that amply smothers them are both made in the same pan. I've taken a liking to pulling out my cast iron skillet for this recipe, but a sturdy nonstick skillet works great too. Fried Apples (page 103), cool Southern Slaw (page 101), and Broccoli Bacon Mac and Cheese (page 113) are all awesome sides.

MAKES 2 SERVINGS

¾ teaspoon onion powder

¾ teaspoon garlic powder

⅛ teaspoon salt

Slight pinch of cayenne pepper

2 (about 6-oz each) bone-in center-cut pork chops

2 tablespoons all-purpose flour

¼ teaspoon thyme

2 teaspoons canola oil

½ cup reduced-sodium chicken broth

¼ cup buttermilk

Black pepper, to taste

1. In a wide flat bowl, combine the onion and garlic powder, salt, and cayenne. Moisten the chops with water and rub ½ teaspoon of the spice mix onto one side. Add the flour and thyme to the spices in the bowl and mix well. Lightly dredge the pork chops in the flour mixture, tapping off the excess.

2. In a small bowl (or a large measuring cup), whisk remaining flour mix into the broth. Set aside.

3. Heat oil in a medium nonstick skillet over medium-high heat. Add pork chops and brown them well, cooking for about 2 minutes on each side. Remove pork chops from pan (they will be returned to finish cooking), and set aside. Whisk broth mixture again, pour into skillet, simmer until it thickens, and then whisk in buttermilk.

4. Return the pork chops to the skillet and simmer in the gravy for 3 to 4 minutes, turning once or twice, until the pork registers 145°F and the gravy is thickened to your liking.

Marlene Says: I love boneless, center-cut pork chops for their leanness and quicker cooking time, but opt for bone-in if you want to ensure a more tender chop.

NUTRITION INFORMATION PER SERVING (1 CHOP WITH GRAVY): Calories 265 | Carbohydrate 6 g (Sugars 2 g) | Total Fat 11 g (Sat Fat 3 g) | Protein 31 g | Fiber 0 g | Sodium 350 mg | Food Exchanges: 4 Lean Meat, ½ Starch | Weight Watcher Smart Point Comparison: 9

Chicken Fried Chicken
With Cream Gravy

SEE PAGE 54

WHEN A FAMOUS SOUTHERN-RAISED TELEVISION "FOODIE" HOST tells you that after tasting your dish he went home and made it himself, you know you hit the mark. Hearing it made me want to do the happy dance! Since this recipe first appeared in Eat More of What You Love, I've made it many times—often halving the recipe when it's just my husband and me (I simply halve the crumb mixture and use the full buttermilk soaking mixture). I've also tested "frying" the chicken in my air fryer, with delicious results—and now you can, too.

MAKES 4 SERVINGS

4 boneless, skinless chicken breasts, about 1 pound

6 tablespoons all-purpose flour, divided

1 large egg white

½ cup low-fat buttermilk

1 teaspoon baking soda

2 cups cornflake cereal, finely crushed

½ teaspoon onion powder

½ teaspoon garlic powder

⅜ teaspoon black pepper

¼ teaspoon dried thyme

⅛ teaspoon salt

1 tablespoon canola oil

Cream Gravy

1. Preheat the oven to 350°F. (To air-fry see page 54.) Gently pound the chicken to ¼-inch thickness. Set aside.

2. Place 2 tablespoons flour in a shallow bowl. In another shallow bowl whisk together egg white, buttermilk, and baking soda. In a third shallow bowl, mix remaining 4 tablespoons flour with next 6 ingredients (cornflake crumbs through salt).

3. Coat chicken with flour, dip into egg mixture, allowing excess egg to drip off, and coat with crumbs. Heat oil in a large non-stick skillet over medium-high heat. Add chicken and cook until undersides are golden brown. Spray top with cooking spray and turn. Cook 2 minutes and transfer pan to oven for 5 to 6 minutes or until cooked through.

4. While the chicken is baking prepare the Cream Gravy (next page). To serve, place each chicken "steak" on a plate and top with ¼ cup gravy.

CREAM GRAVY

1 slice center-cut bacon, cut in half

2 tablespoons all-purpose flour

1 cup reduced-sodium chicken broth

⅛ teaspoon black pepper

Pinch of thyme

3 tablespoons nonfat half-and-half

Pinch of salt (optional)

1. In a small saucepan, cook the bacon over moderate heat, turning until crisp. Remove the bacon, mince, and set aside.

2. Add flour to pan and slowly whisk in ½ cup of broth, stirring until smooth. Add remaining broth and pepper. Finely crush thyme between your fingers and into the gravy. Bring to a boil, reduce heat, and simmer for 3 to 4 minutes, whisking occasionally until gravy thickens.

3. Whisk in the nonfat half-and-half and the minced cooked bacon and simmer 1 more minute. Adjust salt to taste.

DARE TO COMPARE: Winner, winner, chicken dinner! At the Cotton Patch Café an order of Chicken Fried Chicken with cream gravy has 629 calories and 2,020 milligrams of sodium. Add a side of sweet potato casserole and cinnamon apples and the plate total jumps to 1,100 calories and almost a day's worth of carbs. A serving of my sweet potato casserole and fried apples added to this plate clocks in with less than half the calories—and just one-third of the carbs.

NUTRITION INFORMATION PER SERVING (1 BREAST WITH GRAVY): Calories 280 | Carbohydrate 22 g (Sugars 3 g) | Total Fat 8 g (Sat Fat 1 g) | Protein 29 g | Fiber 1 g | Sodium 600 mg | Food Exchanges: 3 ½ Lean Meat, 1 ½ Starch | Weight Watcher Smart Point Comparison: 6

Broccoli Bacon Mac and Cheese

THERE'S NO PLACE "SIDES" (OR BACON!) ARE MORE REVERED than in the South, where "meat-plus-three" diners dot the landscape, offering guests a choice of a "meat" entrée and three sides. I'm not sure if this mac and cheese laced with tender broccoli would count as one or two sides, but the pop of color and extra flavor the broccoli brings to the quintessential comfort food is a definite plus. Made on the stovetop, this recipe takes just 20 minutes. Oh yeah, it's also topped with bacon!

MAKES 6 SERVINGS

2 cups dry large elbow macaroni

3 cups fresh broccoli florets

¾ cup low-fat evaporated milk

½ cup reduced-sodium chicken broth

2 teaspoons cornstarch

½ teaspoon dry mustard

¾ teaspoon garlic salt with parsley

½ teaspoon onion powder

⅛ teaspoon black pepper

1¼ cups shredded reduced-fat sharp cheddar cheese, divided

3 tablespoons real bacon bits

1. Cook the pasta according to the package directions, adding the broccoli for the last 3 minutes of cooking. Drain, transfer back to the pot, and set aside.

2. While the pasta is cooking, make the sauce. Combine the next 7 ingredients (evaporated milk through pepper) in a small saucepan over medium heat, and whisk it until it comes to a low boil and thickens. Turn off heat, add 1 cup cheese, and whisk until the sauce is smooth.

3. Pour the cheese sauce over the pasta and broccoli and stir to combine, heating gently if needed to re-warm pasta. (If desired, transfer to a serving dish.) Lightly stir in or top the dish with remaining ¼ cup cheese, sprinkle with the bacon bits, and serve.

DARE TO COMPARE: A single cup of macaroni and cheese can have as much as 700 calories and 30 grams of fat. This satisfying creamy cheesy "mac" has less than half the usual carbs and one-third of the typical calories. A 1½-cup serving with a green salad on the side would make a great lunch.

NUTRITION INFORMATION PER SERVING (1 CUP): Calories 215 | Carbohydrate 26 g (Sugars 5 g) | Total Fat 6 g (Sat Fat 3 g) | Protein 14 g | Fiber 2 g | Sodium 410 mg | Food Exchanges: 1½ Lean Meat, 1 Starch, 1 Vegetable, | Weight Watcher Smart Point Comparison: 6

Small Batch Red Velvet Cupcakes

BAKING CAN BE A TRICKY BUSINESS. When I tried to create a smaller batch of my delicious one-bowl Red Velvet Cupcakes by simply halving the original recipe, it did not yield the results you richly deserve (to be honest, I'm still not quite sure why). With additional testing, this brand-new recipe gave me six tender, sweet, perfectly rounded cupcakes. Two beloved Southern ingredients—buttermilk and mayonnaise—make them marvelously moist and baking them low in the oven produces the ideal rise. My beloved Whipped Cream Cheese Frosting tops them beautifully.

MAKES 6 SERVINGS

1 large egg

6 tablespoons buttermilk

2 tablespoons light mayonnaise

2 tablespoons canola oil

⅓ cup granulated sweetener*

1 tablespoon brown sugar

2 teaspoons red food coloring

1 teaspoon vanilla

¾ cup cake flour

1 tablespoon cocoa powder

¼ teaspoon baking powder

¼ teaspoon baking soda

⅛ teaspoon salt

Whipped Cream Cheese Frosting (see Marlene Says)

*See page 36 for sweetener options.

1. Position a baking rack in the lower third of the oven and preheat the oven to 325°F. Line a nonstick 6-cup muffin tin with cupcake liners and lightly spray them with nonstick baking spray.

2. In a medium bowl, whisk egg until double in volume. Whisk in next 7 ingredients (buttermilk through vanilla), and then sift in flour, cocoa and baking powder, baking soda, and salt directly into the bowl and whisk until smooth.

3. Scoop the batter into prepared muffin cups and bake for 15 to 17 minutes, or until the center springs back when lightly touched or toothpick comes out clean. Cool completely and top with Whipped Cream Cheese Frosting.

Marlene Says: *For* **WHIPPED CREAM CHEESE FROSTING,** *in a small bowl with an electric mixer, beat together 2 tablespoons each reduced-fat and nonfat cream cheese with 2 tablespoons granulated no-calorie sweetener until smooth. Fold in ⅔ cup of light whipped topping.*

NUTRITION INFORMATION PER SERVING (1 CUPCAKE WITH FROSTING): Calories 160 | Carbohydrate 16 g (Sugars 4 g) | Total Fat 8 g (Sat Fat 2 g) | Protein 4 g | Fiber 1 g | Sodium 225 mg | Food Exchanges: 1 Carbohydrate, 1 Fat | Weight Watcher Smart Point Comparison: 5

Peanut Butter Icebox Pie

COOL, CREAMY, SOUTHERN ICEBOX PIES BEAT THE HEAT by keeping both the diners and the kitchen cool. And when they say "easy as pie," this is the pie they are talking about! Simply beat, fold, spoon, and chill for a spell to create this ridiculously rich-tasting, chocolate-crusted, creamy, two-step peanut butter pie (now that was a mouthful). Concerned about calories or carbs? Worry no more. This sweet gem has one-third the usual calories, less than half the carbs, and 75% less saturated fat, making it a cool treat for all.

MAKES 10 SERVINGS

½ cup peanut butter

4 ounces light tub-style cream cheese

4 ounces nonfat cream cheese, softened

½ cup granulated sweetener*

¼ cup low-fat milk

½ teaspoon vanilla extract

1 ¾ cups light whipped topping, thawed

1 store-bought Oreo Crust

1 tablespoon sugar-free chocolate ice cream topping

See page 36 for sweetener options.

1. In a large mixing bowl, using an electric mixer, cream the peanut butter and cream cheeses. Add the sweetener, milk, and vanilla, and beat until smooth. Fold in the whipped topping, and spoon the mixture into the crust.

2. Warm the chocolate topping and drizzle across the top in a decorative fashion. Refrigerate for at least 1 hour before serving.

DARE TO COMPARE: A traditional recipe for this Southern staple delivers a hefty 600 calories, 50 grams of carbohydrate, 16 grams of saturated fat—and 24 points—per slice.

NUTRITION INFORMATION PER SERVING: Calories 220 | Carbohydrate 19 g (Sugars 9) | Total Fat 13 g (Sat Fat 4 g) | Protein 7 g | Fiber 1 g | Sodium 280 mg | Food Exchanges: 1 Carbohydrate, 1 Medium-Fat Meat, 1 Fat | Weight Watcher Smart Point Comparison: 8

Peach and Cherry Cobbler

COLORFUL SWEET CHERRIES DOT THE PEACHY FILLING in this last Southern-style gem. Cobblers come with two different types of tops, either crumb-based or piecrust. This one is fashioned with the latter to take advantage of convenient foolproof refrigerated dough. I've also elected to make it fuss-free and year-round-friendly by using frozen fruit, but fresh peaches also work beautifully (use 4 cups peeled and sliced when fresh). I love it served warm with a small scoop of light vanilla ice cream.

MAKES 7 SERVINGS

24 ounces frozen peach slices (about 6 cups)

1 1/3 cups frozen dark sweet cherries

1 1/2 teaspoons vanilla

1/3 cup no-calorie sweetener*

1 tablespoon cornstarch

1/2 package refrigerated piecrust (I like Pillsbury)

1 large egg white, beaten

1 1/2 teaspoons granulated sugar

*See page 36 for sweetener options.

1. Preheat oven to 425°F. Coat a 7 x 11-inch or 2-quart baking dish with nonstick cooking spray.

2. In a large bowl, gently toss together peach slices, cherries, vanilla, and 2 tablespoons water. Add sweetener and cornstarch and toss to evenly coat fruit, spoon into baking dish, and set aside.

3. On a lightly floured surface, roll out piecrust to 12-inch diameter, then, using a sharp knife, trim about 1/2 inch of the edge on all four sides to create a rounded 11-inch square. Cut the crust into nine 1-inch-thick strips and place on top of the fruit in an alternating basket weave pattern to build a lattice crust using four strips for the length and five strips for the width (trimming to fit). Brush the piecrust with the egg white and sprinkle evenly with the sugar.

4. Bake for 40 to 45 minutes, until crust is golden brown, edges are bubbling, and peaches are tender when checked with a fork (they will soften slightly more once out of the oven).

> **DARE TO COMPARE:** A serving of peach cobbler at Texas-based Cotton Patch Café (without ice cream) has 534 calories. Counting carbs? It has 94 grams with 62 grams of sugar. Counting points? It has 20!

NUTRITION INFORMATION PER SERVING (SCANT 3/4 CUP): Calories 160 | Carbohydrate 27 g (Sugars 13 g) | Total Fat 6 g (Sat Fat 2 g) | Protein 4 g | Fiber 3 g | Sodium 145 mg | Food Exchanges: 1 Starch, 1 Fruit, 1 Fat | Weight Watcher Smart Point Comparison: 4

MEXICAN FAVORITES

MEXICAN FAVORITES

Huevos Racheros

5-Minute Red Chili Sauce

10-Minute Chicken Taquitos with
Creamy Avocado Salsa

Cheesy Chili Nachos

Shrimp Tostadas

Quick & Easy Queso Dip

Speedy Smothered Chicken Burritos

Chili's-Style Beef Fajitas

Better Burrito Bowls

Carnitas-Style Shredded Pork

Baja-Style Fish Tacos

Cilantro-Lime Fiesta Rice

Supremely Simple Refried Beans

Ice Cream–Stuffed Churro Tacos or Tostadas

Margaritas for Two, Two Ways

For the Love of

GLUTEN-FREE RECIPES

If you or someone you love is on a gluten-free diet or has sensitivity to gluten, it's comforting to know that most of Mother Nature's finest (and healthiest) foods are naturally gluten-free. Yep, fruits, vegetables, lean meats, seafood, beans, nuts, and eggs—as well as nutrient-rich dairy products and oils—are all gluten-free. Because I love to cook with these healthful ingredients, I'm excited to share that a great number of the recipes in this book are already G-free. Better yet, all but a handful of the remaining recipes can be made gluten-free using one simple ingredient swap! Here's a handy guide to assist you in cooking and eating gluten-free with this book.

GLUTEN-FREE RECIPES

When made according to the recipe*, these recipes are deliciously G-free!

COFFEEHOUSE, DONUT & SMOOTHIE SHOPS: Coffee Coolatta, McCafé-Style Frosty Caramel & Mocha Frappés, Strawberry Banana Smoothie, DIY Cold-Brew Mocha Iced Coffee, Almond Joy Hot Chocolate | **FAST-FOOD FIX:** Chicken, Apple, and Pecan Salad with Balsamic Vinaigrette, Air-Fried Seasoned Fries, Better-Than-Ever Thick and Creamy Milkshakes | **AMERICAN COMFORT:** Spinach & Mushroom Benedict Omelette, Hot Artichoke Spinach Dip, Classic Cobb Salad, Loaded Mashed Potatoes | **SOUTHERN KITCHEN:** Easy Southern Slaw, Cracker Barrel–Style Fried Apples, Shrimp & Cheesy Grits, Cajun Catfish with Homemade Tartar Sauce | **MEXICAN:** Huevos Rancheros, 5-Minute Red Chili Sauce, 10-Minute Chicken Taquitos with Creamy Avocado Salsa, Shrimp Tostadas, Quick & Easy Queso Dip, Chili's-Style Beef Fajitas, Better Burrito Bowls, Carnitas-Style Shredded Pork, Cilantro-Lime Fiesta Rice, Supremely Simple Refried Beans, Margaritas for Two, Two Ways | **ASIAN:** Stir-Fried Shrimp with Snow Peas, Pork Fried Rice | **ITALIAN:** Elana's Toscana Soup, 15-Minute Bruschetta Mussels, Chicken Marsala, Slow-Cooker Braised Beef Ragu, Shrimp Fra Diavolo, Chicken Caprese | **STEAKHOUSE:** Spectacular Wedge Salad with Balsamic Drizzle, Classic Shrimp Cocktail, Scampied Surf & Turf, Perfectly Cooked Steakhouse Fillet Topped Your Way, Succulent Lobster Tails with Seasoned Butter, Simply Steamed Lemon Butter Broccoli, Lawry's-Style Creamed Spinach, Creamy All-Purpose Mashed Potatoes | **CAFÉ BAKERIES—MORE SOUPS, SALADS, SANDWICHES & SWEETS:** Overnight Creamy Oats with Fruit and Nuts, Strawberry Chicken Poppy Seed Salad, My La Madeleine Tomato Basil Soup | **DIY RECIPE BUILDERS:** Quick 'N' Easy Breakfast & Italian Sausage, Pico de Gallo, Blue Cheese Dressing, Pickled Onions, Ranch Dressing Four Ways, Homemade Marinara, 1-Minute Hollandaise or Béarnaise Sauce, Chocolate Sauce Three Ways, All-Purpose Raspberry Sauce

When using the first ingredient if there is an option. Check labels on packaged goods, such as chicken broth and oats, to ensure the brand you buy is gluten-free.

GLUTEN-FREE WITH SIMPLE SWAPS

Virtually all the recipes in the book can be made gluten-free by swapping an ingredient or two. Better yet, today's vast array of gluten-free products makes it easier—and tastier—to do so than ever before. Here are some substitution and shopping tips.

ALL-PURPOSE FLOUR OR BAKING MIX: For thickening and light coatings on meat, substitute cornstarch (using half as much when used as a thickener instead of flour). Alternately, and for baking, I like Cup4Cup brand gluten-free "flour" due to its taste, texture, and structure. Use it anywhere flour is called for in both sweet and savory recipes and enjoy Red Velvet Pancakes with Cream Cheese Drizzle, Warm Chocolate Brownie Sundaes, Chicken 'N' Waffles, Easy Eggplant Parmesan, and Luscious Lemon Cream Cake. Bisquick Gluten Free Pancake & Baking Mix works great for the Quick 'N' Easy Blueberry Banana Breakfast Loaf, Cheddar Bay and Rosemary Parmesan Biscuits, and Weeknight Chicken and Dumplings.

BREAD AND BREADCRUMBS: Gluten-free bread can easily be found in most markets. For burgers, you can also go bunless by wrapping burgers like the Classic Quarter-Pound Burger with Special Sauce or Western Bacon Chicken Sandwich in lettuce leaves. For breadcrumbs, make your own, or purchase one of the many, including panko breadcrumbs available for Crispy Chicken Strips with Ranch Dressing, Extra Crispy Onion Rings, and Longhorn-Style Parmesan-Crusted Chicken.

GRAHAM CRUST/REGULAR CRUST: Swap in gluten-free chocolate cookies, graham crackers, or a ready-made graham-cracker crust for the Peanut Butter Icebox Pie, No-Bake Key Lime Pie Cups, New York Cheesecake with Raspberry Sauce, and Individual Black Bottom Cheesecakes for four. The remaining ingredients are gluten-free!

PASTA: Gluten-free pastas vary greatly in taste and texture. I find the best include corn, like Barilla brand and Schär (a good-tasting gluten-free brand). Make the simple swap and dig into pasta dishes like Cheesecake Factory–Style Cajun Jambalaya Pasta, Broccoli Bacon Mac & Cheese, Chicken Broccoli Alfredo, and Lazy Day Lasagna.

SOY SAUCE: Simply swap out soy sauce with tamari sauce for 10-Minute Wonton Soup, P.F. Chang's–Style Chicken Lettuce Wraps, Take-Out Teriyaki, Sweet & Sour Pork for Two, Better Beef & Broccoli, Mimi's Café Asian Chicken Salad, and Brown Sugar Bourbon Salmon.

TORTILLAS: I like Mission Brand Gluten-Free tortillas. They look and taste like regular flour tortillas and crisp perfectly. Use them to make a tasty Stephen's Taco Bell Chicken Quesadilla, Speedy Smothered Chicken Burritos, Ice Cream–Stuffed Churro Tacos, or Fast-Fix Pizza Margherita for One. La Tortilla brand is great for burritos and wraps.

Huevos Rancheros

AS IN AUTHENTIC MEXICAN RESTAURANTS, simplicity reigns in my version of this comfort dish. Fast-fix renditions often substitute salsa for ranchero sauce, but after testing the recipe multiple ways, my easy, flavorful 5-Minute Red Chili Sauce (oppostie page) was deemed muy bueno! In Mexico refried beans are usually served on the side—here many prefer them on the tortilla—I leave the choice up to you. Finely grated feta cheese is a perfect stand-in for less commonly-sold crumbly salty Mexican cotija.

MAKES 2 TO 4 SERVINGS

½ cup 5-Minute Red Chili Sauce (page 123)

4 (6-inch) corn tortillas

4 large eggs

Salt and black pepper, to taste

½ cup warm Supremely Simple Refried Beans (page 139) or fat-free canned*

2 tablespoons grated feta or Mexican cotija cheese

Cilantro sprigs (optional)

1. Make (or warm) the red chili sauce.

2. Place a large nonstick skillet over high heat. Spray tortillas with nonstick cooking spray and one by one (or more if your pan is big enough) cook tortillas a minute on each side, or until they soften, and then begin to crisp. Stack tortillas on a plate, cover, and set aside.

3. Spray skillet with cooking spray and crack eggs into pan. Season with salt and pepper to taste, and cook until whites are firm but yolks still soft, or to your taste. (I add a tablespoon of water to the skillet and cover it to allow the eggs to steam during the last minute or so.)

4. To assemble, if desired, spread 2 tablespoons beans onto each tortilla. Top with an egg and spoon 2 tablespoons of chili sauce onto the white portion of the egg (it's traditional to leave the yolk uncovered). Sprinkle with ½ tablespoon cheese, and garnish with cilantro, if desired. Serve with warmed beans on the side if you have not spread them on the tortilla.

Marlene Says: *Beans are a great way to add fiber to your morning. One-quarter cup of refried beans is enough to top two tortillas, but may feel a bit small as a side. Each additional quarter cup adds 60 calories, 10 grams of carb, and 3 grams of fiber.*

NUTRITION INFORMATION PER SERVING (EACH): Calories 160 | Carbohydrate 15 g (Sugars 1 g) | Total Fat 7 g (Sat Fat 2 g) | Protein 10 g | Fiber 3.5 g | Sodium 350 mg | Food Exchanges: 1 Medium-Fat Meat, 1 Starch, ½ Fat | Weight Watcher Smart Point Comparison: 2

5-Minute Red Chili Sauce

IT MAY BE HARD TO BELIEVE THAT IN FIVE SHORT MINUTES you can make a richly flavored chili sauce better than any you can buy in a can, but you absolutely can! In addition to smothering burritos (see page 131) and creating saucy Huevos Rancheros, this skinny, fat-free sauce can be used for everything from saucing chicken or beef for tacos and enchiladas to spooning it over a Mexican-inspired omelette. Once made, it will keep for at least a week in the refrigerator.

MAKES ABOUT 1 CUP

¼ teaspoon garlic powder

2 ¼ teaspoons chili powder

1 teaspoon all-purpose flour

½ teaspoon ground cumin

½ teaspoon sugar

¼ teaspoon dried oregano

Pinch of salt, or to taste

½ cup tomato sauce

1. Place a small saucepan over medium heat and add all the ingredients except the tomato sauce. Stir until fragrant, about 30 seconds.

2. Whisk in the tomato sauce and ½ cup of water to the spice mixture, stir well, and simmer on low for 2 to 3 minutes or until the sauce thickens slightly.

NUTRITION INFORMATION PER SERVING (SCANT ¼ CUP): Calories 15 | Carbohydrate 3 g (Sugars 2 g) | Total Fat 0 g (Sat Fat 0 g) | Protein 1 g | Fiber 1 g | Sodium 230 mg | Food Exchanges: Free Food | Carbohydrate Choices: 0 | Weight Watcher Smart Point Comparison: 0

10-Minute Chicken Taquitos With Creamy Avocado Salsa

SEE PAGE 54

I MAKE THESE AMAZINGLY CRISPY TAQUITOS in no time flat by "frying" them in my air fryer for five minutes, but you can also bake them for 10 short minutes instead. If that were not enough, the made-in-a-flash blenderized avocado salsa is a standout on its own. Compared to guacamole, not only does it stretch the deliciousness and yield of one avocado, it also lowers the calories. Perfect for taquitos, tacos, or salads—or as a dip for chips—it's my new favorite taqueria sauce.

MAKES 4 SERVINGS

TAQUITOS

8 thin corn tortillas*

1½ cups cooked shredded chicken breast

1 (4-ounce) can diced roasted green chilies (optional)

½ cup reduced-fat Mexican cheese blend

8 teaspoons chopped green onions

AVOCADO SALSA

1 medium ripe avocado (about ¾ cup mashed)

2 tablespoons lime juice

¾ teaspoon garlic salt with parsley

¼ teaspoon onion powder

Pinch of pepper

*I use Mission brand thin corn tortillas. They do not break as easily as other brands upon rolling.

1. Preheat oven to 400°F. Line a baking sheet with foil and spray with cooking spray. (To air-fry see page 54.)

2. To make the taquitos, microwave 2 tortillas at a time on high for 30 seconds. Spread 3 tablespoons chicken near the front edge of a tortilla, top with 2 teaspoons chilies, if desired, 1 tablespoon cheese and 1 teaspoon green onions. Roll tortilla over meat into a tight roll and place seam-side down on baking sheet (or plate if air-frying). Repeat with remaining tortillas.

3. Spray taquitos lightly with cooking spray and bake for 10 minutes or until tortillas are crisp. (They will crisp slightly more upon cooling for a minute or two.)

4. While taquitos are baking, combine all of the salsa ingredients and 1¼ cups water in a blender and puree until smooth. (Alternatively, use a large container or jar and an immersion blender.) Adjust water for desired thickness. Serve taquitos with sauce.

DARE TO COMPARE: An order of four crispy Chicken Taquitos at the Cheesecake Factory, served with avocado cream and salsa verde, has 1140 calories and 65 grams of fat. You'll find my recipe for Pico de Gallo on page 243.

NUTRITION INFORMATION PER SERVING: (2 TAQUITOS WITH 2 TABLESPOONS SAUCE): Calories 190 | Carbohydrate 18 g (Sugars 0 g) | Total Fat 3 g (Sat Fat 1 g) | Protein 18 g | Fiber 2 g | Sodium 200 mg | Food Exchanges: 1½ Lean Meat, 1 Starch, ½ Fat | Weight Watcher Smart Point Comparison: 4

Cheesy Chili Nachos

MY INCREDIBLE QVC FOOD STYLIST, CAROLE, has made hundreds of my recipes for on-air presentation. This is one of her (and my) all-time favorites. Perfectly seasoned meaty "chili" sits atop crunchy tortilla chips and is then draped in "liquid gold." After presenting the nachos on TV, Carole and I promptly dig into them, thrilled not only by the wonderful mix of texture and taste, but also because we can enjoy them guilt-free! Garnish with green onion, cilantro, or sour cream if you please.

MAKES 4 SERVINGS

8 ounces lean ground turkey

¾ cup diced onion

½ cup diced red bell pepper

½ cup fire-roasted diced tomatoes

1½ teaspoons chili powder

1 teaspoon cumin

Pinch of cayenne pepper

½ cup canned black beans, rinsed and drained

2 teaspoons margarine or butter

2 teaspoons all-purpose flour

½ cup reduced-sodium chicken broth

Pinch of garlic powder

1 cup shredded reduced-fat cheddar cheese

3 ounces reduced-fat tortilla chips (about 25 chips)

1. Spray a medium nonstick skillet with cooking spray and place over medium-high heat. Add the ground turkey, onion, and red bell pepper to the pan and cook for 10 minutes, breaking meat apart with a spoon until the meat is browned and the vegetables are soft.

2. Stir in next 4 ingredients (tomatoes through cayenne) and stir thoroughly. Add ½ cup water, reduce heat to low, cover, and cook for 10 minutes, stirring occasionally. Stir in beans and heat until warmed; cover, and remove from heat.

3. In a small saucepan over low heat, melt margarine, add flour, and whisk until smooth. Whisk in chicken broth and garlic powder, bring to a simmer, and whisk for 1 minute, or until sauce thickens. Remove from heat and whisk in cheese ½ cup at a time.

4. Spread the chips onto a serving platter. Spoon the chili mixture evenly onto the chips, drizzle with the cheese sauce, and add any additional desired toppings.

> **DARE TO COMPARE:** Typical of most restaurant nacho appetizers, the Chili Cheese Nachos at Applebee's have 1,680 calories, 107 grams of fat, 133 grams of carbohydrates, and 3,850 milligrams of sodium!

NUTRITION INFORMATION PER SERVING (ABOUT 6 LOADED CHIPS): Calories 160 | Carbohydrate 12 g (Sugars 4 g) | Total Fat 7 g (Sat Fat 2 g) | Protein 13 g | Fiber 3 g | Sodium 260 mg | Food Exchanges: 2 Lean Meat, 1 Starch | Weight Watcher Smart Comparison: 9 (with 99% lean ground turkey: 5)

Shrimp Tostadas

SEND YOUR PALATE ON A TRIP TO COASTAL MEXICO, where I was first introduced to this type of light, colorful, and oh-so-tasty tostada. You'll be treated to a crispy-edged tortilla, layered with creamy beans and plump tender shrimp (using my new favorite cooking method), mingled with fresh salsa and a splash of citrus—topped off with creamy slices of avocado. As an appetizer or for smaller appetites, a single tostada is adequately filling, but as they are so light and tasty, for a meal I usually eat two.

MAKES 2 TO 4 SERVINGS

1⅛ teaspoons salt, divided

8 ounces large shrimp (21 to 25 count), peeled and deveined

Juice of 1 medium orange (about ⅓ cup)

Juice of 1 large lime (about ¼ cup)

⅓ cup diced, seeded, and peeled cucumber

⅓ cup finely chopped red onion

1 tablespoon finely diced jalapeño (optional)

4 corn tortillas

1 large tomato, seeded and diced

1 tablespoon chopped cilantro, plus leaves for garnish

½ cup warm Supremely Simple Refried Beans (page 139) or fat-free canned

½ medium avocado, sliced

1. Combine 3 cups of water and 1 teaspoon of salt in a medium pot and bring to a boil over high heat. Add the shrimp and immediately remove from heat. Let shrimp sit for 3 minutes, or until just cooked through; drain, and transfer shrimp to a cutting board.

2. Chop shrimp into ½-inch pieces and place in a medium bowl. Add orange and lime juice, and ⅛ teaspoon salt, and stir. Stir in cucumber, onions, and jalapeño, if desired. Let sit for about 15 minutes to allow flavors to meld.

3. While shrimp is marinating, heat a medium skillet over high heat, spray tortillas with nonstick cooking spray, and one by one (or more if your pan is big enough) cook tortillas a minute or so on each side, until they soften, and then partially crisp. Stack tortillas on a plate, cover, and set aside.

4. Stir the tomato and cilantro into the shrimp mixture. To make each tostada, spread 2 tablespoons beans onto a tortilla and top with ⅓ cup of the shrimp mixture. Garnish tostada with a few slices of avocado and cilantro leaves.

Marlene Says: *When buying shrimp, look for the "count," rather than descriptions of size, like small, medium, or large, which may vary by brand. The count tells you how many shrimp are in each pound. The smaller the count, the larger the shrimp!*

NUTRITION INFORMATION PER SERVING: Calories 165 | Carbohydrate 20 g (Sugars 4 g) | Total Fat 4 g (Sat Fat 0.5 g) | Protein 13 g | Fiber 4 g | Sodium 260 mg | Food Exchanges: 1½ Lean Meat, 1 Starch, ½ Vegetable, ½ Fat | Weight Watcher Smart Point Comparison: 2

Quick & Easy Queso Dip

IF YOU LOVE QUESO, YOU KNOW HOW ADDICTIVE the warm, melty Mexican cheese sauce is. That's why I'm thrilled to say that when it comes to ooey, gooey, flavor-packed queso, this version delivers the goods! You can assemble the ingredients ahead of time, but for the best quality, prepare it just before serving. When serving as a dip, keep calories in check by serving veggie dippers, warm corn tortillas, and/ or baked tortilla chips. As a sauce, spoon over nachos, fajitas, taquitos, carnitas, or even burgers!

MAKES 6 SERVINGS

¾ cup reduced-sodium chicken broth

½ cup low-fat milk

2 teaspoons cornstarch

¾ teaspoon garlic salt

¼ teaspoon ground cumin

1 cup shredded reduced-fat cheddar cheese

1 (4-ounce) can fire-roasted diced green chilies

⅓ cup shredded reduced-fat mozzarella cheese

½ cup seeded, chopped tomato, or Pico de Gallo (page 243)

1. In a medium saucepan, whisk together the first 5 ingredients (broth through cumin) over medium heat, until bubbles form and the mixture thickens.

2. Reduce heat and stir in cheddar cheese until smooth. Drain or spoon off excess juice from green chilies and add to dip. Stir until evenly incorporated, move off the heat, add mozzarella, and stir just until cheese melts.

3. Pour the queso into a bowl, top with chopped tomatoes, and serve immediately.

DARE TO COMPARE: An order of White Spinach Queso at Chili's serves up 1,510 calories, 93 grams of fat and 3,630 milligrams of sodium. It's meant for sharing, but even eating half of it will have you gobbling down a meal's worth of calories before your entrée ever arrives.

NUTRITION INFORMATION PER SERVING (¼ CUP): Calories 90 | Carbohydrate 4 g (Sugars 3 g) | Total Fat 4 g (Sat Fat 3 g) | Protein 10 g | Fiber 1 g | Sodium 280 mg | Food Exchanges: 1 Medium-Fat Meat | Weight Watcher Smart Point Comparison: 3

Speedy Smothered Chicken Burritos

MY FAMILY LOVES TEX-MEX and they are big fans of stuffed, saucy, smothered burritos (or, as Baja Fresh calls them, enchilados). To get them on the table pronto, I start with rotisserie chicken meat, which I dress up with canned fire-roasted tomatoes, black beans, and warm Mexican spices. I then slather the assembled burritos with rich chili sauce and adorn them with cheese and more toppings. Let's just say you get the whole enchilada with these bodacious smothered burritos.

MAKES 2 SERVINGS

6 tablespoons warm 5-Minute Red Chili Sauce (page 123)

½ teaspoon chili powder

½ teaspoon ground cumin

¼ teaspoon dried oregano

¼ teaspoon garlic salt

½ cup fire-roasted tomatoes

½ cup canned black beans, rinsed and drained

1 cup shredded chicken breast

2 (8-inch) light high-fiber flour tortillas

1½ cups shredded lettuce

3 tablespoons shredded reduced-fat Mexican blend cheese

2 tablespoons light sour cream

½ cup chopped fresh tomato (optional)

1. Make the chili sauce. Set aside.

2. While sauce is simmering, combine chili powder, cumin, oregano, and garlic salt in a medium nonstick skillet and place over medium heat. Warm spices for 30 seconds, then add the fire-roasted tomatoes. Mash large tomato pieces with a fork, heat for 1 minute to blend spices, add beans, and fold in chicken.

3. Microwave tortillas on high for 20 to 30 seconds to soften and warm. Place ½ cup lettuce on each tortilla, leaving 1 inch uncovered at one end, and top with ½ cup chicken filling. Fold in empty end, and then sides to form a burrito with one end open.

4. Place burritos onto serving plates. Blanket each with 3 tablespoons very warm chili sauce and immediately sprinkle with cheese. (If you want the cheese meltier, heat the burrito in the microwave for 30 seconds.) Top each with ¼ cup lettuce and a dollop of sour cream and chopped tomatoes, if desired.

DARE TO COMPARE: An Enchilado Chicken Nacho Burrito at Baja Fresh has 1,590 calories, 32 grams of saturated fat, and 3,760 grams of sodium. It includes queso and rice. A quarter cup of rice would add 50 calories, a quarter cup of my queso 90. Add both, and you still would need to eat four of these to equal the calories of one of theirs!

NUTRITION INFORMATION PER SERVING: Calories 270 | Carbohydrate 34 g (Sugars 4 g) | Total Fat 6 g (Sat Fat 3 g) | Protein 27 g | Fiber 11 g | Sodium 650 mg | Food Exchanges: 3 Very Lean Meat, 2 Starch, 1 Vegetable | Weight Watcher Smart Point Comparison: 4

Chili's-Style Beef Fajitas

ONE OF MY FAVORITE MEXICAN RESTAURANT ENTRÉES is a piping-hot fajita platter with lightly caramelized strips of peppers and onions. Chili's Grill & Bar is known for their sizzling fajitas, but what isn't widely known is that a single order of beef fajitas with all the fixins clocks in with over 1,600 calories and a staggering 5,660 milligrams of sodium! My recipe offers the same fabulous flavors of their signature dish for a whole lot less, and you get to pick the fixins.

MAKES 6 SERVINGS

¼ cup lime juice

5 teaspoons olive oil, divided

1½ teaspoons minced garlic, divided

2 teaspoons reduced-sodium soy sauce

½ teaspoon liquid smoke

½ teaspoon cumin

½ teaspoon cayenne pepper

¼ teaspoon chili powder

1½ pounds flank or sirloin steak

1 large onion, sliced

3 medium bell peppers cut into ½-inch slices

2 tablespoons sweet vermouth or water

¼ teaspoon salt

Warm tortillas (for serving)

¾ cup store-bought salsa or Pico de Gallo (page 243)

1. For the marinade, whisk together the lime juice, 2 tablespoons water, 3 teaspoons oil, 1 teaspoon minced garlic, and next 5 ingredients (soy sauce through chili powder). Place steak in a large bowl or ziplock bag, top with the marinade, cover or seal, and refrigerate for at least 30 minutes or up to 24 hours.

2. Heat a grill to medium-high. Grill the steak for 4 to 5 minutes on each side, or until cooked to medium rare or medium (130°F to 135°F with a meat thermometer). Cover and set aside.

3. While steak is cooking, heat remaining 2 teaspoons oil in a large nonstick pan over medium-high heat. Add onions and peppers and sauté, stirring frequently, for 6 to 8 minutes, or until crisp tender. Add ½ teaspoon of garlic and sauté for an additional minute. Add sweet vermouth (or water) and salt, and continue stirring until vegetables are soft and slightly caramelized.

4. Once the steak has rested 10 minutes, slice against the grain into very thin slices. Tuck the meat into warm tortillas with the onions and peppers and serve with salsa.

NUTRITION INFORMATION PER SERVING (WITHOUT TORTILLAS): Calories 210 | Carbohydrate 8 g (Sugars 4 g) | Total Fat 9 g (Sat Fat 3 g) | Protein 26 g | Fiber 2 g | Sodium 380 mg | Food Exchanges: 3 Lean Meat, 1 Vegetable | Weight Watcher Smart Point Comparison: 4

Better Burrito Bowls

LIKE MOST FOLKS, MY SON STEPHEN FIGURED IF he ditched the tortilla and ordered his burrito in a bowl he would be making a healthier choice and saving calories. To his surprise, he found the calories, carbs, and sodium in his bowl still really stacked up! This big bowl has mouthwatering layers of bean-and-corn-studded rice, sizzling peppers and onions, your choice of protein, lettuce, fresh pico de gallo, and creamy avocado, with 50% of the calories, 67% less fat, and a fraction of the sodium of an in-kind bowl. A better bowl indeed!

MAKES 2 SERVINGS

1⅓ cups Cilantro-Lime Fiesta Rice (page 138)

1 medium onion, sliced

1 medium bell pepper, sliced

1 teaspoon canola oil

1 garlic clove, minced

1 tablespoon sweet vermouth or water

⅛ teaspoon salt

1 cup cooked shredded chicken, carnitas, or beef

⅔ cup shredded lettuce

½ cup Pico de Gallo (page 243) or store-bought salsa

½ medium ripe avocado, sliced

2 tablespoons light sour cream (optional)

1. Prepare or warm leftover rice. Set aside.

2. Place onions and peppers in a large microwave-safe bowl and cook on high for 2 minutes.

3. Heat the oil in a large nonstick skillet over medium-high heat. Add onion mixture and garlic, and cook for 3 to 4 minutes, or until peppers are crisp-tender, stirring occasionally. Add vermouth (or water) and salt. Continue to cook, stirring occasionally, for 5 minutes, or until onions and peppers are soft and slightly caramelized.

4. In 2 bowls, layer half the rice, onions and peppers, and then the meat. Top each with lettuce, pico de gallo or salsa, sliced avocado, and sour cream, if desired.

DARE TO COMPARE: A chicken burrito bowl at Chipotle, layered with rice, beans, corn, peppers and onions, chicken, lettuce, salsa, and guacamole, has 855 calories and 1,590 grams of sodium. Using Carnitas-Style Shredded Pork (page 134) adds 60 calories and 5 grams of fat.

NUTRITION INFORMATION PER SERVING (1 BOWL WITH CHICKEN): Calories 320 | Carbohydrate 39 g (Sugars 6 g) | Total Fat 9 g (Sat Fat 1 g) | Protein 22 g | Fiber 8 g | Sodium 560 mg | Food Exchanges: 2 Lean Meat, 2 Vegetable, 1½ Starch, 1 Fat | Weight Watcher Smart Point Comparison: 2

Carnitas-Style Shredded Pork

MOIST AND TENDER WITH CRISPY EDGES, Mexican-style shredded pork is divine, whether served on a plate or tucked into a taco, enchilada, or burrito—but that heavenly taste usually comes with a hefty nutritional price. Fortunately, I've found a way to significantly reduce the fat in this classic meat dish without losing texture or flavor. This recipe yields about four cups of tender meat. Be sure to use some of it for the pork carnitas variation of my Better Burrito Bowls and Speedy Smothered Chicken Burritos.

MAKES 8 SERVINGS

2 to 2 ½ pounds boneless pork loin roast

1 teaspoon ground cumin

¾ teaspoon dried oregano

1 teaspoon onion powder

½ teaspoon black pepper

2 smashed garlic cloves

1 bay leaf

½ medium orange, halved

1 teaspoon garlic salt

1. Preheat the oven to 300°F. Slice the pork loin vertically and then horizontally to make four even pieces.

2. Spray a large ovenproof pot with cooking spray and place over high heat. Sear pork until all sides are brown, remove from pot, and set aside. Reduce heat to medium, add ½ cup water, and stir to deglaze pot.

3. Combine cumin, oregano, onion powder, and pepper in a small bowl. Coat pork with spice mixture and return to pot with garlic and bay leaf. Squeeze juice of the orange into pot (removing any seeds), and add the spent orange pieces and 1 ½ cups water. Cover pot, place in the oven, and cook for 1 ½ hours, or until meat shreds easily with a fork.

4. Transfer the pork to a cutting board, discard bay leaf and orange, and using two forks shred the meat apart and spread it onto a baking sheet. Simmer and reduce the liquid in the pot until it is thick enough to coat a spoon. Pour ½ cup of the liquid over the meat to moisten it, and toss. Just before serving, turn on the broiler, sprinkle meat with garlic salt, place pan in top third of the oven, and broil for 3 to 4 minutes, or until the edges of the meat are browned and slightly crisped.

> **DARE TO COMPARE:** A single carnitas taco topped simply with onions, cilantro, and salsa at Una Mas Mexican Grill has 460 calories with a hefty 27 grams (or more than half its calories) from fat.

NUTRITION INFORMATION PER SERVING (½ CUP): Calories 140 | Carbohydrate 0 g (Sugars 0 g) | Total Fat 5 g (Sat Fat 2 g) | Protein 22 g | Fiber 0 g | Sodium 145 mg | Food Exchanges: 2 ½ Lean Meat | Weight Watcher Smart Point Comparison: 2

Baja-Style Fish Tacos

WHEN I WAS FIRST introduced to Baja-style fish tacos in San Diego in 1987, Rubio's was the only place that was serving them. Now it's hard not to find them on a Mexican restaurant menu. The must-haves for me that really set Baja-style tacos apart are the creamy white sauce and the finely shredded cabbage. To keep them fresh tasting and light, rather than battering and frying the fish I simply coat it with a flavorful flour mix and pan-sauté. I dare you not to get hooked on these.

MAKES 4 SERVINGS

3 tablespoons light mayonnaise

3 tablespoons plain nonfat Greek yogurt

¾ teaspoon garlic salt, divided

⅛ teaspoon Tabasco sauce

1 pound white fish (about 4 fillets)

2 tablespoons all-purpose flour

½ teaspoon chili powder

½ lime, cut into wedges

1 tablespoon canola oil

8 (6-inch) thin corn tortillas

2 cups finely shredded cabbage

Fresh cilantro for garnish

½ cup salsa or Pico de Gallo (page 243)

1. In a small bowl, whisk together the mayonnaise, yogurt, 3 tablespoons water, ⅛ teaspoon of the garlic salt, and the Tabasco.

2. Pat fish fillets dry. In a shallow bowl, combine flour, chili powder, and remaining garlic salt. Squeeze lime wedges over fish, and dredge in flour mixture. Heat oil in a large nonstick skillet over medium-high heat. Pan-sauté the fish for 3 minutes on each side, or until slightly browned and fully cooked.

3. Stack the tortillas, wrap them in a damp paper towel, and microwave on high for 1 minute.

4. Assemble the tacos by dividing each piece of fish between two tortillas. Tuck the cabbage into the tacos, drizzle 1 tablespoon of sauce over fish and cabbage, and garnish with cilantro. Serve with salsa and wedges of lime.

DARE TO COMPARE: Batter up! With 330 calories, 28 grams of carb, and 20 grams of fat (and just 9 grams of protein), one battered Original Fish Taco at Rubio's has more calories than two of these!

NUTRITION INFORMATION PER SERVING (2 TACOS): Calories 290 | Carbohydrate 31 g (Sugars 4 g) | Total Fat 7 g (Sat Fat 1 g) | Protein 27 g | Fiber 5 g | Sodium 500 mg | Food Exchanges: 3 Very Lean Meat, 1½ Starch, ½ Vegetable, 1 Fat | Weight Watcher Smart Point Comparison: 5

Cilantro-Lime Fiesta Rice

SUBTLY SEASONED WITH A HINT OF LIME AND FRESH CILANTRO, Chipotle's Cilantro Lime Rice a favorite among diners. Not only is it a tasty side dish, it's also a flavorful filling and layering component for many of their entrées. The addition of fiber-rich black beans, colorful red peppers, and sweet corn makes this rice dish healthier and an even more versatile side, filler, and layering ingredient for all your Mexican-inspired needs—like my Better Burrito Bowls (page 133)! Once made, it keeps for days.

MAKES 4 SERVINGS

⅔ cup dry instant brown rice (see Marlene Says)

¾ cup canned black beans, rinsed and drained

¼ cup frozen corn, thawed

⅓ cup diced red bell pepper

1 medium green onion, white and green parts, finely diced

Juice of 1 medium lime

2 tablespoons chopped cilantro

¼ teaspoon salt

1. Cook the rice according to package directions. Remove from heat and fluff with a fork.

2. Immediately add the beans, corn, red peppers, green onions, and lime juice to the rice, and toss gently to combine. Cover and let sit for 3 to 4 minutes to warm the added ingredients. Remove cover, stir in cilantro and salt.

Marlene Says: *Please note, when preparing instant brown rice, the ratio of water to rice varies by brand. I use Uncle Ben's Instant Brown Rice that combines ⅔ cup dry rice cooked with 1¼ cups water to yield about 2 cups cooked. Follow package instructions of the brand you are using to make 2 cups of cooked rice.*

NUTRITION INFORMATION PER SERVING (¾ CUP): Calories 135 | Carbohydrate 27 g (Sugars 1 g) | Total Fat 1 g (Sat Fat 0 g) | Protein 4 g | Fiber 4 g | Sodium 250 mg | Food Exchanges: 1½ Starch | Weight Watcher Smart Point Comparison: 1

Supremely Simple Refried Beans

THESE EASY 10-MINUTE UN-FRIED BEANS ARE TASTIER (with less sodium) than any in a can and healthier (with less fat) than any from a taqueria. Serve these creamy frijoles for breakfast with Huevos Rancheros (page 122), for lunch on a Shrimp Tostada (page 128), or for dinner alongside Carnitas-Style Shredded Pork (page 135) or Baja-Style Fish Tacos (page 136). I make them most often with black beans; pinto beans are more traditional.

MAKES 4 SERVINGS

1 teaspoon olive oil

⅓ cup chopped green onions

1 teaspoon jarred minced garlic

½ teaspoon chili powder

¼ teaspoon ground cumin

1 (15-ounce) can reduced-sodium black or pinto beans

¼ teaspoon oregano

⅛ teaspoon salt, or to taste

1. In a medium saucepan, heat the oil over medium heat. Add the green onions and garlic, and sauté for 2 to 3 minutes, or until the onion is soft.

2. Add the chili powder and cumin, stir to warm, then add the beans (with their liquid) and oregano. Cook for 5 minutes on low, stirring occasionally. Add 2 tablespoons of water, and using an immersion blender or potato masher, mash the beans until roughly smooth. Add more water, if needed for desired consistency, and adjust salt to taste.

Marlene Says: *"Seasoned" is another way to say additional salt. Seasoned canned refried beans average close to 600 milligrams a serving and restaurant versions even more. Salt will need to be adjusted based on the brand of beans you buy.*

NUTRITION INFORMATION PER SERVING (⅓ CUP): Calories 90 | Carbohydrate 17 g (Sugars 1 g) | Total Fat 1 g (Sat Fat 0 g) | Protein 5 g | Fiber 7 g | Sodium 190 mg | Food Exchanges: 1 Starch | Weight Watcher Smart Point Comparison: 0

Ice Cream–Stuffed Churro Tacos or Tostadas

IMPRESSIVE AND UTTERLY IRRESISTIBLE, these sweet treats are also easy to make! While the directions may look long, shaping the crispy taco shells is not difficult, and, once frozen, they keep for weeks. Or, if you prefer, simply create crispy cinnamon-and-sugar-laced tostada shells instead. Either way, you and your guests will be amazed at how delectable the combination of a crunchy cinnamon-and-sugar-laced tortilla and creamy, sweet ice cream can be.

MAKES 4 SERVINGS

1 tablespoon granulated sugar

¾ teaspoon cinnamon

4 (6-inch) low-carb flour tortillas*(I like Mission Carb Balance)

2 cups light reduced-sugar or no-sugar-added vanilla ice cream

4 teaspoons sugar-free chocolate or caramel sundae sauce or homemade Chocolate Sauce (page 250)

Note: Not all higher-fiber tortillas crisp well. Mission Carb Balance tortillas do. If you can't find the 6-inch "Fajita" size, buy the "Taco" size and trim them down.

1. Preheat the oven to 375°F. In a small bowl, combine the sugar and cinnamon.

2. **FOR TACOS,** lightly spray both sides of a tortilla with cooking spray, lay flat, and sprinkle 1 side with ½ teaspoon of cinnamon-sugar. Flip tortilla and repeat with ¼ teaspoon of cinnamon-sugar, sprinkling most of it around the outer rim.

3. Loosely roll up 4 sheets of aluminum foil and flatten slightly to make inserts about 4 inches wide and 1½ inches high. Place tortilla with heavier, sugared side down flat onto a baking sheet. Place insert on half of tortilla and fold uncovered side over insert to create a taco shell (leave it short of covering entire bottom half to create "rim" per photo). Press on tortilla lightly to keep insert intact and repeat.

4. Bake for 10 to 12 minutes or until lightly browned and crispy. Slip out foil and let shells cool. With a small spoon, carefully stuff each shell with ½ cup ice cream and drizzle or decorate each with 1 teaspoon chocolate sauce. Freeze until ice-cream firms, or until ready to serve.

5. **FOR TOSTADAS,** lightly spray both sides of a tortilla with cooking spray, lay tortilla flat on a baking sheet, and sprinkle with ¼ teaspoon cinnamon-sugar. Flip tortilla and sprinkle top with ½ teaspoon cinnamon-sugar. Repeat.

6. Bake for 8 to 10 minutes or until lightly browned and crispy. To serve, top each with a ½ cup of ice cream, drizzle with 1 teaspoon chocolate sauce.

NUTRITION INFORMATION PER SERVING (1 TACO OR TOSTADA): Calories 160 | Carbohydrate 27 g (Sugars 8 g) | Total Fat 5 g (Sat Fat 2 g) | Protein 5 g | Fiber 11 g | Sodium 310 mg | Food Exchanges: 1½ Carbohydrate, 1 Fat | Weight Watcher Smart Point Comparison: 5

Margaritas for Two, Two Ways

IF YOU FEEL THAT A FIESTA ISN'T A TRUE FIESTA without an icy-cold margarita, this recipe is for you. While I love margaritas, sugary mixers with lime flavoring don't excite me. What does excite me is fresh lime juice sweetened without the empty calories of sugar (leaving more calories for my favorite Mexican foods!). Shake up a traditional margarita or blend yourself a strawberry margarita when you are in the mood for one that is frozen and fruity. Cheers!

MAKES 2 SERVINGS

3 ½ ounces tequila

2 ounces fresh lime juice

5 teaspoons granulated sweetener (or 3 packets)*

¼ teaspoon orange extract

Lime wedges for rim and garnish (optional)

Coarse sea salt for glass rim (optional)

*See page 36 for sweetener options.

1. Pour the first 4 ingredients (tequila through orange extract) into a shaker filled ⅔ full with ice. Cover and shake well.

2. If desired, wet the rim of 2 rocks or 6-ounce glasses with a lime wedge and dip rims into salt. Fill glasses half full of ice, strain drink into glasses, and garnish with optional lime wedges.

Marlene Says: *To make a* **FROZEN STRAWBERRY MARGARITA,** *add the first 4 ingredients above to a blender along with ¾ cup crushed ice, and 4 to 5 whole frozen strawberries, and blend until smooth. To serve, pour into margarita glasses (with salted rims, if desired), and garnish with optional lime wedges. (Adds 10 calories, 2 grams of carbohydrate, and 1 point.)*

NUTRITION INFORMATION PER SERVING: Calories 120 | Carbohydrate 2 g (Sugars 1 g) | Total Fat 0 g (Sat Fat 0 g) | Protein 0 g | Fiber 0 g | Sodium 0 mg | Food Exchanges: 2 Fat | Weight Watcher Smart Point Comparison: 4

ASIAN INSPIRATION

ASIAN INSPIRATION

10-Minute Wonton Soup

P.F. Chang's–Style Chicken Lettuce Wraps

Take-Out Teriyaki

General Tso's Chicken

Sweet & Sour Pork for Two

Panda-Style Mushroom Chicken

Stir-Fried Shrimp with Snow Peas

Better Beef & Broccoli

Quicker-Than-Takeout Orange Chicken

P.F. Chang's-Style Mongolian Beef

Pork Fried Rice

20-Minute Loaded Veggie Lo Mein

Sweet & Spicy Glazed Green Beans

Chinese Almond Cookies

Asian-Inspired Dishes

With their enticing array of sweet, spicy, salty, sour, and savory flavors, Asian-inspired dishes tempt and tantalize our taste buds like no other cuisine. Creating classic and crave-worthy Asian dishes at home is not difficult, but it does require the right combination of flavors (I've done the heavy lifting for you in this regard), and the proper ingredients. Fortunately, when it comes to essential Asian-ingredient pantry staples the number you need is small, the cost is not large, and virtually all can be found in most supermarkets. Unless otherwise noted, all also last almost indefinitely!

SEVEN ESSENTIAL INGREDIENTS

GINGER. Knobby brown pieces of fresh ginger can be found in the produce department. To use, scrape away the thin skin and grate or finely chop for "minced" ginger. Ginger will keep fresh for several weeks in the fridge or up to six months in the freezer. For ease, minced fresh ginger can be bought in tubes or jars. Once opened, it will keep for at least three months in the refrigerator. Powdered ginger is not an equal substitute for fresh.

HOISIN SAUCE. Hoisin sauce is the sauce commonly spread onto the pancakes served with mu shu pork. A thick sweet slightly spicy "barbecue" sauce, it adds a rich, sweet flavor to sauces and stir-fries. Lee Kum Kee and Koon Chun are two preferred brands.

OYSTER OR "OYSTER-FLAVORED SAUCE." This salty, slightly sweet, deeply flavored, savory brown sauce adds an amazing distinctly rich flavor, without any hint of its oyster namesake, to stir-fries and stir-fried rice. Dynasty brand is carried in most supermarkets.

RICE WINE VINEGAR. Rice wine vinegar has a milder flavor and lower acidity level than other vinegars. Choose natural rice wine vinegar rather than seasoned, which is "seasoned" with sugar.

SESAME OIL. Made from crushed sesame seeds, there is no replacement for sesame oil's signature flavor. It lasts indefinitely in the fridge (bring to room temperature for easier measuring).

SHERRY. Head to the liquor department for an inexpensive dry sherry for better flavor (and none of the saltiness) of the "cooking" sherry sold next to bottled dressings.

SOY SAUCE. Made from soybeans, roasted wheat, yeast and salt, soy sauce is essential for sauces, stir-fries, soups, and more. Reduced-sodium versions average 40% less sodium. Kikkoman brand is widely available. Trader Joe brand is another I like. Tamari sauce is the gluten-free substitute.

10-Minute Wonton Soup

YOU MAY NEVER ORDER TAKE-OUT WONTON SOUP AGAIN after making this super-easy and supremely satisfying soup. Frozen wontons are quickly simmered in richly flavored broth for a wonton soup a slurp above the rest. (Or, if you prefer, pork, chicken, or veggie pot stickers can be used instead.) Although I've listed them as optional, a few shrimp significantly perk up the presentation and heartiness and turn this into what is called Wor (or everything) Wonton Soup.

1 (14.5-ounce) can reduced-sodium chicken broth

½ teaspoon jarred minced ginger

½ teaspoon garlic powder

½ teaspoon granulated sugar

1 teaspoon reduced-sodium soy sauce

1 small carrot, peeled and finely diced

10 frozen mini wontons or 4 pot stickers

1 head baby bok choy roughly chopped, or ¾ cup fresh spinach

¼ cup green onions, chopped, divided

6 extra-large shrimp (or 4 ounces, optional)

1 teaspoon sesame oil

1. Place the first 5 ingredients (broth through soy sauce) into a medium pot. Add ½ cup water and heat over medium heat until broth starts to simmer. Add carrot and wontons, cover, and simmer on low for 2 minutes.

2. Add the bok choy, half the green onions, and shrimp, if desired, and simmer soup for an additional 2 minutes. Stir in the sesame oil. Ladle the soup between 2 bowls and garnish with remaining green onions.

Marlene Says: *Three large shrimp (26 to 30 count) add 40 calories, 9 grams of protein, and 0 points. For an even heartier "Wor" Wonton Soup, drop in a few thin slices of uncooked chicken breast along with the shrimp.*

NUTRITION INFORMATION PER SERVING: (1½ CUPS) Calories 140 | Carbohydrate 15 g (Sugars 2 g) | Total Fat: 5 g (Sat Fat 1 g) | Protein 7 g | Fiber 2 g | Sodium 675 mg | Food Exchanges: ½ Starch, ½ Lean Meat, ½ Vegetable, ½ Fat | Weight Watcher Smart Point Comparison: 3

P.F. Chang's–Style Chicken Lettuce Wraps

P.F. CHANG'S IS FAMOUS FOR THEIR WILDLY POPULAR Chang's Lettuce Wraps. The combination of warm minced chicken and vegetables, cloaked in a sweet, salty, savory sauce, and tucked into cool lettuce, hits all the right notes. After enjoying these signature wraps again recently, I hit the kitchen. Made Chang's-style with lean ground chicken, these are my healthiest, easiest, restaurant-worthy lettuce wraps yet. The recipe serves four as an appetizer or two as an entrée. Fresh cool mint is a tasty garnish.

MAKES 4 SERVINGS (16 WRAPS)

2 tablespoons reduced-sodium soy sauce

2 tablespoons granulated sweetener*

2 tablespoons hoisin sauce

1 tablespoon rice wine vinegar

¼ teaspoon red chili flakes

1¼ teaspoons cornstarch

2 teaspoons canola oil

2 teaspoons minced garlic

1 pound ground chicken breast

1 (8-ounce) can water chestnuts, drained and minced

1½ cups finely chopped mushrooms

½ cup finely diced red bell pepper

⅓ cup sliced green onions

1 small peeled carrot

1 large head butter or iceberg lettuce leaves

See page 36 for sweetener options.

1. To make the sauce, in a small bowl or 1-cup measuring cup whisk ¼ cup of water with the first 6 ingredients (soy sauce through cornstarch). Set aside.

2. Heat the oil in a large nonstick skillet or wok over medium-high heat. Add garlic and warm for 15 seconds. Add chicken and sauté, using a large fork or spatula to crumble the meat, for 6 to 8 minutes or until chicken is just no longer pink. Add water chestnuts, mushrooms, bell peppers, and green onions, and cook for 4 to 5 minutes, tossing frequently, until vegetables are tender.

3. Make a well in the center of the pan, add sauce, cook it until it thickens and clears, then stir it into the meat. Grate the carrot into the pan and continue to cook, while stirring, until carrot is incorporated and the sauce thoroughly coats everything.

4. Spoon the meat onto lettuce leaves, or place in a bowl and serve with lettuce leaves and any garnishes.

DARE TO COMPARE: Ounce for ounce, these revised chicken lettuce wraps deliver double the protein with half as much fat and sodium—and 90% less added sugar—than P.F. Chang's Chicken Lettuce Wraps.

NUTRITION INFORMATION PER SERVING (4 WRAPS): Calories 210 | Carbohydrate 16 g (Sugars 3 g) | Total Fat 6 g (Sat Fat 1 g) | Protein 25 g | Fiber 5 g | Sodium 510 mg | Food Exchanges: 3 Lean Meat, 2 Vegetable, ½ Starch | Weight Watcher Smart Point Comparison: 4

Take-Out Teriyaki

IF YOU LOVE TANTALIZING TERIYAKI-SAUCED CHICKEN, beef, or seafood, and it's been off your menu due to its sky-high sugar and sodium stats, you're in luck. This recipe has been designed to satisfy your sweet, sticky, salty, teriyaki sauce cravings happily with half the usual sugar and sodium. I've included directions and nutritional stats for chicken, but serve it on anything you choose! A tablespoon of the sauce has 20 calories, 1 gram of sugar, and 210 milligrams of sodium. It keeps for weeks in the fridge.

MAKES 4 SERVINGS

2 teaspoons cornstarch

¼ cup reduced-sodium soy sauce

¼ cup dry sherry or water

2 tablespoons granulated no-calorie sweetener*

2 tablespoons rice vinegar

1 tablespoon brown sugar

2 teaspoons sesame oil

¼ teaspoon garlic powder

½ teaspoon ground ginger

4 boneless, skinless chicken breasts (about 1¼ pounds)

Black pepper, to taste

See page 36 for sweetener options.

1. To make the teriyaki sauce, in a small saucepan whisk together the cornstarch, ¼ cup water, and next 8 ingredients (soy sauce through ginger). Bring to a simmer over medium heat and simmer for 3 to 4 minutes, stirring occasionally, until thickened and clear. Cover and turn the heat off.

2. Cover chicken breasts with plastic wrap, pound very thin (⅛-inch thickness), and season with pepper to taste. Preheat the broiler with an oven rack in the upper position.

3. Spray a large nonstick ovenproof skillet with cooking spray and place over medium-high heat. Add chicken and sauté for 2 minutes or until underside is golden brown. Turn, and cook 2 more minutes, or until chicken is just cooked through.

4. Cover each breast with 1 tablespoon sauce. Place skillet under broiler for 1 minute, or until the sauce bubbles. Remove from the oven, and place chicken on serving plates. Drizzle each piece (or accompanying vegetables or rice) with an additional tablespoon of teriyaki sauce.

Marlene Says: *Note that soy sauce varies by brand. When testing this recipe, Trader Joe's Reduced Sodium Soy Sauce produced a dark-colored teriyaki sauce, Kikkoman brand, less so. To deepen the color, if desired, add ½ to ¾ teaspoon of Kitchen Bouquet.*

NUTRITION INFORMATION PER SERVING (1 CHICKEN BREAST WITH SAUCE): Calories 190 | Carbohydrate 5 g (Sugars 2 g) | Total Fat 3 g (Sat Fat 0 g) | Protein 31 g | Fiber 0 g | Sodium 520 mg | Food Exchanges: 4 Lean Meat, 1/2 Carbohydrate | Weight Watcher Smart Point Comparison: 1

General Tso's Chicken

IT'S ALWAYS NICE TO HEAR THAT MY RECIPES have made someone happy and this one has afforded me that many times over. I actually had no idea of how very popular General Tso's Chicken is before I created it, but now I do! This is another recipe where the ingredient list may appear long, but, trust me, the steps are simple and grabbing a few more pantry staples is well worth the effort to create a sweet, spicy, much-loved (far healthier) dish that tastes as good, or even better, than takeout.

MAKES 4 SERVINGS

1 cup reduced-sodium chicken broth

3 tablespoons granulated no-calorie sweetener (or 4 packets)*

2 tablespoons low-sodium soy sauce

1 tablespoon cornstarch

1 tablespoon rice vinegar

1 tablespoon brown sugar

1 tablespoon minced garlic

1 tablespoon ketchup

¼ teaspoon red pepper flakes

½ cup sliced onions

3 cups broccoli florets

¼ cup all-purpose flour

¼ teaspoon black pepper

1 pound boneless, skinless chicken breast, cut into 1-inch pieces

1 egg, beaten

2 tablespoons canola oil

*See page 36 for sweetener options.

1. To make the sauce, in a medium bowl combine the first nine ingredients (chicken broth through red pepper flakes). Add onions and set aside.

2. Place broccoli in a microwave-safe bowl. Add 2 tablespoons of water, cover, and microwave for 2 minutes. Set aside.

3. In a small bowl, mix flour and black pepper. Roll chicken in egg, letting excess drip off, and toss with flour. Heat 1 tablespoon oil in a large nonstick wok or skillet over medium-high heat. Add half the chicken and cook 4 to 5 minutes or until well browned and cooked through. Heat remaining oil and repeat. Set chicken aside.

4. Whisk the sauce, add it to the wok, and cook for 1 minute, or until it thickens and clears. Add the chicken and broccoli, and cook 1 to 2 minutes, tossing with sauce to coat.

DARE TO COMPARE: A typical order of General Tso's Chicken, averaged across five restaurants, has 1,300 calories with 3,200 milligrams of sodium, and three days' worth of added sugar.

NUTRITION INFORMATION PER SERVING (1½ CUPS): Calories 300 | Carbohydrate 19 g (Sugars 6 g) | Total Fat 12 g (Sat Fat 1 g) | Protein 29 g | Fiber 3 g | Sodium 510 mg | Food Exchanges: 3½ Lean Meat, 1 Vegetable, 1 Starch, ½ Fat | Weight Watcher Smart Point Comparison: 4

Sweet & Sour Pork for Two

WHEN I WAS IN HIGH SCHOOL, MY ITALIAN MOTHER took Chinese cooking classes. I don't know what inspired her, but I do know our entire family benefited as a result. We were especially delighted when she served sweet and sour chicken or pork. She followed her instructor's guidelines, heavily coating and frying the meat, but of course I take a much lighter approach. My perfectly sweet and tangy sauce is based on hers, and I think you will be just as delighted. This recipe amply serves two.

MAKES 2 SERVINGS

1 medium carrot

3 tablespoons rice vinegar

3 tablespoons granulated sweetener*

2 tablespoons ketchup

2 teaspoons reduced-sodium soy sauce

½ teaspoon minced ginger

1 teaspoon plus 1 tablespoon cornstarch, divided

8 ounces pork tenderloin, cut into ¾-inch pieces

2 teaspoons canola oil

1 green or red bell pepper, cut into 1-inch squares

½ cup onion cut into squares

1 (8-ounce) can sliced water chestnuts, drained

½ cup pineapple chunks, fresh or canned in juice (drained)

*See page 36 for sweetener options.

1. Peel carrot and cut into ½-inch pieces. Place in a small microwave-safe bowl; add 2 tablespoons water, cover, and microwave on high for 3 minutes. Drain and set aside.

2. While carrots are cooking, in a small bowl, whisk together the next 5 ingredients (vinegar through ginger), 1 teaspoon cornstarch, and ¼ cup water. Set aside.

3. Toss pork with remaining tablespoon of cornstarch to coat. Heat 2 teaspoons oil in a large nonstick skillet or wok over medium-high heat. Add pork and cook 2 to 3 minutes, or until well browned on all sides. Add bell pepper and onion and cook for 2 minutes or until they start to soften, then add the carrots and water chestnuts, and cook for another minute to incorporate them.

4. Stir in the pineapple and vinegar mixture, reduce heat to low, and cook for 2 to 3 minutes, stirring constantly, until the sauce thickens and clears.

> **DARE TO COMPARE:** An order of sweet and sour pork from BD's Mongolian Grill delivers (surprisingly) nearly same amount of fat, but it does so with double the calories. If you are watching your blood sugar or count points, watch out. It has five times as much sugar (carbs, and points)!

NUTRITION INFORMATION PER SERVING (1 ½ CUPS): Calories 260 | Carbohydrate 18 g (Sugars 8 g) | Total Fat 9 g (Sat Fat 2 g) | Protein 25 g | Fiber 2 g | Sodium 390 mg | Food Exchanges: 3 ½ Lean Meat, 1 Vegetable, ½ Fruit, ½ Carbohydrate | Weight Watcher Smart Point Comparison: 5

Panda-Style Mushroom Chicken

ORANGE CHICKEN MAY RULE THE ROOST AT PANDA EXPRESS, but one of my favorite entrées is actually their Mushroom Chicken. Soft tender strips of stir-fried chicken breast mingle with mushrooms and crisp-tender zucchini in a light sauce, perfectly balanced with garlic and ginger. I'm thrilled to now have a taste twin—with more protein and less fat—that I can make right at home. This is a quick-fix stir-fry dish!

MAKES 4 SERVINGS

3 tablespoons reduced-sodium soy sauce

1 tablespoon rice vinegar

2 teaspoons granulated sugar

1½ teaspoons minced garlic

1½ teaspoons minced ginger

12 ounces boneless, skinless chicken breast

2 tablespoons cornstarch

2 teaspoons canola oil

2 teaspoons sesame oil

2 medium zucchini sliced into half-moons (about 1 pound)

1 (8-ounce) package sliced mushrooms

1. In a small bowl, combine the first 5 ingredients (soy sauce through ginger) plus 2 tablespoons water. Set aside.

2. Slice chicken across the grain into very thin slices. Place in a large bowl and toss with cornstarch. Add both oils to a wok or large nonstick skillet and place over high heat. Add chicken and cook for 3 to 4 minutes, while tossing, until lightly browned yet barely done. Remove and set aside.

3. Spray the wok with cooking spray, add zucchini, and toss for 1 minute. Add 2 tablespoons of water, cover, and steam zucchini for 1 minute. Uncover, add mushrooms, stir-fry until just softened and lightly browned, then add chicken and sauce mixture. Cook for an additional minute, tossing until the sauce slightly thickens and evenly coats the chicken and vegetables.

NUTRITION INFORMATION PER SERVING (1¼ CUPS): Calories 180 | Carbohydrate 11 g (Sugars 3 g) | Total Fat 6 g (Sat Fat 1 g) | Protein 23 g | Fiber 3 g | Sodium 415 mg | Food Exchanges: 3½ Lean Meat, 1½ Vegetable | Weight Watcher Smart Point Comparison: 2

Stir-Fried Shrimp with Snow Peas

WHILE MUCH OF THE FARE YOU COMMONLY FIND on Asian American menus is heavy in sugar, fat, or calories, this lovely dish is a welcome exception. In this easy 20-minute classic Chinese recipe, fresh snow peas, juicy shrimp, and crunchy water chestnuts are lightly coated in a velvety sauce infused with a hint of garlic and a pop of fresh ginger. Spoon it over a cup of instant brown rice, grab your chopsticks, and sit down to an elegant Asian meal for less than 375 calories.

MAKES 4 SERVINGS

1 pound peeled shrimp, (26 to 30 count)

1 tablespoon sherry

¼ teaspoon salt

3 teaspoons cornstarch, divided

2 teaspoons reduced-sodium soy sauce

1 teaspoon sugar

2 teaspoons canola oil

1 tablespoon minced (or jarred) ginger

1 teaspoon minced garlic

8 ounces snow peas

1 (8-ounce) can sliced water chestnuts, drained

1 teaspoon sesame oil

1. In a large bowl, toss the shrimp with sherry and salt. Add 2 teaspoons cornstarch, toss to coat, and let stand 5 minutes. In a small bowl combine ⅓ cup of water, soy sauce, sugar, and remaining 1 teaspoon cornstarch. Set aside. Remove the strings from the snow peas, if needed.

2. Heat oil in a large nonstick skillet or wok over high heat. Add shrimp, spreading them into a single layer, and cook for 30 seconds, or until the bottoms start to turn pink. Using a spatula, stir-fry shrimp for 1 minute. Add ginger and garlic, toss well, then add the snow peas. Add the soy sauce mixture, to the skillet and cover for 1 minute.

3. Uncover, add water chestnuts and sesame oil, and continue to stir-fry until the snow peas are tender and everything is coated evenly with the sauce.

NUTRITION INFORMATION PER SERVING (1 CUP): Calories 170 | Carbohydrate 9 g (Sugars 3 g) | Total Fat 4 g (Sat Fat 0 g) | Protein 23 g | Fiber 4 g | Sodium 440 mg | Food Exchanges: 3 Lean Meat, 1½ Vegetable, ½ Fat | Weight Watcher Smart Point Comparison: 1

Better Beef and Broccoli

TENDER STRIPS OF BEEF COMBINED WITH fresh steamed broccoli in a savory brown sauce is another popular Chinese restaurant pick. The trick to producing tender beef for this dish is slicing the steak as thin as possible across the grain before coating it with cornstarch and cooking briefly over high heat. Using a very sharp knife and slicing the meat while it's partially frozen assists in getting wafer-thin slices. When coated and cooked this way, inexpensive lean sirloin becomes amazingly melt-in-your-mouth tender.

MAKES 4 SERVINGS

1 pound trimmed sirloin steak

1 tablespoon sherry

2 tablespoons reduced-sodium soy sauce, divided

1 teaspoon fresh minced ginger

1 tablespoon plus 1 teaspoon cornstarch, divided

⅓ cup reduced-sodium beef broth

1 tablespoon hoisin sauce or sugar

½ teaspoon black pepper

1 pound broccoli florets

3 teaspoons canola oil, divided

1 teaspoon minced garlic

1. Slice the meat across the grain into very thin slices. Place it in a bowl and toss well with the sherry, 1 tablespoon soy sauce, and the ginger. Add 1 tablespoon cornstarch, toss again, and set aside. In another small bowl or large measuring cup, combine 1 tablespoon soy sauce, 1 teaspoon of the cornstarch, the beef broth, hoisin, and pepper. Set aside.

2. Heat a wok or a very large nonstick skillet on high. Add the broccoli and ⅓ cup water, cover and steam for 3 to 4 minutes, or until crisp-tender. Remove from wok and set aside.

3. Cook off any remaining water and heat 1 teaspoon of oil over high heat. Add half the beef and half the garlic and quickly stir-fry just until beef is just no longer pink (do not overcook). Remove from wok and set aside. Repeat with remaining garlic and meat.

4. Add the broth mixture to the empty wok and cook over medium heat until the sauce thickens and clears. Add the beef, its juices, and the broccoli back to the skillet and toss to coat.

> DARE TO COMPARE: Analysis by the Center for Science in the Public Interest tags an order of Beef with Broccoli at your typical Asian restaurant with 900 calories and 3,200 milligrams of sodium.

NUTRITION INFORMATION PER SERVING (1 ½ CUPS): Calories 245 | Carbohydrate 8 g (Sugars 3 g) | Total Fat 10 g (Sat Fat 3 g) | Protein 30 g | Fiber 3 g | Sodium 430 mg | Food Exchanges: 3½ Lean Meat, 1 Vegetable | Weight Watcher Smart Point Comparison: 5

Quicker-Than-Takeout Orange Chicken

THIS RECIPE REMAINS ONE OF MY PROUDEST RESTAURANT MAKEOVERS; I'm especially flattered because "addictive" is how readers most often describe it. The Panda Express copycat recipe I fashioned it from called for a full cup of brown sugar and two cups of oil so you can imagine my delight when I created this recipe—with the same irresistible taste—with just two tablespoons of each! Less breading, more tender chicken, and a sauce too tempting to resist, will have you clamoring for more.

⅓ cup light orange juice

3 tablespoons rice vinegar

3 tablespoons lemon juice

2 tablespoons reduced-sodium soy sauce

½ cup granulated no-calorie sweetener*

2 tablespoons brown sugar

1½ tablespoons cornstarch

¼ teaspoon ground ginger

⅛ teaspoon red pepper flakes

1¼ pounds boneless, skinless chicken breast, cut into ¾ inch pieces

1 large egg, beaten

¼ cup all-purpose flour

2 tablespoons canola oil, divided

1 small red bell pepper, cut into ¾-inch squares

1 small onion, cut into ¾-inch squares

See page 36 for sweetener options.

1. To make the sauce, in a medium saucepan, whisk together ½ cup water with the first 9 ingredients (orange juice through pepper flakes). Place over medium-high heat, bring to a low boil, and cook for 1 minute, or until the sauce thickens and clears. Reduce heat to lowest setting just to keep sauce warm.

2. Coat chicken with beaten egg and toss with flour to coat. Heat 1 tablespoon of oil in a large nonstick skillet over medium-high heat. Add half the chicken and cook 4 to 5 minutes, or until well browned on all sides and chicken is cooked through. Transfer to a bowl and repeat with remaining oil and chicken.

3. Add the red pepper and onion to the skillet and cook for 4 to 5 minutes, or until slightly softened. Add the chicken back to the pan with the warm orange sauce, and stir to coat.

DARE TO COMPARE: Panda Express is not the only one serving up over-the-top orange chicken. A regular order of Wei Better Orange Chicken at Pei Wei Asian Diner has 33 grams of protein (like mine) but also 1,020 calories, 48 grams of fat, 71 grams of sugar, and 1,750 milligrams of sodium.

NUTRITION INFORMATION PER SERVING (1 CUP): Calories 290 | Carbohydrate 18 g (Sugars 8 g) | Total Fat 9 g (Sat Fat 1 g) | Protein 33 g | Fiber 0 g | Sodium 360 mg | Food Exchanges: 4 Lean Meat, 1 Starch, ½ Carbohydrate | Weight Watcher Smart Point Comparison: 5

P.F. Chang's–Style Mongolian Beef

FOR MANY TELEVISION HOSTS AND READERS this was the knockoff dish that formally elevated me to the title of "magician in the kitchen." For them, and my two boys, P.F. Chang's sets the bar for what Mongolian Beef should taste like—savory, salty, and sinfully sweet—and this recipe duplicates it to a tee. The "magician" part is that it does so with a mere fraction of the usual calories, fat, and sodium. It took more than a few tries to get this better-at-home recipe right, but it was oh-so-worth-it!

MAKES 4 SERVINGS

3 tablespoons reduced-sodium soy sauce

1 tablespoon dry sherry

¼ cup granulated no-calorie sweetener (or 6 packets)*

1 tablespoon molasses

2 teaspoons cornstarch

1 tablespoon minced garlic

½ teaspoon minced ginger

1 pound lean sirloin steak

1 tablespoon cornstarch

2 teaspoons canola oil

2 medium carrots, cut into matchsticks

1 small red bell pepper, cut into ¼-inch strips

4 stalks green onion, green and white parts, sliced ¼-inch thick on the diagonal

2 teaspoons sesame oil

See page 36 for sweetener options.

1. In a small saucepan, combine the first 7 ingredients (soy sauce through ginger). Add ⅓ cup water and heat for 1 to 2 minutes or until sauce is thick and clear. Remove from heat and set aside.

2. Slice the meat across the grain into very thin slices, and lightly toss with 1 tablespoon cornstarch. Heat oil in a nonstick wok or large sauté pan over high heat; add beef and cook for 30 to 60 seconds or until no longer pink, stirring frequently. Remove beef from pan, and set aside.

3. Add the carrots and bell peppers to the pan and stir-fry for 2 minutes. Add the sauce mixture and green onions, cover, and cook for 2 minutes. Uncover and simmer for 1 minute or until the sauce thickens slightly. Add the meat back to the pan with the sesame oil and toss until well coated.

> **DARE TO COMPARE:** An order of Mongolian Beef at P.F. Chang's China Bistro has 790 calories, 42 grams of fat, and 2,300 milligrams of sodium. If you count points, it has 24.

NUTRITION INFORMATION PER SERVING (1 GENEROUS CUP): Calories 300 | Carbohydrate 15 g (Sugars 6 g) | Total Fat 13 g (Sat Fat 4.5 g) | Protein 32 g | Fiber 2 g | Sodium 490 mg | Food Exchanges: 4 Lean Meat, 1 Vegetable, ½ Carbohydrate, ½ Fat | Weight Watcher Smart Point Comparison: 6

Pork Fried Rice

YOU'D BE HARD PRESSED to think of an Asian dish that conjures up the thought of more fat and calories than pork fried rice, and, unfortunately, it's for good reason. But those days are over. If you love fried rice, it thrills me to tell you that a cup of this flavorful pork-studded rice rings in with four times the protein, double the fiber, half the carbs, and fewer calories than a cup of regular white rice! Plenty of healthy veggies bulk it up—including cauliflower—but I promise you, the only thing you taste when eating is meaty, gingery, flavorful pork-fried-rice perfection.

MAKES 4 SERVINGS

2 teaspoons vegetable oil, divided

1 ½ cups frozen or fresh riced cauliflower

1 large egg, lightly beaten

⅓ cup diced carrots

1 ½ cups chopped fresh mushrooms

1 teaspoon minced ginger (or ½ teaspoon powdered)

4 green onions, chopped, separate green ends

6 ounces lean ground pork

1 (8-ounce) can sliced water chestnuts, drained, and chopped

1 cup cooked rice

2 tablespoons oyster sauce

¼ teaspoon black pepper

½ cup frozen peas, thawed

1. Heat 1 teaspoon oil in a large nonstick pan over high heat. Add cauliflower and let cook for 1 to 2 minutes, without stirring, until the underside is browned. Stir and cook for 30 seconds longer, then push it to the edges of the pan, add the egg, scramble it with a fork until mostly cooked, and stir it into the cauliflower.

2. Add carrots, mushrooms, ginger, and white parts of green onions, stir, and cook for 1 minute. Add pork (breaking it into a few clumps), and, using a fork, work it into the vegetables, breaking it into crumbles as it cooks. When pork is no longer pink, add water chestnuts, rice, and half of green onion tops.

3. Add the oyster sauce, black pepper, and peas, and toss well. Drizzle remaining 1 ½ teaspoons of oil over rice. turn rice over (so oiled rice is on bottom of pan) and cook without stirring for 1 to 2 more minutes, or until underside is nicely browned. Garnish with remaining green onion tops.

DARE TO COMPARE: You'd have to walk for over five hours to burn off the 1,150 calories and 160 grams of carbs in an order of Pork Fried Rice from P.F. Chang's. This recipe serves four as a side, two as a belly-filling entrée!

NUTRITION INFORMATION PER SERVING (1 CUP): Calories 185 | Carbohydrate 20 g (Sugars 3 g) | Total Fat 6 g (Sat Fat 1 g) | Protein 16 g | Fiber 5 g | Sodium 340 mg | Food Exchanges: 1 Starch | Weight Watcher Smart Point Comparison: 4

20-Minute Loaded Veggie Lo Mein

HEL-LO LO MEIN! THE main difference between lo mein and chow mein is that lo mein uses a soft noodle and chow mein noodles are traditionally crispy or fried. I've chosen to go the softer route here, pairing the noodles with oodles of vegetables. The ingredient list is my longest, but rest assured that the only things you need to slice or dice are a single red pepper and a few green onions. Enjoy it as is, or swap in any meat or seafood of your choice. Leftovers make a marvelous lunch.

MAKES 4 SERVINGS

5 ounces whole-grain spaghetti or linguini

4 teaspoons sesame oil, divided

½ cup reduced-sodium chicken broth

2 tablespoons reduced-sodium soy sauce

1½ tablespoons oyster sauce

2 teaspoons granulated sugar

1 teaspoon cornstarch

½ teaspoon ginger (or 1 teaspoon fresh)

¼ teaspoon black pepper, or more to taste

1 medium red bell pepper, thinly sliced

1 (8-ounce) package sliced mushrooms

1 tablespoon jarred minced garlic

2½ cups packaged shredded coleslaw mix

8 ounces sugar snap peas

½ cup green onion, thinly sliced

1. Cook the pasta al dente according to the package directions. Drain very well, shaking to remove all excess water, and toss with 1 teaspoon sesame oil.

2. While pasta cooks, combine next 7 ingredients (broth through black pepper), and set aside.

3. Heat 2 teaspoons sesame oil in a large nonstick skillet or wok over medium-high heat. Add red pepper and stir-fry for 2 minutes. Add mushrooms and garlic and stir-fry for 3 to 4 minutes or until mushrooms start to soften. Add coleslaw mix, stir-fry for 1 minute to soften, then add pea pods, and 1 tablespoon water, cover and steam for 1 minute. Uncover, stir-fry off any water, add soy sauce mixture, and cook until sauce starts to thicken.

4. Add the pasta, last teaspoon of sesame oil, and toss until well mixed and pasta is hot. Top with green onions and serve.

DARE TO COMPARE: Oodles of noodles! Don't let the vegetables fool you. A serving of vegetable Lo Mein at Pei Wei has 1,059 calories with a hefty 146 grams of carbohydrate and 3,460 milligrams of sodium!

NUTRITION INFORMATION PER SERVING (1½ CUPS): Calories 215 | Carbohydrate 38 g (Sugars 8 g) | Total Fat 5 g (Sat Fat 1 g) | Protein 8 g | Fiber 7 g | Sodium 540 mg | Food Exchanges: 1½ Starch, 1½ Vegetable, 1 Fat | Weight Watcher Smart Point Comparison: 5

Sweet & Spicy Glazed Green Beans

ORDERING A VEGGIE SIDE AT AN ASIAN RESTAURANT to balance out heavier dishes seems like a great idea—until you get a hold of the nutritional stats. While seemingly a healthy choice, a side of green beans can have over 500 calories! Luckily, you don't have to choose between good health and good taste. These nutritious beans are swimming in enough sweet, spicy, garlicky sauce to turn a veggie hater into a veggie lover.

MAKES 4 SERVINGS

2 teaspoons canola oil

1 pound fresh green beans, washed

1 ½ teaspoons minced garlic

2 tablespoons reduced-sodium soy sauce

1 tablespoon balsamic vinegar

1 tablespoon brown sugar

1 teaspoon cornstarch

¼ teaspoon red chili flakes

Sesame seeds for garnish (optional)

1. Heat the oil in a large nonstick skillet over medium-high heat. Add the green beans and stir-fry for about 2 minutes to sear the beans. Add the garlic and cook for 10 to 15 seconds.

2. Pour in ¼ cup water and immediately cover skillet. Steam beans for 4 to 5 minutes, or until crisp tender. Meanwhile, in a small bowl, whisk ¼ cup water with next 5 ingredients (soy sauce through chili flakes).

3. Remove the lid from the skillet, add the soy sauce mixture, and cook for 1 to 2 minutes, tossing, until the sauce thickens slightly and the beans are cooked to your liking.

> **DARE TO COMPARE:** With a whopping 530 calories, 40 grams of fat, 23 grams of sugar, and 1,580 milligrams of sodium, a side order of Chili Garlic Green Beans at P.F. Chang's clocks in with as many calories, twice the sugar and sodium, and three times the fat as a side order of their fried rice.

NUTRITION INFORMATION PER SERVING (¼ RECIPE): Calories 70 | Carbohydrate 12 g (Sugars 6 g) | Total Fat 2.5 g (Sat Fat 0 g) | Protein 3 g | Fiber 2 g | Sodium 240 mg | Food Exchanges: 1 Vegetable, ½ Carbohydrate | Weight Watcher Smart Point Comparison: 2

Chinese Almond Cookies

TRADITIONAL CRUNCHY CHINESE ALMOND COOKIEs are not just pretty to look at, the almond in the center is thought to bring good luck. In my quest for healthy, I ditched the traditional lard and added almond flour to lower the carbs and up the delicate, nutty flavor. While these cookies have less than one teaspoon of sugar per serving, the only comments I received when I took them to a family dinner were compliments. Lucky me.

3 tablespoons shortening

3 tablespoons butter

½ cup granulated sweetener*

¼ cup granulated sugar

2 large eggs, divided

2 teaspoons almond extract

1 cup all-purpose flour

½ teaspoon baking soda

¾ cup almond flour or meal, or sliced almonds**

18 sliced or whole almonds

See page 36 for sweetener options.

1. Preheat oven to 350°F. Line a baking sheet with a silicone baking sheet, if desired.

2. In a medium bowl, with an electric mixer, beat shortening, butter, granulated sweetener, and sugar for 1 minute or until light and fluffy. Add 1 egg white and almond extract and beat for 1 more minute. Add flour, baking soda, and almond meal to bowl, and blend just until dough comes together.

3. Roll rounded tablespoons of dough into balls and place onto baking sheet 2 inches apart. Using the bottom of a glass, press dough flat (dough will be slightly sticky, a light spray of cooking spray on the glass can be used). Beat remaining egg with 1 teaspoon water and brush cookies with egg.

4. Press an almond slice in the middle of each cookie and bake for 12–14 minutes or until lightly browned and bottoms are able to lift off cleanly. Let cookies cool for a few minutes on the baking sheet and then move to a wire rack to finish cooling.

Marlene Says: **To make your own almond meal, place sliced almonds in a food processor and process to a fine meal.*

NUTRITION INFORMATION PER SERVING (1 COOKIE): Calories 95 | Carbohydrate 8 g (Sugars 3 g) | Total Fat 6 g (Sat Fat 1 g) | Protein 2 g | Fiber 1 g | Sodium 45 mg | Food Exchanges: ½ Carbohydrate, 1 Fat | Weight Watcher Smart Point Comparison: 3

ITALIAN CLASSICS

ITALIAN CLASSICS

In-a-Flash Caesar Salad for Two

Elana's Toscana Soup

15-Minute Bruschetta Mussels

Fast-Fix Pizza Margherita for One

Chicken Marsala

Chicken Broccoli Alfredo

Slow-Cooker Braised Beef Ragu

Lazy Day Lasagna

Shrimp Fra Diavolo

Chicken Caprese

Easy Eggplant Parmesan

Tender Turkey Meatballs with Marinara

Stovetop Rigatoni with Sausage and Peppers

Luscious Lemon Cream Cake

Tiramisu

In-a-Flash Caesar Salad for Two

ALL HAIL, CAESAR! CAESAR SALAD MAY NOT HAVE ORIGINATED IN ROME, but that doesn't mean it's not the emperor of salads. I've never dined at an Italian restaurant that didn't offer it (or a steakhouse or café for that matter). Fortunately, I don't have to leave home to enjoy one whenever the urge strikes. The creamy dressing is quickly whisked together and the garlic croutons are made in a flash under the broiler. Less than 10 minutes is all it takes for a Caesar salad worth saluting.

MAKES 2 SERVINGS

1 slice sourdough bread

⅛ teaspoon garlic salt

1 tablespoon lemon juice

1 tablespoon extra-virgin olive oil

2 tablespoons plain nonfat or low-fat Greek yogurt

¾ teaspoon Worcestershire sauce

½ teaspoon minced garlic or ⅛ teaspoon garlic powder

¼ teaspoon anchovy paste (optional)

¼ teaspoon black pepper

3 tablespoons grated Parmesan cheese, divided

4 cups torn or chopped romaine lettuce

1. Place a rack in the center of the oven and turn on the broiler.

2. Slice bread into a dozen ¾-inch cubes and spread evenly on a baking sheet. Spray lightly with cooking spray, sprinkle with garlic salt, and gently toss. Place in oven and broil until tops are brown. Flip croutons, and repeat. Turn off the broiler, and leave croutons in warm oven.

3. In a small bowl, whisk together the next 7 ingredients (lemon juice through pepper), plus 2 tablespoons Parmesan cheese.

4. Lightly toss lettuce with dressing and divide between 2 plates. Top with croutons and sprinkle each with remaining Parmesan and additional pepper, if desired.

> **DARE TO COMPARE:** With 590 calories, 54 grams of fat, and 964 milligrams of sodium, a Carrabba's side Caesar Salad adds a meal's worth of calories and sodium and almost a day's worth of fat to your meal.

NUTRITION INFORMATION PER SERVING (1 SALAD): Calories 150 | Carbohydrate 12 g (Sugars 2 g) | Total Fat 9 g (Sat Fat 2 g) | Protein 8 g | Fiber 2 g | Sodium 270 mg | Food Exchanges: 1 Vegetable, 1 Fat, ½ Lean Meat, ½ Starch | Weight Watcher Smart Point Comparison: 4

Elana's Toscana Soup

ONE OF MY EXCEPTIONAL KITCHEN ASSISTANTS, ELANA, shared with me that she was once a server at an Olive Garden restaurant where she had served countless bowls of Toscana soup. "Perfect," I thought as we grabbed our spoons and dug into making a clone of the enormously popular soup using my lean homemade Italian Sausage (page 242). One spoonful and I think you will agree we hit the mark! Better yet, with ingredients assembled, you can be eating this tasty zuppa in just 20 minutes.

MAKES 4 SERVINGS

8 ounces Italian Sausage (page 242), or store-bought

¼ teaspoon red pepper flakes

1 teaspoon olive oil

½ cup chopped onions

4 cups reduced-sodium chicken broth

1 (8-ounce) russet potato

½ teaspoon liquid smoke

2 cups kale leaves, stems removed

⅔ cup nonfat half-and-half or low-fat evaporated milk

1 tablespoon cornstarch

1. Spray a medium soup pot with cooking spray, and place over medium heat. Add the sausage and red pepper flakes, stir to break up the meat into large crumbles, and cook just until browned. Remove and set aside.

2. Add oil and onions to pot, and cook onions for 5 minutes, or until translucent (adding a little broth as needed to prevent onion from burning). While onions cook, cut potato in half lengthwise, lay flat, then cut into ¼-inch slices. When onion is translucent, stir in liquid smoke.

3. Add the broth and potatoes, cover and cook 4 minutes. Uncover, add kale, and cook for 5 minutes, or until kale is just tender. Combine half-and-half with cornstarch and add to pot, along with the sausage. Simmer for 1 additional minute and serve.

Marlene Says: *Both half-and-half and evaporated milk produce a soup very close to that at the restaurant. Half-in-half has the edge in color; evaporated milk in taste. Be careful not to oversimmer the soup as the potato slices break down easily once cooked.*

NUTRITION INFORMATION PER SERVING (1 ½ CUPS): Calories 190 | Carbohydrate 17 g (Sugars 5 g) | Total Fat 5 g (Sat Fat 1.5 g) | Protein 18 g | Fiber 3 g | Sodium 610 mg | Food Exchanges: 2 Lean Meat, 1 Vegetable, 1 Starch | Weight Watcher Smart Point Comparison: 4

15-Minute Bruschetta Mussels

FOR ME, SEEING THE WORD BRUSCHETTA CONJURES UP the wonderful taste and aroma of freshly diced tomatoes mingled with fragrant basil and garlic, spooned over toasted crostini. I love it when the same fragrance and taste are paired with steamed mussels. If you are hesitant about cooking mussels at home, I urge you to give it a try, as they are both inexpensive and easy to cook. This recipe serves four as a starter, or two as a light meal with a salad and the bread (to mop up the sumptuous juices).

MAKES 2 TO 4 SERVINGS

1 teaspoon olive oil

3 tablespoons finely chopped shallots or onions

2 teaspoons minced garlic (about 3 cloves)

⅓ cup white wine

¼ cup reduced-sodium chicken broth

1½ pounds mussels

¾ cup fresh chopped tomatoes

2 tablespoons julienned fresh basil

1½ teaspoons butter

Toasted bread (optional)

1. Rinse and clean the mussels under running water, tapping any mussels that are slightly open. Discard any that are not fully closed after being tapped and rinsed.

2. Heat the oil in a large flat pot or a high-sided skillet with a tight-fitting lid over low heat. Add shallots and cook for 1 to 2 minutes or until just softened. Add garlic and cook for 30 seconds to warm. Add wine and broth, bring to a simmer, and add mussels.

3. Cover and steam mussels for 3 to 4 minutes or until most have opened. Sprinkle fresh tomatoes and basil onto opened mussels, cover, and steam for 1 to 2 more minutes or until all mussels are opened and tomatoes are warm.

4. Using a slotted spoon, transfer mussels from the pot into a serving bowl or bowls. Swirl butter into the pot and simmer on low for about 30 seconds. Pour broth over mussels and serve with toasted bread, to mop up the juices, if desired.

> **DARE TO COMPARE:** The Tuscan Mussels at Maggiano's Little Italy have 530 calories and 30 grams of fat, not terrible for a meal out. At Bertucci's Italian Restaurant, a steamed-mussel appetizer clocks in with 1,600 calories with 71 grams of fat and 2,810 milligrams of sodium. This recipe easily beats them both!

NUTRITION INFORMATION PER SERVING (FOR 4): Calories 120 | Carbohydrate 6 g (Sugars 3 g) | Total Fat 4 g (Sat Fat 1 g) | Protein 12 g | Fiber 0 g | Sodium 310 mg | Food Exchanges: 1½ Lean Meat | Weight Watcher Smart Point Comparison: 1

Fast-Fix Pizza Margherita for One

MY SON JAMES WAS STUNNED TO FIND OUT the perfectly thin crispy crust for his mouthwatering margherita-style pizza was none other than a low-carb high-fiber tortilla. Not only is this pizza—made with fresh creamy mozzarella, juicy diced tomato, and fragrant basil—low in carbs, high in fiber, and blood sugar–friendly—it also bakes in mere minutes. Pair it with my In-a-Flash Caesar Salad (page 168) and you'll have lunch or dinner on the table before you can say "buon appetito."

MAKES 1 SERVING

1 high-fiber tortilla (like Mission Carb Balance*)

1 tablespoon pizza sauce

1 ounce sliced fresh mozzarella (or ¼ cup shredded)

1 tablespoon diced fresh tomato

1 tablespoon chopped or slivered fresh basil

Pinch of dried oregano

1. Preheat the oven to 425°F. Place the tortilla on a baking pan and spray lightly with nonstick cooking spray. Bake for 4 minutes or until lightly crisped.

2. Remove tortilla from oven and spread with pizza sauce. Break fresh mozzarella into small pieces and distribute evenly over sauce. Sprinkle with tomato, basil, and oregano.

3. Return to oven and bake for 4 to 5 minutes, or until cheese is melted and crust is crispy.

Marlene Says: *While all higher-fiber, lower-carb tortillas work for wraps, not all brands crisp well; Mission Carb Balance (and their Gluten-Free ones), and traditional flour tortillas, do.*

NUTRITION INFORMATION PER SERVING: Calories 200 | Carbohydrate 20 g (Sugars 1 g) | Total Fat 9 g (Sat Fat 4 g) | Protein 10 g | Fiber 11 g | Sodium 460 mg | Food Exchanges: 1 Starch, 1 Medium-Fat Meat, ½ Fat | Weight Watcher Smart Point Comparison: 7

Chicken Marsala

THIS CLASSIC ITALIAN RESTAURANT STAPLE IS A FAVORITE OF MINE. To make it, chicken is traditionally dredged in flour and then sautéed in oil, butter, or both. Sadly, far too many restaurants ratchet up the amount of fat, turning what can be a lovely light dish into a heavy meal. Instead, I use cornstarch to create melt-in-your-mouth tender chicken and just enough oil and butter to create a light, luscious sauce that lets the Marsala shine. Serve it with thin spaghetti and a glass of Chianti for a trattoria-worthy meal.

MAKES 4 SERVINGS

4 boneless, skinless chicken breasts (about 1 ¼ pounds)

⅜ teaspoon salt

½ teaspoon black pepper, divided

4 teaspoons cornstarch, divided

2 teaspoons olive oil

1 (8-ounce) package sliced mushrooms

¼ cup finely chopped shallots

⅔ cup reduced-sodium chicken broth

⅔ cup Marsala

2 teaspoons butter

2 tablespoons minced parsley

1. Cover the chicken breasts in plastic wrap and gently pound flat to ¼-inch thickness. Season chicken with salt and ¼ teaspoon pepper and coat one side of each breast with cornstarch (about ¾ teaspoon each).

2. Heat the oil in a large nonstick skillet over medium-high heat. Add chicken cornstarch-side down and cook for 3 to 4 minutes or until well browned. Turn and cook for 2 to 3 more minutes or until almost, but not quite cooked through. Transfer to a plate and keep warm.

3. Reduce heat to medium. Add mushrooms to pan and cook for 2 minutes. Add shallots and cook for 3 minutes or until softened; add broth, and simmer until liquid has reduced by half.

4. Whisk the remaining teaspoon of cornstarch into Marsala and add it to skillet with remaining ¼ teaspoon pepper. Simmer until slightly thickened and clear. Swirl in the butter, and add the chicken back to the skillet. Turn heat to low, cover, and cook for 2 to 3 minutes, turning chicken to coat with sauce. To serve, top chicken with Marsala sauce and garnish with parsley.

NUTRITION INFORMATION PER SERVING (1 BREAST WITH SAUCE): Calories 255 | Carbohydrate 9 g (Sugars 5 g) | Total Fat 8 g (Sat Fat 1.5 g) | Protein 33 g | Fiber 1 g | Sodium 350 mg | Food Exchanges: 4 Lean Meat, ½ Vegetable | Weight Watcher Smart Point Comparison: 3

Chicken Broccoli Alfredo

ALFREDO. NEED I SAY more? I originally fashioned this chicken broccoli Alfredo pasta dish after one at a local trattoria, and it quickly became a reader favorite. It's an easy, last-minute recipe, guaranteed to cure any decadent Alfredo cravings. With so many requests for smaller recipe yields, however, I retested the recipe, made a few tweaks, and scaled the number of servings down to four. (A recipe for four is perfect for four, or two for dinner and then lunch for two!). The taste is as luscious as ever.

MAKES 4 SERVINGS

6 ounces linguine or penne

3 cups broccoli florets

⅔ cup low-fat milk

1 tablespoon cornstarch

⅔ cup reduced-sodium chicken broth

3 tablespoons light cream cheese

1 teaspoon garlic powder

¼ teaspoon black pepper

¼ teaspoon salt

⅓ cup grated Parmesan cheese

2 cups shredded cooked chicken breast

Grated Parmesan, for garnish (optional)

1. Cook the pasta according to the package directions, adding the broccoli during the last 3 minutes of cooking. Drain, place back into the pot, cover, and set aside.

2. In a medium saucepan, whisk the milk and cornstarch until smooth. Whisk in the broth and place over low heat. Add the cream cheese, garlic powder, and pepper. Bring to a low simmer and cook until the sauce thickens, about 3 minutes. Whisk in the Parmesan and cook for 1 to 2 more minutes, or until sauce is smooth.

3. Toss the cooked pasta and broccoli with the sauce and place on a platter or plates. Top with the chicken and garnish with a couple tablespoons of grated Parmesan, if desired.

DARE TO COMPARE: Lean meat and vegetables in pasta dishes add protein and veggie goodness (which help curb carbs). Your typical restaurant chicken broccoli Alfredo dish undoes all the extra goodness as it dishes up 1,200 calories, two days' worth of saturated fat, and over 2,000 milligrams of sodium.

NUTRITION INFORMATION PER SERVING: Calories 325 | Carbohydrate 36 g (Sugars 5 g) | Total Fat 7 g (Sat Fat 3.5 g) | Protein 27 g | Fiber 4 g | Sodium 540 mg | Food Exchanges: 3 Lean Meat, 2 Starch, 1 Vegetable, ½ Fat | Weight Watcher Smart Point Comparison: 7

Slow-Cooker Braised Beef Ragu

WHEN YOU'RE CRAVING A SUNDAY FAMILY SUPPER with Sunday "gravy," make this beefy ragu. The heavenly aroma will have your family thinking you've been cooking all day, like an Italian nonna, while it cooks itself in a slow cooker. The slow cooking delivers the perfect Old World taste of tomatoey goodness and melt-in-your-mouth braised beef. Combining it in a skillet with cooked pappardelle before serving is an Old World tradition, but simply serving atop pasta works too. To complete the meal, I suggest a Caesar salad (page 168), warm bread, and a Luscious Lemon Cream Cake (page 186).

MAKES 8 SERVINGS

1 teaspoon olive oil

1 ½ pounds trimmed beef stew meat

1 cup diced carrots

1 cup diced celery

¾ cup red wine

1 (24-ounce) jar (or 2 ½ cups) marinara sauce

1 (8-ounce) package sliced mushrooms

1 ½ cups reduced-sodium beef broth

1 bay leaf

½ teaspoon red pepper flakes (optional)

2 tablespoons tomato paste

¼ teaspoon salt, plus more to taste

Black pepper to taste

1. In a large pot over high heat, heat the oil, add the meat, brown on all sides, remove, and set aside. In the same pot, cook the carrots and celery for 5 to 8 minutes or until softened. Deglaze the pot with the wine, scraping browned bits off the bottom of the pan with a wooden spoon.

2. Transfer vegetables to slow cooker, add next 5 ingredients (marinara through red pepper flakes), along with meat and accumulated juices, and stir to combine. Cook on low for 6 to 8 hours or high for 3 to 4 hours, or until meat is tender enough to shred with a fork.

3. Using 2 forks, break up the meat, and stir in the tomato paste. Cook for 10 to 15 more minutes or until paste is fully incorporated into warm sauce. Season with salt and black pepper to taste.

DARE TO COMPARE: The Braised Beef Bolognese at the Olive Garden served over pasta has 1,040 calories and six times as much fat and sodium. Served with ¾ cup of pasta, a portion of this dish has 330 calories.

NUTRITION INFORMATION PER SERVING (¾ CUP): Calories 180 | Carbohydrate 11 g (Sugars 4 g) | Total Fat 7 g (Sat Fat 2 g) | Protein 17 g | Fiber 3 g | Sodium 420 mg | Food Exchanges: 2 Lean Meat, 1 ½ Vegetable | Weight Watcher Smart Point Comparison: 5

Lazy Day Lasagna

I TRULY LOVE THIS RECIPE. Before I wrote Eat More of What You Love, *if you told me my favorite way to cook lasagna would be in a slow cooker, I would have never believed you. Yet now it is. Not only is it the quickest and easiest way I know (it takes less than 20 minutes to assemble with no boiling required), it's one of most delicious. The noodles come out soft and tender, the cheese filling extra creamy, and the mozzarella on top perfectly stringy. For my homemade marinara recipe see page 248.*

15 ounces low-fat ricotta cheese

1 ½ cups low-fat cottage cheese

6 tablespoons grated Parmesan cheese, divided

¾ teaspoon dried oregano, divided

1 (24-ounce) jar marinara sauce (or about 2 ½ cups)

7 traditional lasagna noodles, uncooked

⅔ cup shredded part-skim mozzarella cheese, divided

1. In a medium bowl, combine the ricotta, cottage cheese, 2 tablespoons water, ¼ cup Parmesan, and ½ teaspoon oregano.

2. Pour marinara into a medium bowl or a large measuring cup. Rinse jar with ½ cup water (unless marinara is already very thin) and stir it into marinara. Spread ½ cup onto the bottom of a 4- to 6-quart slow cooker.

3. Place half the lasagna noodles on top of the sauce, breaking noodles to fit (don't worry if small spaces are uncovered). Cover noodles with half the cheese mixture (about 1 ½ cups), then top with 1 cup sauce, and repeat.

4. Sprinkle the sauce with mozzarella, remaining oregano, and remaining Parmesan. Cook for 3 to 3 ½ hours on low or until fork-tender. Turn off heat and let sit at least 15 minutes before serving.

Marlene Says: *For* **SAUSAGE SLOW COOKER LASAGNA**, *brown 8 ounces of homemade Italian Sausage (page 242) or lean store-bought. Mix the sausage with 2 cups of the marinara and use it for the layering in Step 3. (Adds 50 calories and 2 grams fat per serving.)*

NUTRITION INFORMATION PER SERVING (⅙ OF THE LASAGNA, OR 1 GENEROUS CUP): Calories 320 | Carbohydrate 35 g (Sugars 12 g) | Total Fat 8 g (Sat Fat 7 g) | Protein 24 g | Fiber 2 g | Sodium 690 mg | Food Exchanges: 3 Lean Meat, 2 Carbohydrate, ½ Fat | Weight Watcher Smart Point Comparison: 7

Shrimp Fra Diavolo

WHILE THERE IS DEBATE ON WHETHER this classic "devil" dish truly came from Italy or if immigrants in America invented it, there's no debate that this seafood-studded dish with a kick is wickedly delicious. Compared to restaurant versions, I'm more generous with the succulent shrimp and a bit more reserved with the spicy red pepper, but feel free to adjust it to your taste. I love this served simply in a bowl with crusty bread to sop up the sauce, but it's also wonderful served over pasta or cooked spaghetti squash.

MAKES 2 SERVINGS

1 ½ teaspoons olive oil

½ cup onion, sliced and then sliced quartered

2 garlic cloves, thinly sliced

12 ounces frozen or ½ pound thawed extra-large shrimp

½ teaspoon red pepper flakes

½ teaspoon dried oregano

½ cup white wine (or broth)

1 cup crushed canned tomatoes

Pinch of salt, to taste

2 tablespoons fresh chopped Italian parsley

1. Place the oil in a medium sauté pan over medium-high heat. Add the onion and sauté 3 to 4 minutes. Add the garlic and warm for 30 seconds. Add the shrimp and sauté each side for 2 minutes, or until just slightly browned.

2. Add the next 4 ingredients to the pan (pepper flakes through tomatoes), cover the pan, and cook for 5 minutes or until flavors have melded. Add a pinch of salt to taste, if desired, and top with parsley.

Marlene Says: *I find this spicy little dish perfect for an at-home candlelit dinner. Pair it with a Caesar Salad (page 168), some good bread, and a bottle of Chianti.*

NUTRITION INFORMATION PER SERVING: Calories 220 | Carbohydrate 7 g (Sugars 3 g) | Total Fat 5 g (Sat Fat 0 g) | Protein 30 g | Fiber 2 g | Sodium 380 mg | Food Exchanges: 4 Very Lean Meat, 1 Vegetable, 2 Fat | Carbohydrate Choices: ½ | Weight Watcher Smart Point Comparison: 1

Chicken Caprese

CHICKEN TOPPED WITH THE INGREDIENTS OF A CAPRESE SALAD—fresh mozzarella, tomato, red onion, and basil—is a common entrée at many Italian-American restaurants. What's interesting is that the restaurant that I found offering the most impressive variation was not Italian, but Applebee's. Their dish of warm grilled red onion and tomato slices topped with melted cheese nestled between tender slices of garlic-flavored chicken breasts and drizzled with a balsamic reduction was delicious and visually impressive. It requires a bit of multitasking but the result is worth it.

MAKES 2 SERVINGS

¼ cup balsamic vinegar

2 teaspoons brown sugar

1 medium red onion, cut into 4 thick slices

4 thick slices of tomato

4 very thin slices fresh mozzarella cheese (about 3 ounces)

2 (4-ounce) boneless skinless chicken breasts

¾ teaspoon garlic salt

½ teaspoon dried basil leaves

½ teaspoon pepper

2 tablespoons thinly sliced fresh basil

1. In a small pot, simmer the vinegar and brown sugar over medium heat, for 3 to 4 minutes, stirring occasionally, or until it reduces by half and is thick and syrupy (watch carefully near the end of cooking—it can quickly burn). Remove from the heat and set aside.

2. Preheat the broiler. Line a baking sheet with foil, spray with cooking spray, and place onion slices onto pan. Brush onion with 2 teaspoons balsamic reduction and broil for 2 to 3 minutes per side or until slightly browned. Remove from broiler, move onion to the side, add tomato slices to same baking sheet, top tomato slices with cheese, and set aside.

3. Cover chicken breasts in plastic wrap and gently pound to ⅛-inch thickness. Season with garlic salt, basil, and pepper. Spray a nonstick skillet with cooking spray and place over medium-high heat. Add chicken and sauté for 2 to 3 minutes per side, until well browned and cooked through. Remove from pan and tent chicken with foil to keep warm

4. Place the baking sheet under the broiler for 1 minute, or until cheese melts and onion is hot. Slice each breast in half on the diagonal. To serve, arrange and overlap chicken breast with the onion and tomato slices on plates. Drizzle with remaining balsamic reduction and garnish with basil.

NUTRITION INFORMATION PER SERVING: Calories 285 | Carbohydrate 15 g (Sugars 11 g) | Total Fat 9 g (Sat Fat 4.5 g) | Protein 35 g | Fiber 2 g | Sodium 430 mg | Food Exchanges: 4½ Lean Meat, 1 Vegetable, ½ Carbohydrate | Weight Watcher Smart Point Comparison: 3

Easy Eggplant Parmesan

CHICKEN AND EGGPLANT PARMESAN ARE TWO OF THE MOST POPULAR DISHES at any Italian American eatery; they are also two of the least healthy. Thickly breaded, deeply fried, and smothered with cheese, the chicken or eggplant doesn't stand a chance. Eggplant, unfortunately, is especially susceptible to soaking up fat. Fortunately, it can be baked instead with absolutely mouthwatering results. I get rave reviews every time I serve this dish—even from eggplant haters.

MAKES 4 SERVINGS

1 medium globe eggplant (about 1 pound)

½ teaspoon salt

½ cup breadcrumbs

½ cup panko crumbs

1 large egg

⅓ cup flour

¼ teaspoon red pepper flakes (optional)

1 ½ cups marinara sauce

1 cup shredded part-skim mozzarella

2 tablespoons grated Parmesan cheese

2 tablespoons chopped fresh basil (optional)

1. Preheat oven to 425°F. Generously spray a 9 x 13 baking dish with cooking spray.

2. Slice eggplant (with skin) into ¼-inch slices. Place eggplant in a bowl, toss with salt, and let sit for 10 minutes. Rinse eggplant with water and pat dry.

3. In a shallow bowl, mix together breadcrumbs and panko crumbs. In another shallow bowl, beat egg until frothy. Place flour in third bowl. Coat eggplant with flour, then egg (letting excess drip off), and then breadcrumb mixture. Place eggplant on a baking sheet and bake for 20 minutes, turning slices over after 10 minutes.

4. If desired, add the pepper flakes to the marinara. Place ¾ cup of the sauce in the baking dish and lay the eggplant slices on top, slightly overlapping them. Top with remaining sauce, sprinkle with mozzarella, and then Parmesan. Cover with foil and bake for 15 minutes or until cheese melts. Garnish with basil, if desired.

> **DARE TO COMPARE:** An order of Eggplant Parmesan at Romano's Macaroni Grill, (served with a moderate amount of pasta) has 1,340 calories, including 90 grams of fat!

NUTRITION INFORMATION PER SERVING: Calories 225 | Carbohydrate 23 g (Sugars 5 g) | Total Fat 9 g (Sat Fat 0 g) | Protein 14 g | Fiber 3 g | Sodium 620 mg | Food Exchanges: 2 Vegetable, 1 Starch, 1 Medium-Fat Meat, 1 Fat | Weight Watcher Smart Point Comparison: 5

Tender Turkey Meatballs with Marinara

THESE ARE MY NEW FAVORITE MEATBALLS and, I hope now, yours too. To make them, instead of using dry breadcrumbs, I soak bread in liquid (like Rao's famed Italian restaurant), then add plenty of Parmesan and Italian spices. I roll them into good-sized balls and smother them with "doctored" store-bought marinara to finish the cooking. Big, saucy, and tender, these restaurant-style meatballs are ready within thirty minutes. Enjoy them with spaghetti, or any other way you please.

MAKES 12 MEATBALLS

2 slices white or wheat bread

1 pound lean ground turkey

1 large egg, beaten

2 tablespoons grated onion

1 tablespoon dried parsley

1 ½ teaspoons dried oregano, divided

¾ teaspoon garlic powder, divided

½ teaspoon salt

¼ teaspoon black pepper

1 ½ cups jarred marinara

¼ cup red wine (optional, but recommended)

1. Crumble the bread into very small pieces in a large bowl. Add ¼ cup water, and mash together. Add the next 8 ingredients (turkey through pepper), including 1 teaspoon dried oregano and ½ teaspoon garlic powder, and mix until combined. With wet hands form twelve 1 ¾-inch meatballs, using a scant ¼ cup meatball mixture for each (a ¼ cup scoop works well).

2. Spray a large nonstick skillet with nonstick cooking spray and heat over medium heat. Add meatballs to pan and cook until bottoms are well browned. Carefully turn over (they will be soft) and brown the other side. When the 2 sides are browned, add marinara along with remaining ½ teaspoon oregano, ¼ teaspoon garlic powder, and wine, if using, and carefully stir the sauce.

3. Cover the skillet and cook meatballs by simmering on low for 10 minutes, spooning sauce over meatballs once or twice, until cooked through (or 150°F).

Marlene Says: *One traditional restaurant 2-ounce Italian-style meatball made with pork and beef has 190 calories, 17 grams of fat, and 390 milligrams sodium. These mouthwatering meatballs are also approximately 2 ounces and only 70 calories each, without sauce.*

NUTRITION INFORMATION PER SERVING (PER MEATBALL WITH 2 TABLESPOONS SAUCE): Calories 80 | Carbohydrate 4 g (Sugars 2 g) | Total Fat 3 g (Sat Fat 1 g) | Protein 9 g | Fiber 1 g | Sodium 210 mg | Food Exchanges: 1¼ Lean Meat | Weight Watcher Smart Point Comparison: 2

Stovetop Rigatoni with Sausage and Peppers

THIS HEARTY DISH GOT A BIG TWO THUMBS-UP! Savory sausage with sweet sautéed peppers and onions are always a hit, and this creamy, cheesy pasta dish takes them to a whole other level. My inspiration for the rich-tasting sauce came by way of Olive Garden and the multitude of variations on their beloved baked ziti that combine Alfredo sauce and marinara. Keeping to the stovetop, instead of "oven-baking" is faster and ensures more creaminess and less cleanup.

MAKES 4 SERVINGS

2 cups dry rigatoni

2 teaspoons oil

1 cup chopped onions

1 medium green pepper, chopped

8 ounces Homemade Italian Sausage (page 242) or store-bought

1 1/2 cups marinara

1/3 cup nonfat half-and-half

1 tablespoon light cream cheese

1/2 teaspoon garlic powder

3 tablespoons grated Parmesan, divided

1/4 cup chopped fresh basil (optional)

1/2 cup shredded light mozzarella

1. Cook the pasta according to the package directions for al dente pasta and set aside.

2. While the pasta cooks, heat oil in a large nonstick skillet over medium-high heat. Add onions and peppers and cook for 3 to 4 minutes, or until they just begin to soften. Add sausage and continue to cook, breaking up the meat into pieces with a spoon, until sausage is just about cooked, onions translucent, and peppers almost tender.

3. Add marinara to skillet and stir. Add half-and-half, cream cheese, garlic powder, and 2 tablespoons Parmesan, and stir until everything is combined. Stir in 2 tablespoons basil, if desired. Add pasta, and stir to combine. (If desired, you can transfer pasta to a baking dish now.)

4. Top pasta with mozzarella, sprinkle with remaining tablespoon Parmesan, cover, and heat on low for 1 to 2 minutes, or until cheese melts (alternatively bake covered at 350°F for 15 to 20 minutes). Garnish with remaining basil before serving, if desired.

DARE TO COMPARE: The Taylor Street Baked Ziti at Maggiano's Little Italy (also made with sausage), has a staggering 1,410 calories, 76 grams of fat, and 4,060 milligrams of sodium (and 45 points!).

NUTRITION INFORMATION PER SERVING (1 1/2 CUPS): Calories 350 | Carbohydrate 42 g (Sugars 3 g) | Total Fat 10 g (Sat Fat 3 g) | Protein 26 g | Fiber 7 g | Sodium 380 mg | Food Exchanges: 4 Very Lean Meat, 1 Vegetable, 2 Fat | Weight Watcher Smart Point Comparison: 3

Luscious Lemon Cream Cake

OR SHOULD I SAY LEMON DREAM CAKE? Just like traditional Lemon Cream or limoncello cakes, this cake boasts moist, tender white cake encasing a heavenly rich-tasting lemon filling. My dinner guests, who gave it "crave" reviews, had no idea the cake had one-third of the usual calories and sugar and 80% less fat than similar cakes. I love to garnish it with fresh berries. If you want to get really fancy, add Raspberry Sauce (page 252).

MAKES 8 SERVINGS

CAKE

3 large eggs, room temperature

½ teaspoon vanilla

¼ cup granulated sugar

¼ cup granulated no-calorie sweetener*

⅔ cup cake flour

½ teaspoon baking powder

FILLING

¼ cup tub-style reduced-fat cream cheese

¼ cup nonfat cream cheese, room temperature

¼ cup plus 1 tablespoon granulated sweetener, divided*

2 tablespoons fresh lemon juice, divided

1½ teaspoons lemon zest

1¾ cups thawed light whipped topping, divided

1 teaspoon powdered sugar

See page 36 for sweetener options.

1. Preheat the oven to 350°F. Spray an 8-inch round cake pan with nonstick baking spray, line with wax paper or parchment paper, and spray it again.

2. In a large bowl with an electric mixer, beat eggs and vanilla on high for 1 minute. Add sugar and sweetener, and beat for 5 minutes, or until very thick and fluffy. Sift cake flour and baking powder into bowl in 2 additions, folding them in gently with a spatula until just incorporated. Spoon batter into prepared pan and bake for 14 to 16 minutes, or until center springs back when lightly touched. Remove from oven and cool on a wire rack.

3. While cake bakes, with an electric mixer, beat cream cheeses until smooth. Add ¼ cup sweetener, 1 tablespoon lemon juice, and lemon zest, and beat until smooth. Fold in 1¼ cups whipped topping and refrigerate.

4. Combine remaining tablespoon each of lemon juice and sweetener and ¼ cup water. Using a sharp serrated knife, slice cooled cake in half. Brush bottom half with lemon mixture, place on a plate, top evenly with filling, and then the cake top. Just before serving, dust top with powdered sugar and garnish with remaining topping and berries if desired.

DARE TO COMPARE: A piece of Lemon Cream Cake at Olive Garden has 550 calories with 31 grams of fat and 45 grams (or 11 teaspoons) of sugar.

NUTRITION INFORMATION PER SERVING: Calories 175| Carbohydrate 23 g (Sugars 13 g) | Total Fat 5 g (Sat Fat 3 g) | Protein 7 g | Fiber 0 g | Sodium 210 mg | Food Exchanges: 1½ Carbohydrate, 1 Fat | Weight Watcher Smart Point Comparison: 6

Tiramisu

TIRAMISU IS ARGUABLY THE BEST KNOWN—AND MOST DESIRED—Italian dessert. The combination of mascarpone (ultra-rich Italian cream cheese), heavy cream, egg yolks, and sugar, not surprisingly, is as decadent as it is delicious. As someone who loves tiramisu, I'm proud to say I've served this one to many a guest and not one ever thought it anything other than decadent. As a hostess, what's not to love about a quick, effortless, sinful-tasting dessert everyone can completely enjoy?

MAKES 6 SERVINGS

4 ounces mascarpone cheese*

4 ounces nonfat cream cheese, room temperature

¼ cup low-fat ricotta cheese

2 tablespoons light sour cream

½ cup plus 3 tablespoons no-calorie granulated sweetener, divided**

¾ cup thawed light whipped topping

1 tablespoon instant coffee

1 tablespoon brandy (optional)

1 (3-ounce) package soft ladyfingers

1 teaspoon cocoa powder, preferably Dutch-process

½ ounce semisweet chocolate, shaved (optional)

**See page 36 for sweetener options.*

1. In a medium mixing bowl, beat the cheeses, sour cream, and ½ cup sweetener with an electric mixer until creamy and smooth. Fold in the light whipped topping and set aside.

2. Place ¾ cup water in a small, microwave-safe bowl or saucepan. Add instant coffee, remaining 3 tablespoons of sweetener, and brandy, if desired, and heat on high for 1 minute.

3. To assemble, line the bottom of a 1-quart baking dish with half the ladyfingers and brush them well with half the coffee mixture. Top with half the cheese mixture, spread until smooth, and repeat. Sift the cocoa powder on top and top with the shaved chocolate, if desired. Refrigerate for at least 4 hours before serving.

Marlene Says: *I love the flavor of rich Italian mascarpone, but you can replace it with 4 ounces light tub-style cream cheese and 2 tablespoons light sour cream.*

NUTRITION INFORMATION PER SERVING (⅙ OF RECIPE): Calories 160 | Carbohydrate 9 g (Sugars 3 g) | Total Fat 11 g (Sat Fat 4 g) | Protein 5 g | Fiber 1 g | Sodium 135 mg | Food Exchanges: ½ Carbohydrate, 1 Lean Meat, 2 Fat | Weight Watcher Smart Point Comparison: 8

STEAKHOUSE & SEAFOOD

STEAKHOUSE & SEAFOOD

Spectacular Wedge Salad with Balsamic Drizzle

Classic Shrimp Cocktail

Crab Cakes with Creamy Dill Sauce

Longhorn-Style Parmesan-Crusted Chicken

Brown Sugar Bourbon Salmon

Scampied Sirloin and Shrimp

Perfectly Cooked Filet Topped Your Way

Succulent Lobster Tails with Seasoned Butter

Simply Steamed Lemon Butter Broccoli

Lawry's-Style Creamed Spinach

Creamy All-Purpose Mashed Potatoes

Chef Judy's Molten Lava Cakes

No-Bake Key Lime Pie Cups

New York Cheesecake with Raspberry Sauce

Individual Black Bottom Cheesecakes for Four

A PERFECTLY SEARED STEAK

If you're a steak lover, here's some sizzling news. You don't need a restaurant-quality kitchen or special equipment to prepare a restaurant-quality steak. The trick is in knowing the techniques steakhouse chefs use when preparing tender, flavorful steaks. Purchase a good-quality steak—lean or well marbled—and follow these five easy steps, and I guarantee you'll always serve a stellar steak.

FIVE EASY STEPS TO THE PERFECT STEAK

1. TAKE THE CHILL OFF. A cold steak doesn't cook evenly. By the time the middle of a cold steak is cooked, the outside will be overdone and tough. Take steaks out of the fridge at least 30 minutes, and up to one hour, before cooking.

2. SEASON WELL. Salt and pepper are the two must-haves for any steak (and I say a pinch of garlic powder never hurts). For the best sear and flavor, season steaks either a minimum of one hour before or immediately before cooking (not in between).

3. HEAT IT UP. Whether grilling a steak or cooking it classic steakhouse style (see page 202), start the cooking process by searing steaks over very high heat to create a flavorful crust on both sides.

4. USE A MEAT THERMOMETER. The pros do. If you overcook your steak, you can't fix it. Instant-read thermometers are inexpensive, easy to use, and quick. To determine doneness, use the chart below. The internal temperature of the steak will rise 5°F as it rests.

5. LET IT REST. Resting the steak after cooking, allows the juices to redistribute and the muscle fibers to relax. A 5- to 10-minute rest can decrease juices lost by as much as 40%!

DESIRED DONENESS	COOK UNTIL IT REGISTERS	FINAL REST TEMPERATURE
BEEF		
Medium-Rare	125 to 130°F	130 to 135°F
Medium	135 to 140°F	140 to 145°F
Medium-Well	145 to 155°F	150 to 160°F
PORK		
Medium	140 to 145°F	145 to 150°F
Well Done	150 to 155°F	155 to 160°F

*Note: for food safety, the government recommends steak be cooked to a minimum temperature of 145°F.

For the Love of
SEAFOOD

From tantalizing appetizers like shrimp cocktail and crab cakes to enticing entrées, such as sumptuous salmon and luxurious lobster, steakhouses are as famous for their seafood as they are for steak. Yet while most of us don't think twice about cooking steak at home; this is often not the case with fish and shellfish. I find this unfortunate, as seafood is not only one of the easiest and quickest foods to cook, it's one of the healthiest for you too! The Dietary Guidelines for Americans recommends consuming fish twice a week as part of a healthy diet. Fresh, frozen, or canned, it doesn't matter which. Here are a few good reasons to eat and cook foods from the sea:

SIX SWIMMINGLY GOOD REASONS TO LOVE SEAFOOD

1. FISH AND SHELLFISH ARE FABULOUS FOR YOUR HEART, BLOOD VESSELS, AND CIRCULATION. When eaten regularly, the omega-3 fatty acids in fish can help reduce the risk of a heart attack by as much as 40%. Aim for two servings a week of oil-rich fish like salmon or tuna.

2. SEAFOOD IS GOOD FOR YOUR BRAIN—AND MOOD! Research shows that people who eat more fish are less likely to suffer from dementia and memory loss. As a feel-good food, seafood not only improves your mood, it lowers your risk for depression.

3. FISH AND SHELLFISH CAN PROTECT YOUR EYES. Studies show that people who eat at least two servings of omega-3-rich fish per week are less likely to develop macular degeneration.

4. SEAFOOD CAN HELP YOU LOSE WEIGHT, AND LOOK GREAT! Fish (especially white fish) and shellfish are packed with satisfying high-quality protein and nutrients and yet are incredibly low in unhealthy fat and calories.

5. SEAFOOD IS CONVENIENT AND ECONOMICAL. Fresh fish is fabulous, while freezer-friendly and canned fish and shellfish can't be beat for satisfying, last-minute, shop-the-pantry meals.

6. FISH AND SHELLFISH ARE INCREDIBLY VERSATILE. From steakhouse faves like Crab Cakes with Creamy Dill Sauce and Longhorn-Style Sweet Bourbon Salmon to Southern-style Shrimp and Cheesy Grits, Mexican-inspired Baja-Style Fish Tacos, and Italian-flavored 15-Minute Bruschetta Mussels, fish and shellfish offer an amazing range of delectable textures and tastes.

Spectacular Wedge Salad with Balsamic Drizzle

A WEDGE SALAD IS A STEAKHOUSE MUST-HAVE. The Blue Cheese Wedge Salad served at Outback Steakhouse inspired this one. What sets it apart, and why I just had to share it again, is the sweet balsamic reduction that dazzles when you drizzle it over an impressive wedge of cool iceberg lettuce topped with tomatoes, diced onion, bacon, and homemade blue cheese dressing. So good! (The slim nutrition stats amaze me still.) If you're not a blue cheese fan, simply swap it out for Homestyle Ranch (page 247).

MAKES 4 SERVINGS

¼ cup balsamic vinegar

2 teaspoons brown sugar

1 medium head iceberg lettuce

¾ cup Blue Cheese Dressing (page 244), or reduced-calorie store-bought

1 cup chopped tomatoes

¼ cup medium diced red onion

8 teaspoons real bacon bits

1. To make the balsamic drizzle, stir the vinegar and brown sugar together in a small pot, and simmer over medium heat for 4 to 6 minutes, or until thick and syrupy and reduced by one-half. (Watch carefully—once reduced, the syrup can quickly burn.) Remove from the heat and set aside.

2. Cut the head of lettuce into quarters lengthwise, and cut the core out of each wedge. Place wedges on plates, remove a small amount of lettuce to make a slightly rounded well, and pour 3 tablespoons of dressing over each wedge.

3. Top each wedge with ¼ cup tomatoes and 1 tablespoon diced onion. Sprinkle 2 teaspoons of bacon bits across each salad, then drizzle 2 teaspoons of the balsamic reduction back and forth across the salad (if it has gotten too sticky or thick, add a small amount of water and/or re-warm).

DARE TO COMPARE: According to Outback Steakhouse, their Blue Cheese Wedge Salad has 530 calories, 43 grams of fat, 22 grams of sugar, and 1,090 milligrams of sodium. An independent analysis conducted by Tufts University tagged it with 1,035 calories. Either way, you can enjoy it at home for a whole lot less!

NUTRITION INFORMATION PER SERVING (1 WEDGE): Calories 120 | Carbohydrate 13 g (Sugars 10 g) | Total Fat 5 g (Sat Fat 2.5 g) | Protein 7 g | Fiber 2 g | Sodium 370 mg | Food Exchanges: 1½ Vegetable, 1 Fat | Weight Watcher Smart Point Comparison: 4

Classic Shrimp Cocktail

YOU ARE OFF TO A PERFECT START WHEN YOU START YOUR MEAL with a shrimp cocktail, as it's one of the healthiest items on a steakhouse menu. Even greater is that it's also one of the easiest dishes to replicate at home. As soon I drop the shrimp in boiling water, I turn off the heat to keep them tender. To add depth and round out the flavor of the usual ketchup horseradish cocktail sauce mixture, I add a splash of Worcestershire. Your taste buds will be saying "cheers"!

MAKES 4 SERVINGS

1½ teaspoons salt

1 pound shrimp (21 to 25 count), peeled and deveined with tails left on

¼ cup plus 2 tablespoons ketchup

1½ to 2 teaspoons horseradish

1½ teaspoons Worcestershire sauce

1½ teaspoons lemon juice

1. Combine 6 cups of water and salt in a large pot and bring to a boil over high heat. Add the shrimp and immediately remove from heat. Let shrimp sit for 3 minutes, or until nicely pink and firm to the touch. Drain, and immediately place shrimp in a bath of ice water. Let sit until completely chilled.

2. In a small bowl combine remaining ingredients with 1 tablespoon water. Drain shrimp, pat dry, and serve with cocktail sauce.

Marlene Says: *At fine-dining restaurants, shrimp cocktail is all about the presentation. I suggest using extra-large or jumbo shrimp. Placing the shrimp around the rim of individual cocktail glasses or on ice in your prettiest glass dish elevates this to a five-star appetizer.*

NUTRITION INFORMATION PER SERVING (5-6 SHRIMP): Calories 105 | Carbohydrate 7 g (Sugars 3 g) | Total Fat 1 g (Sat Fat 0 g) | Protein 18 g | Fiber 0 g | Sodium 360 mg | Food Exchanges: 2½ Very Lean Meat | Weight Watcher Smart Point Comparison: 1

Crab Cakes with Creamy Dill Sauce

FIRST-CLASS CRAB CAKES MADE WITH LUMP CRABMEAT are always a treat, but those made in five-star restaurants often come at a high price, both in cost and calories. These cakes use just enough mayo and breadcrumbs to hold the patties together, allowing the sweet crabmeat to take center stage. I oven-bake them, then like Morton's Steakhouse, I serve them with a mustard-tinged mayonnaise. The silky smooth 1-Minute Béarnaise Sauce on page 249 also pairs wonderfully.

MAKES 6 CRAB CAKES

CRAB CAKES

16 ounces lump crabmeat

1 scant cup breadcrumbs, divided

2 egg whites, lightly beaten

3 tablespoons light mayonnaise

2 tablespoons chopped parsley

2 teaspoons Worcestershire sauce

¾ teaspoon Old Bay seasoning

Black pepper, to taste

SAUCE

¼ cup plain low-fat yogurt

2 tablespoons light mayonnaise

¾ teaspoon prepared yellow mustard

1½ teaspoons fresh minced dill (or ½ teaspoon dried)

Pinch of sugar

1. Place a baking sheet in the oven and preheat to 400°F.

2. Place the crabmeat and ½ cup breadcrumbs in a large bowl. Add remaining crab cake ingredients and gently combine, taking care to keep large pieces of crab. Using wet hands shape the mixture into 6 patties (about ½ cup crab mix each). Place remaining crumbs on a plate or flat bowl and lightly coat both sides with crumbs.

3. Carefully remove hot baking sheet from oven. Lightly spray crab cakes with cooking spray, place on pan, and cook about 5 minutes per side, turning once, lightly spraying them with cooking spray again, or until lightly browned and warmed through.

4. While crab cakes are baking, whisk together sauce ingredients, adding 2 to 3 teaspoons of water to thin sauce to desired consistency.

DARE TO COMPARE: An appetizer of a single jumbo crab cake with mustard mayonnaise at Morton's has 690 calories. Two of these tasty crab cakes with sauce has 260.

NUTRITION INFORMATION PER SERVING (1 CRAB CAKE WITH SAUCE): Calories 130 | Carbohydrate 9 g (Sugars 0 g) | Total Fat 4 g (Sat Fat 0.5 g) | Protein 16 g | Fiber 2 g | Sodium 320 mg | Food Exchanges: 2 Very Lean Meat, ½ Starch | Weight Watcher Smart Point Comparison: 2

Longhorn-Style Parmesan-Crusted Chicken

WHEN FOLKS FLOCK TO A STEAKHOUSE TO ORDER CHICKEN, you know it has to be good. To recreate Longhorn's famous Parmesan Crusted Chicken, ranch dressing and two kinds of cheese are used to create gooey, cheesy layers atop tender chicken before it's smothered in buttery, cheesy garlic bread-crumbs. If this wonder of a chicken dish sounds deliciously decadent-tasting, it is. Pair it with Creamy All-Purpose Mashed Potatoes (page 208) and steamed broccoli for a waistline and wallet-friendly dinner that's guaranteed to have your family flocking to the table.

MAKES 4 SERVINGS

¼ cup Homestyle Ranch Dressing (page 247) or reduced-calorie store-bought

6 tablespoons shredded Parmesan cheese, divided

⅓ cup panko breadcrumbs

½ teaspoon garlic salt

2 teaspoons melted butter

4 boneless, skinless chicken breasts (about 1 pound)

¼ teaspoon black pepper

¾ cup shredded reduced-fat mozzarella cheese

1. In a small bowl, combine the dressing and 3 tablespoons Parmesan. In another small bowl, combine the remaining 3 tablespoons Parmesan, breadcrumbs, garlic salt, and melted butter.

2. Position oven rack in middle of oven. Gently pound chicken to ½-inch thickness. Coat a large ovenproof nonstick skillet with cooking spray and place over medium-high heat. Season chicken with pepper and cook for 2 to 3 minutes per side, or until well browned and just cooked through. Turn on the broiler.

3. Spread each breast with 1 generous tablespoon of the dressing, evenly top with 3 tablespoons mozzarella, and sprinkle with 2 tablespoons Parmesan breadcrumbs. Move the chicken to the oven and broil for 2 to 3 minutes, or until the cheese is melted and crumbs are nicely browned.

DARE TO COMPARE: This entrée clocks in with the exact same amount of protein as the 6-ounce serving of Parmesan Crusted Chicken at Longhorn Steakhouse, with half the calories, 75% less saturated fat and sodium, and 4 points instead of 14!

NUTRITION INFORMATION PER SERVING (1 BREAST): Calories 225 | Carbohydrate 6 g (Sugars 1 g) | Total Fat 8 g (Sat Fat 4 g) | Protein 36 g | Fiber 0 g | Sodium 440 mg | Food Exchanges: 4½ Lean Meat | Weight Watcher Smart Point Comparison: 4

Brown Sugar Bourbon Salmon

IF YOU PREFER SURF OVER TURF, this succulent salmon supper is for you. My husband and sons adored the flavors of this Longhorn Steakhouse favorite. Just like at the restaurant, a splash of bourbon is used to create the sweet, tangy, brown sugar marinade. To plate the salmon restaurant-style, serve it over brown rice alongside mixed vegetables. The recipe can easily be doubled to serve four.

MAKES 2 SERVINGS

2 tablespoons bourbon*

1½ tablespoons brown sugar

1½ tablespoons reduced-sodium soy sauce

1 tablespoon lime juice

1 garlic clove, minced

½ teaspoon powdered ginger (or 1½ teaspoons fresh grated)

2 (5-ounce) salmon fillets

2 tablespoons chopped green onions

1. In a 1-cup microwave-safe measuring cup, whisk together first 6 ingredients (bourbon through ginger). Place salmon in a ziplock bag or a bowl, top with 3 tablespoons of the sauce, and let marinate for 15 minutes. (If salmon has skin, lay the nonskin side of the fish into the sauce.)

2. Coat a nonstick skillet with nonstick cooking spray and place over medium-high heat. Add salmon and cook for 3 to 4 minutes per side, or until well browned on both sides. Alternately, heat a grill to medium hot, spray grates with cooking spray, and grill the fish for 3 to 4 minutes per side.

3. Place the measuring cup with the remaining sauce in the microwave and heat for 30 to 45 seconds (it should reduce slightly). Place salmon fillets on plates, drizzle with the remaining sauce, and garnish with green onions.

Marlene Says: *The flavor of the bourbon itself does not stand out, but you can use apple juice with ⅛ teaspoon of vanilla if you wish.*

NUTRITION INFORMATION PER SERVING (1 FILET WITH SAUCE): Calories 235 | Carbohydrate 7 g (Sugars 5 g) | Total Fat 10 g (Sat Fat 1 g) | Protein 28 g | Fiber 0 g | Sodium 300 mg | Food Exchanges: 4 Medium-Fat Meat | Weight Watcher Smart Point Comparison: 2

Scampied Sirloin and Shrimp

HERE'S AN IMPRESSIVE YET SPEEDY SURF-AND-TURF DINNER FOR TWO—that's economical too. Pairing steak with shrimp is a steakhouse tradition. Here, sirloin steak gets the royal treatment when topped with butterflied, buttery, steak-seasoned shrimp. Cooking the steak in a skillet allows you to take advantage of the "fond" (the caramelization of the meat left in the pan), which seasons the shrimp and creates a flavorful "scampi" pan sauce.

MAKES 2 SERVINGS

10 ounces sirloin steak (about ⅔ pound)

¾ teaspoon garlic powder, divided

¼ teaspoon salt

⅛ teaspoon black pepper

6 shrimp (21 to 25 count), peeled and deveined with tails left on

2 teaspoons butter

3 tablespoons white wine or reduced-sodium chicken broth

Chopped parsley for garnish

1. Let the steak come to room temperature and cut in half to make 2 steaks. Combine ½ teaspoon garlic powder, salt, and pepper. Just before cooking, season steaks with spice mixture.

2. Coat a large nonstick skillet with cooking spray and place over medium-high heat. Add steaks and cook for 2 minutes, or until bottom is well browned. Turn steaks, cook another 2 minutes, then turn again and cook for 1 minute until steaks are medium-rare (130°F), or to your liking.

3. Transfer steaks to a plate, cover with foil, and set aside. With a sharp knife, slice shrimp along the backside to partially "butter-fly" them. Add butter to hot skillet, then shrimp, and cook for 1 to 2 minutes per side, or until firm.

4. Move the steaks to serving plates and top each with three shrimp (or place two on top and one on the side). Add steak juices from plate along with remaining garlic powder and wine to skillet, swirl to combine with pan drippings, let reduce slightly, and pour sauce over steaks. Garnish with parsley.

Marlene Says: *Cold steaks are tough steaks. Be sure to let the steak sit out for at least 30 minutes and up to one full hour before cooking. Pat dry before seasoning.*

NUTRITION INFORMATION PER SERVING (1 STEAK WITH SHRIMP): Calories 290 | Carbohydrate 0 g (Sugars 0 g) | Total Fat 12 g (Sat Fat 6 g) | Protein 40 g | Fiber 0 g | Sodium 420 mg | Food Exchanges: 5½ Lean Meat | Weight Watcher Smart Point Comparison: 6

Perfectly Cooked Filet Topped Your Way

COOKING A STEAK STEAKHOUSE–STYLE IS NOT DIFFICULT. First you sear the outside of the steak on the stovetop to create a crust and seal in the juices, then you move it to the oven to finish cooking the center. Because filets are known for tenderness more than flavor, they often get topped or sauced. On this page, I give you two options, a buttery pan jus or a delectable Blue Cheese Topping (see Marlene Says). Or, for the royal French treatment, serve your steak with 1-Minute Béarnaise (page 249).

MAKES 2 SERVINGS

2 (5- to 6-ounce) trimmed filet mignon steaks (1 ¼ to 1 ½ inch thick)

¼ teaspoon salt (kosher or large grind recommended)

⅛ teaspoon black pepper

⅛ teaspoon garlic powder

BUTTERY PAN JUS

¼ cup reduced-sodium beef broth

Pinch of black pepper

1 teaspoon butter

1. Remove steaks from refrigerator at least 30 minutes before cooking. Preheat the oven to 400°F.

2. Combine salt, pepper, and garlic powder. When ready to cook, sprinkle each steak with half of the seasoning mixture. Heat a well-seasoned, cast-iron, or other ovenproof stainless-steel skillet very lightly coated with oil over medium-high heat until VERY hot. Add steaks and sear 2 minutes per side. (If desired, prepare blue cheese topping—see Marlene Says—while steaks cook so you can top your steaks before they move to the oven.)

3. Transfer pan to the oven and finish cooking for 7 to 8 minutes for a medium-rare steak (130–135°F), or to your liking.

4. Remove pan from the oven and transfer steaks to a warm plate to rest. For the buttery jus, place pan over medium heat, add beef broth, and a pinch of black pepper. Simmer broth until reduced by half. Stir in butter and top each steak with half of the buttery jus (adds 15 calories, 1.5 grams fat).

Marlene Says: For **BLUE CHEESE TOPPING**: *In a small bowl, combine 1 tablespoon EACH light cream cheese, crumbled blue cheese, plain nonfat yogurt or light sour cream, and 1 tablespoon white portion of chopped green onion (save green part for garnish). Before moving steak to oven, place a heaping tablespoon onto each steak and cook as in Step 3. Garnish with chopped green onion tops. (Adds 35 calories, 2 grams of fat, 2 grams protein).*

NUTRITION INFORMATION PER SERVING (1 FILET): Calories 215 | Carbohydrate 0 g (Sugars 0 g) | Total Fat 9 g (Sat Fat 4 g) | Protein 28 g | Fiber 0 g | Sodium 210 mg | Food Exchanges: 4 Lean Meat | Weight Watcher Smart Point Comparison: 5

Succulent Lobster Tails with Seasoned Butter

MY GOAL TO GIVE YOU EASY, SUCCULENT, RESTAURANT-STYLE LOBSTER, healthfully, meant I had to boil, bake, and steam more lobster tails than I'd ever even eaten in my entire life (or so it seemed). To that end (pun intended), I found steaming the tail a quick and easy way to produce succulent meat. Butterflying the tail takes a bit of practice, but it's totally worth it for the gorgeous presentation and the ability to brush the lobster with the heavenly seasoned butter. One five-ounce tail is perfect for surf and turf; two for a lavish, low-cal meal.

MAKES 2 SERVINGS

1 tablespoon butter

½ teaspoon lemon juice

⅛ teaspoon paprika

⅛ teaspoon garlic powder

Scant ⅛ teaspoon salt

Pinch of black pepper

2 (5-ounce) Maine lobster tails

Lemon wedges for garnish

1. In a small microwave-safe bowl, combine the first 6 ingredients (butter through pepper). Set aside. With the top shell up, using kitchen shears, cutting as close to the shell as possible, cut down the center of the shell to the base of the tail leaving the fin tip intact.

2. Flip tail over, make a slight snip at the top of the underside, and insert your finger between the thin shell and meat to separate meat from shell. Flip tail back over and slip a thin knife between sides of shell and meat to separate meat from top shell.

3. Using both hands, pry open the shell, and gently pull meat up and out of shell (leaving far fin end attached). Close empty shell and lay meat on top. Repeat with remaining tail.

4. Place a large skillet on the stove, add 1 inch of water, and bring to a low simmer. Add the tails, meat side up, to the pan, cover, and steam lobster for 4 to 5 minutes, or until meat reaches 140°F. While the lobster is steaming, microwave the butter mixture on high for 30 seconds. Remove lobster from skillet, place onto a paper towel to dry bottoms, then place them on plates, brush with butter sauce, and serve.

DARE TO COMPARE: The typical restaurant serving of clarified butter has 350 calories and 24 grams of saturated fat; the most outrageous, serves up a stunning 800 calories and three days' worth of saturated fat!

NUTRITION INFORMATION PER SERVING (1 TAIL): Calories 115 | Carbohydrate 0 g (Sugars 0 g) | Total Fat 5 g (Sat Fat 3 g) | Protein 13 g | Fiber 0 g | Sodium 370 mg | Food Exchanges: 2 Very Lean Meat, 1 Fat | Weight Watcher Smart Point Comparison: 1

Simply Steamed Lemon Butter Broccoli

IF YOU ARE LOOKING FOR AN EASY, FUSS-FREE SIDE that works with just about any entrée, this is it! In as few as five minutes, you have a restaurant-worthy plate partner that pairs with all of the recipes in this chapter, and beyond. Steaming the broccoli in the microwave, which keeps the broccoli gorgeously green, also means less prep and less cleanup—and I really love that!

MAKES 4 SERVINGS

1 pound broccoli florets

1 tablespoon butter

1 tablespoon fresh lemon juice

⅜ teaspoon seasoned salt

½ teaspoon grated lemon zest

2 tablespoons grated Parmesan cheese (optional)

1. Place the broccoli in a large microwave-safe bowl. Add ¼ cup water, cover tightly with plastic wrap, and microwave on high for 4 minutes.

2. While broccoli is cooking, place butter, lemon juice, and salt in a small microwave-safe cup or bowl. Remove broccoli and set aside. Microwave butter mixture on high for 30 seconds, or until butter melts. Add the lemon zest.

3. Uncover broccoli, carefully drain excess water, and toss well with lemon-butter sauce. Sprinkle with Parmesan before serving, if desired.

Marlene Says: *While I often focus on what my recipes do not have, it's good to know that they offer good nutrition too. For example, a single serving of this side delivers 3 healthy grams of fiber, along with 180% of your daily need for vitamin C and 35% of the RDA of vitamin A.*

NUTRITION INFORMATION PER SERVING (¾ CUP): Calories 60 | Carbohydrate 6 g (Sugars 2 g) | Total Fat 3 g (Sat Fat 2 g) | Protein 3 g | Fiber 3 g | Sodium 190 mg | Food Exchanges: 1 Vegetable, ½ Fat | Weight Watcher Smart Point Comparison: 1

Lawry's-Style Creamed Spinach

MY GOAL WHEN CREATING THIS RECIPE was a luscious, flavorful, silky creamed spinach—and nothing less would do. It took me a lot of tries, but in the end I found the secret to creating the silkiness I wanted was cooking the spinach separately before adding it to the rich, creamy, bacon-y sauce (mimicked by way of liquid smoke). Parmesan cheese adds that final flourish of cheesy flavor. I am proud to say I deliciously met my goal.

MAKES 6 SERVINGS

2 (10-ounce) packages frozen chopped spinach

2 teaspoons butter

½ cup finely chopped shallots or onions

2 garlic cloves, minced

2 teaspoons cornstarch

1½ cups low-fat milk

½ teaspoon liquid smoke

3 tablespoons light cream cheese

¾ teaspoon reduced-sodium seasoned salt

¼ teaspoon fresh ground black pepper

2 tablespoons grated Parmesan cheese

1. Place the spinach in a large microwave-safe bowl, add ½ cup of water, cover, and microwave on high for 9 minutes. Move the spinach to a strainer and using a small pot lid or plate, press down on it firmly, until the spinach is almost dry.

2. In a large nonstick skillet over medium heat, melt the butter; add the shallots, and cook until soft, about 3 minutes. Add garlic and sauté for 1 minute. Whisk together cornstarch, milk, and liquid smoke, add to pan, bring to a simmer, and cook for 2 minutes or until slightly thickened. Reduce heat to low and stir in cream cheese, seasoned salt, and pepper, and cook until smooth.

3. Increase the heat to medium and stir in spinach, turning to coat with sauce. Cook for 2 to 3 minutes or until thoroughly coated and creamy (if adding the spinach creates excess water, continue cooking until the water is cooked off). Stir in Parmesan cheese and serve.

DARE TO COMPARE: Like Morton's and Ruth's Chris steakhouses, the Capital Grille steakhouse serves sides for sharing (for two or three). A side order of creamed spinach dishes up 980 calories and 80% of them are from fat (and not the good kind).

NUTRITION INFORMATION PER SERVING (½ CUP): Calories 100 | Carbohydrate 10 g (Sugars 6 g) | Total Fat 3 g (Sat Fat 1.5 g) | Protein 8 g | Fiber 3 g | Sodium 290 mg | Food Exchanges: 1 Vegetable, ½ Low-Fat Milk, ½ Fat | Weight Watcher Smart Point Comparison: 3

Creamy All-Purpose Mashed Potatoes

WHAT'S A STEAKHOUSE ENTRÉE WITHOUT A SIDE OF CREAMY, buttery mashed potatoes? These super-creamy mashed potatoes are the perfect "steak" mates for every steak, chicken, or fish supper. Cauliflower curbs the carbs (the trick to no one noticing is to blend it 50/50 mix with regular potatoes), while cream cheese and a swirl of butter deliver the type of dreamy mash we all adore. They're luscious, but also light enough so you can enjoy that slice of cheesecake, too!

MAKES 4 SERVINGS

3 medium Yukon Gold potatoes, about 12 ounces, peeled and cubed

3 garlic cloves, peeled

2 cups frozen or fresh riced cauliflower, about 12 ounces

⅓ cup finely diced green onion tops

2 tablespoons light cream cheese

2 tablespoons low-fat milk

¼ teaspoon salt, or to taste

⅛ teaspoon pepper

1 tablespoon butter

1. Place the potatoes and garlic in a large pot of water, bring to a boil, and cook for 5 minutes. Add the cauliflower and cook an additional 10 minutes, or until the potatoes and cauliflower are tender.

2. Drain potato mixture in a fine-mesh colander or strainer. Remove excess water by pressing down firmly on the mixture with a pot lid or small plate.

3. Transfer the potato-cauliflower mixture back to the pot and add the onion tops, cream cheese, milk, salt, and pepper. Using a hand masher or electric mixer, process until smooth. Adjust salt to taste and swirl in the butter.

Marlene Says: *Look for riced cauliflower in the produce or freezer section of your market. An advantage to frozen is that it works equally well and keeps for months in your freezer.*

NUTRITION INFORMATION PER SERVING (⅔ CUP): Calories 115 | Carbohydrate 17 g (Sugars 3 g) | Total Fat 4 g (Sat Fat 2 g) | Protein 3 g | Fiber 3 g | Sodium 240 mg | Food Exchanges: 1 Starch, 1 Vegetable | Weight Watcher Smart Point Comparison: 3

Chef Judy's Molten Lava Cakes

WITH THEIR MELTY CHOCOLATY CENTERS, these dark chocolate lava cakes are the real deal. To serve, simply dust them with powdered sugar and and/or a squirt of whipped cream along with a tangle of fresh berries for no-fuss decadence. Hershey's Special Dark chocolate bars work well and are an easy-to-find chocolate option. With other chocolates, use two-ounces of chocolate for the batter, and one-ounce, divided, for pressing in the centers, or melt one-third cup semi-sweet chocolate chips for the batter and press a square or two of chocolate in each center.

MAKES 4 SERVINGS

2 (1.45-ounce) Hershey's Special Dark bars (or 1 [6.8-ounce] bar), divided*

1 tablespoon butter

2 tablespoons low-fat milk

1 teaspoon vanilla extract

3 large eggs, room temperature, separated

2 tablespoons cocoa powder, preferably Dutch-processed

2 tablespoons all-purpose flour

1 tablespoon granulated sugar

1 tablespoon powdered sugar (optional for dusting)

*You will not use all of the larger bar.

1. Preheat the oven to 400°F. Set the oven rack to the lower third of oven. Lightly coat four 6-ounce ramekins with cooking spray.

2. Reserve either 8 squares of chocolate from the small bars, or 2 from the large one. In a medium, microwave-safe bowl, microwave butter and remaining chocolate on high for 60 seconds, or until chocolate is mostly melted. Remove and stir until smooth. Whisk in milk, vanilla, and egg yolks until smooth. Sift in cocoa powder and flour, and whisk to combine.

3. In a medium bowl, with an electric mixer on high speed, beat the egg whites until foamy. Gradually add granulated sugar and beat to soft peaks. Fold ⅓ of the egg whites into the chocolate mixture to lighten, and then gently fold in remaining whites.

4. Divide the batter among the ramekins. If using small chocolate bars, press 2 squares into the center of each cake. With larger bar, cut each square in half and press into each cake. Bake for 8 to 9 minutes, or until tops are just firm to the touch and the cakes still jiggle slightly in the center. Let cool for 2 minutes and serve immediately with a dusting of powdered sugar, if desired.

> **DARE TO COMPARE:** A single chocolate lava cake can add another 900 calories to your steakhouse dinner, including two days' worth of added sugar, a day's worth of fat, and an entire meal's worth of carbohydrates.

NUTRITION INFORMATION PER SERVING (1 LAVA CAKE): Calories 210 | Carbohydrate 21 g (Sugars 15 g) | Total Fat 12 g (Sat Fat 7 g) | Protein 7 g | Fiber 2 g | Sodium 85 mg | Food Exchanges: 1½ Carbohydrate, 1 Lean Meat, 1½ Fat| Weight Watcher Smart Point Comparison: 9

No-Bake Key Lime Pie Cups

TAKE A PEEK AT A STEAKHOUSE DESSERT TRAY, and chances are sitting prettily between the chocolate and cheesecake, you'll find citrusy, little key lime pie cups. Their popularity should come as no surprise because it's hard to pass up such a tempting offering. Tart, sweet, and refreshing—they are also the perfect size after a big dinner. What most diners don't know is that these "mini" treats often have mega-calories. With only 155 calories, and less than a teaspoon of added sugar each, my no-bake key lime beauties are the perfect finish to your at-home steakhouse dinner.

MAKES 4 SERVINGS

6 tablespoons finely crushed graham crackers

3 tablespoons granulated sweetener, divided*

1 tablespoon butter, melted

¼ cup key lime juice

1½ teaspoons granulated sugar

¾ teaspoon unflavored gelatin powder

¼ cup light tub-style cream cheese, softened

½ cup plain nonfat Greek yogurt

1–2 drops green food coloring (optional)

Grated zest of 1 lime

½ cup plus 6 tablespoons light whipped topping, divided

Fresh berries for garnish (optional)

See page 36 for sweetener options.

1. In a small bowl, stir together the graham cracker crumbs, 1 tablespoon sweetener, and butter. Stir in about 1 teaspoon water, or just enough for crumbs to hold shape when pressed together. Lightly press into four 6-ounce glass cups, using about 2 tablespoons each. Set aside.

2. In a small microwave-safe bowl, combine lime juice and sugar. Sprinkle gelatin on top and let sit 5 minutes. Microwave for 20 seconds on high, stir, and set aside.

3. In a medium bowl, with an electric mixer on low speed, beat cream cheese, yogurt, food coloring, if desired, remaining 2 tablespoons sweetener, and key lime juice mixture until smooth. Fold in lime zest and ½ cup whipped topping.

4. Spoon the filling on top of crumbs. Chill for at least 1 hour or until filling sets. To serve, top each with 1½ tablespoons topping and fresh berries, if desired.

DARE TO COMPARE: With 570 calories, 23 grams of fat, and 66 grams of sugar, a Key Lime Pie Mini Parfait at Outback Steakhouse has 4X the calories (and points), 5X the carbohydrates and 6X times the sugar of these delectable pie cups.

NUTRITION INFORMATION PER SERVING (1 KEY LIME CUP): Calories 155 | Carbohydrate 15 g (Sugars 10 g) | Total Fat 8 g (Sat Fat 5 g) | Protein 9 g | Fiber 0 g | Sodium 85 mg | Food Exchanges: 1 Carbohydrate, 1 Fat | Weight Watcher Smart Point Comparison: 7

New York Cheesecake with Raspberry Sauce

DENSE, RICH, CREAMY New York cheesecake delivers decadence in every bite. To create the same luxurious taste and texture, sans the guilt, is rather tricky. Light cream cheese and cottage cheese have long been go-tos for me, but I've discovered that Greek yogurt works fantastically, too. The trick is to use one that is very thick and creamy and has a smooth sour cream taste (see page 30). Baking the cheesecake in a water bath is also a must. Love chocolate? Chocolate sauce (page 250) can replace the raspberry.

MAKES 12 SERVINGS

2 tablespoons margarine or butter, melted

1 cup graham cracker crumbs

1 ¼ cups plus 2 tablespoons granulated sweetener, divided*

1 ½ cups low-fat cottage cheese

12 ounces light tub-style cream cheese, room temperature

2 ½ tablespoons cornstarch

2 ½ teaspoons vanilla extract

3 large eggs, beaten, room temperature

1 cup nonfat or reduced-fat Greek yogurt (I use Fage brand)

All-Purpose Raspberry Sauce (page 252)

*See page 36 for sweetener options.

1. Preheat the oven to 325°F. Coat an 8-inch round cake pan with nonstick cooking spray. (If you use a springform pan, tightly wrap it with heavy-duty foil to make it waterproof.)

2. Place melted margarine in the pan, add graham cracker crumbs, and 2 tablespoons of sweetener, combine, and press crumbs firmly onto bottom of pan. Bake for 10 minutes and set aside.

3. Place cottage cheese in food processor and process until completely smooth. Add cream cheese, 1 ¼ cups sweetener, cornstarch, and vanilla, and process just until smooth. Pour mixture into a bowl and whisk in eggs one half at a time, whisking just until blended. Stir in yogurt.

4. Place prepared pan inside a 9 x 13-inch pan (or larger) with 2- to 3-inch sides. Pour batter into smaller pan and place in oven. Pour hot water into larger pan until it reaches halfway up the sides of the cheesecake. Bake for 50 to 60 minutes, or until sides of cake appear firm but center still jiggles slightly.

5. Remove the cheesecake from the oven and water bath and cool to room temperature. Place in the refrigerator and chill at least 6 hours before serving. Serve each piece with 2 tablespoons raspberry sauce.

DARE TO COMPARE: A piece of Outback Cheesecake with raspberry sauce packs 1,040 calories, two days' worth of saturated of fat, and 20 teaspoons of sugar. (Count points? It's 50!)

NUTRITION INFORMATION PER SERVING (1 SLICE WITH SAUCE): Calories 190 | Carbohydrate 16 g (Sugars 8 g) | Total Fat 8 g (Sat Fat 4 g) | Protein 10 g | Fiber 3 g | Sodium 320 mg | Food Exchanges: 1 ½ Lean Meat, 1 Carbohydrate, 1 Fat | Weight Watcher Smart Point Comparison: 6

Individual Black Bottom Cheesecakes for Four

A FULL-SIZED CHEESECAKE IS A BEAUTIFUL THING TO BEHOLD, but let's face it, unless you are entertaining guests, 12 servings of cheesecake is a lot to have around. This recipe solves that dilemma, and deliciously so, as it serves just four (or yourself four times!). Not only is the yield less, so is the time it takes to make it. Oh, and the crust is dark chocolate. These will keep well in the fridge for a week. Fresh berries are great garnishes.

MAKES 4 SERVINGS

2 teaspoons margarine or butter, melted

½ cup chocolate graham cracker crumbs

1 teaspoon cocoa powder (I use Dutch-process)

7 tablespoons granulated sweetener, divided*

⅔ cup low-fat cottage cheese

½ cup light tub-style cream cheese

1 tablespoon cornstarch

¾ teaspoon vanilla extract

1 large egg, beaten

½ cup light sour cream

Fresh raspberries or strawberries (optional)

All-Purpose Raspberry Sauce (optional, page 252)

*See page 36 for sweetener options.

1. Preheat the oven to 275°F. Spray four 6-ounce ramekins with nonstick cooking spray.

2. Place melted margarine in a small bowl, add crumbs, cocoa powder, and 1 tablespoon sweetener, combine, and press 2 rounded tablespoons of crumbs onto the bottom of each ramekin. Bake for 10 minutes and set aside.

3. Place cottage cheese in a food processor and process until completely smooth. Add cream cheese, 6 tablespoons sweetener, cornstarch, and vanilla, and process briefly just until smooth. Pour mixture into a bowl and whisk in egg, whisking just until blended (adding air to the batter increases the likelihood of cracking). Stir in the sour cream with a large spoon.

4. Place the ramekins on a baking sheet and bake for 30 minutes, or until the middle is barely set. Cool to room temperature, then place in the refrigerator and chill at least 4 hours before serving. Top with fresh berries and/or raspberry sauce, if desired.

NUTRITION INFORMATION PER SERVING (1 CHEESECAKE): Calories 190 | Carbohydrate 14 g (Sugars 8 g) | Total Fat 9 g (Sat Fat 4 g) | Protein 12 g | Fiber 0 g | Sodium 360 mg | Food Exchanges: 1 Lean Meat, 1 Carbohydrate, 1 Fat | Weight Watcher Smart Point Comparison: 6

CAFÉ BAKERIES—MORE SOUPS, SALADS, SANDWICHES & SWEETS

CAFÉ BAKERIES—MORE SOUPS, SALADS, SANDWICHES & SWEETS

Spinach & Artichoke Breakfast Bakes

Overnight Creamy Oats with Fruit and Nuts

Mimi's Café Asian Chicken Salad

Strawberry Chicken Poppy Seed Salad

My La Madeleine Tomato Basil Soup

Easy Southwest Chicken Chili

Panera-Style Broccoli Cheddar Soup

Turkey Ranch Wrap

Tuna Tartine (aka My Favorite Toasted Tuna Sandwich)

Grown-Up Grilled Cheese

Chocolate Chip Muffies

Baker's Dozen Peanut Butter Scotchies

James' Lemon Blueberry Bars

Fresh Orange Scones

Spinach & Artichoke Breakfast Bakes

IN A SEA OF QUICK-SERVICE BREAKFAST FARE, Panera Bread's Baked Egg Soufflés rise to the top. To create them, Panera places a small spoonful of eggs into the middle of a generous portion of croissant dough. My take on the spinach and artichoke variation amps up the creamy filling and tops it with cheesy convenient crescent dough instead. If you prefer a Spinach & Bacon Breakfast Bake, simply swap out the artichokes for two tablespoons of real bacon bits.

MAKES 4 SERVINGS

¾ cup fresh spinach

2 tablespoons light tub-style cream cheese

3 tablespoons plain nonfat Greek yogurt or light sour cream

4 large eggs, room temperature, divided

3 tablespoons finely diced artichoke hearts

2 tablespoons shredded reduced-fat cheddar cheese

¾ teaspoon baking powder

¼ teaspoon garlic powder

Dash of Tabasco or ⅛ teaspoon black pepper

3 tablespoons grated Parmesan or Romano cheese, divided

1 (8-ounce) can reduced-fat crescent-rolls dough*

*You will only use half of the crescent dough for this recipe. The remaining dough can be rolled and baked along with the soufflés. The crescent rolls will take a few more minutes to finish baking.

1. Preheat the oven to 325°F. Spray four 6-ounce ramekins with cooking spray and place on a baking sheet. Place spinach in a small bowl and microwave for 30 seconds, or until fully wilted. Drain off any water, blot spinach dry with a paper towel, and finely chop it.

2. In a medium bowl, whisk together cream cheese and yogurt until very smooth. Whisk in one egg until smooth, or until only flecks of cream cheese remain. Whisk in 2 more eggs, artichoke hearts, cheddar cheese, baking and garlic powders, Tabasco, spinach, and 2 tablespoons Parmesan. Divide mixture among ramekins and bake for 8 minutes, or just until the tops only are no longer liquid.

3. While soufflés are baking, quickly unroll crescent dough and lay flat. Cut dough in half widthwise (setting one half aside)*, press seams together, cut into 4 squares, and fold in the tips at the 4 corners. Beat remaining egg with 1 teaspoon water and brush onto dough. Dust each with ¾ teaspoon Parmesan cheese.

4. As soon as just the tops of the soufflés are set, gently place a dough square on top of each, increase the oven temperature to 350°F, and bake for another 8 to 10 minutes, or until soufflés are puffed and tops are golden brown. Do not overbake.

DARE TO COMPARE: A Panera Spinach & Artichoke Soufflé serves up 520 calories, three times the fat, and five times the saturated fat. I'll take this bake!

NUTRITION INFORMATION PER SERVING (1 SOUFFLÉ): Calories 195 | Carbohydrate 14 g (Sugars 3 g) | Total Fat 10 g (Sat Fat 4 g) | Protein 13 g | Fiber 1 g | Sodium 420 mg | Food Exchanges: 1½ Medium-Fat Meat, 1 Starch, ½ Fat | Weight Watcher Smart Point Comparison: 4

Overnight Creamy Oats with Fruit and Nuts

AMERICA'S MOST POPULAR HOT BREAKFAST CEREAL has gone cold! Yes, creamy chilled oatmeal for breakfast is now all the rage. Instead of cooking the oats, uncooked oats are soaked overnight in water or milk until thick and velvety. (The Swiss have been serving oats this way for hundreds of years.) The trick to the perfect texture is to quickly toast the oats before soaking. Doing so gives you oh-so-creamy—instead of pasty—oats. Sweet, fruity, and a little bit nutty, these make-ahead oats are chill-icious.

MAKES 1 SERVING

⅓ cup old-fashioned rolled oats

¼ cup plain nonfat Greek yogurt

1½ tablespoons granulated sweetener (or 2 packets) *

½ teaspoon cinnamon

Pinch of salt

⅓ cup frozen (unthawed) or fresh mixed berries

1 teaspoon light maple-flavored syrup

1 teaspoon sliced or chopped nuts

*See page 36 for sweetener options.

1. Sprinkle oats into a small nonstick skillet. Heat over medium heat for 1 to 2 minutes or until oats are lightly browned and smell toasty.

2. In a small (8-ounce) Mason jar, other container with lid, or bowl, combine oats, yogurt, sweetener, cinnamon, and salt. Add ½ cup of water and stir well.

3. Top with berries, drizzle with syrup, cover (if made in a bowl, oats do not require covering unless desired) and let sit overnight. Just before serving (or grabbing to go), sprinkle with nuts.

Marlene Says: *Greek yogurt adds a wallop of hunger-satisfying protein and extra creaminess stealthily (meaning you won't taste it in the finished oat cereal). While fresh berries are always a treat, I prefer frozen berries here as they release delicious sweet juice onto the oats as they thaw.*

NUTRITION INFORMATION PER SERVING: Calories 185 | Carbohydrate 29 g (Sugars 7 g) | Total Fat 3 g (Sat Fat 0 g) | Protein 11 g | Fiber 5 g | Sodium 160 mg | Food Exchanges: 1 Starch, ½ Lean Meat, ½ Fruit, ¼ Nonfat Milk | Weight Watcher Smart Point Comparison: 4

Mimi's Café Asian Chicken Salad

MIMI'S CAFE IS A CASUAL RESTAURANT FOUND ACROSS THE WESTERN and Southern portion of the United States. The "French-inspired" Mimi's offers a wide selection of dishes; ironically, one the most revered is their Asian Chicken Chopped Salad. To make this salad, I buy no-sugar-added mandarin oranges, packaged in individual serving cups. When drained, each one contains the perfect amount for this salad. Use one here and another for the Strawberry Chicken Poppy Seed Salad on page 223.

MAKES 2 SERVINGS

DRESSING

2 tablespoons rice vinegar

1 tablespoon sesame oil

1 ½ tablespoons granulated sweetener*

1 tablespoon reduced-sodium soy sauce

2 teaspoons ketchup

1 teaspoon grated fresh ginger

2 tablespoons sliced almonds

SALAD

2 cups chopped romaine lettuce

1 cup shredded cabbage

1 medium red bell pepper, chopped

¼ cup chopped cilantro

¼ cup green onion, sliced at an angle

⅓ cup mandarin oranges, drained

1 cup shredded chicken breast

See page 36 for sweetener options.

1. For the dressing, in a small bowl, whisk together the first 6 ingredients (vinegar through ginger). Set aside.

2. Place almonds in a small skillet over low heat and toast for about 2 to 3 minutes, or until the almonds are lightly browned. In a medium bowl, combine lettuce, cabbage, bell pepper, cilantro, and half the green onion. Add orange segments and chicken and lightly toss.

3. Pour the dressing over the salad and toss lightly to coat. Garnish with the toasted almonds and remaining green onions.

DARE TO COMPARE: At Mimi's, a salad like this has a "restaurant-modest" 520 calories and 28 grams of sugar. Mimi's however serves it with a muffin. The salad meal has 1,096 calories and triple the sugar. At home **YOU** choose your sides.

NUTRITION INFORMATION PER SERVING (1 SALAD): Calories 250 | Carbohydrate 15 g (Sugars 8 g) | Total Fat 10 g (Sat Fat 1 g) | Protein 24 g | Fiber 5 g | Sodium 290 mg | Food Exchanges: 3 Lean Meat, 2 Vegetables, 1 Fat | Weight Watcher Smart Point Comparison: 1

Strawberry Chicken Poppy Seed Salad

WHEN I TOLD A FRIEND I WAS CREATING A VARIATION ON A PANERA SALAD, she blurted out, "Is it the Strawberry Poppy Seed Salad?" Truth be told, this super popular seasonal salad is one of Panera's better-for-you options, but why go out and buy one when it's a snap to make at home? Crisp lettuce, tender chicken, sweet strawberries, blueberries, and mandarin orange slices are topped with crunchy pecans and drizzled with an addictive poppy seed dressing. It's every bite as good as the original!

MAKES 2 SERVINGS

DRESSING

1 ½ tablespoons light orange juice

1 ½ tablespoons light mayonnaise

1 tablespoon rice vinegar

1 teaspoon granulated sugar

½ teaspoon Dijon mustard

¼ teaspoon poppy seeds

SALAD

3 ½ cups chopped romaine lettuce

½ cup sliced fresh strawberries

⅓ cup mandarin oranges, drained

¼ cup fresh blueberries

⅔ cup chopped cooked chicken breast

2 tablespoons toasted pecans

1. For the dressing, in a small bowl, whisk together the dressing ingredients. Set aside.

2. Divide lettuce between 2 plates or flat bowls. Divide the strawberries, oranges, and blueberries between each plate, tucking fruit into the lettuce. Drizzle each salad with 2 tablespoons dressing, top with ⅓ cup chicken, and garnish with pecans.

Marlene Says: Go ahead and use this poppy seed dressing on other salads. It has just 40 calories, 2.5 grams of fat, 4 grams of carbohydrate, and 120 milligrams of sodium per 2-tablespoon serving.

NUTRITION INFORMATION PER SERVING (1 SALAD): Calories 230 | Carbohydrate 16 g (Sugars 10 g) | Total Fat 8 g (Sat Fat 0.5 g) | Protein 24 g | Fiber 4 g | Sodium 350 mg | Food Exchanges: 2 Lean Meat, 1 Fruit, 1 Vegetable, 1 Fat | Weight Watcher Smart Point Comparison: 3

My La Madeleine Tomato Basil Soup

LA MADELEINE FRENCH BAKERY & CAFÉ IS HAPPY TO SHARE that their customers love their *"iconic" signature tomato basil soup, so much that it's also sold in jars—but what a tale its label tells. The first ingredient is tomatoes with puree (like this recipe), then cream, and LOTS of butter. To recreate the silky creaminess, I use nonfat half-and-half and cornstarch. To get the biggest bang from the requisite butter, I swirl it in last—as the last thing in the pot is the first thing you taste!*

MAKES 4 SERVINGS

1 (14.5-ounce) can no-salt-added crushed tomatoes in puree

1 ½ cups tomato juice

½ cup reduced-sodium chicken broth

½ teaspoon onion powder

½ teaspoon garlic powder

⅛ teaspoon black pepper

¼ cup slivered fresh basil, divided

⅔ cup nonfat half-and-half

2 ½ teaspoons cornstarch

1 ½ tablespoons butter

1. In a medium soup pot, combine the first 6 ingredients (tomatoes through pepper) plus 2 tablespoons basil, and place over medium-high heat. Bring to a simmer, cover, reduce the heat to medium-low, and simmer for 10 minutes to meld flavors.

2. Whisk together half-and-half and cornstarch, and add to soup. Simmer on low for 2 minutes, or until slightly thickened. (Do not let it boil vigorously.)

3. Just before serving, swirl in the butter and garnish with remaining 2 tablespoons basil.

DARE TO COMPARE: According to the jar, an 8-ounce serving of La Madeleine Tomato Basil Soupe has 360 calories, and an entire day's worth of saturated fat.

NUTRITION INFORMATION PER SERVING (1 CUP): Calories 120 | Carbohydrate 16 g (Sugars 9 g) | Total Fat 4 g (Sat Fat 3 g) | Protein 4 g | Fiber 2.5 g | Sodium 410 mg | Food Exchanges: 2 Vegetable, 1 Fat, ½ Carbohydrate | Weight Watcher Smart Point Comparison: 3

Easy Southwest Chicken Chili

SIMILAR TO THE WHITE CHICKEN CHILI THAT USED TO BE SERVED in bread bowls at St. Louis Bread Company, this is one of my favorite recipes, as it couldn't be easier or faster to make, especially if you have cooked chicken on hand. You can also make it with turkey as they do at Cosi's; the only other difference is that theirs includes colorful yellow corn and jalapeños for a bit of subtle heat.

MAKES 6 SERVINGS

2 teaspoons canola oil

1 medium onion, diced

1 teaspoon minced garlic

1½ teaspoons ground cumin

¾ teaspoon dried oregano

⅛ teaspoon cayenne pepper

1 (14-ounce) can, or 2 cups, reduced-sodium chicken broth

1 (4-ounce) can chopped green chilies

2 (15-ounce) cans Great Northern beans, drained

3 cups shredded chicken breast

⅓ cup fresh chopped cilantro, for garnish

1 cup reduced-fat Mexican blend shredded cheese (optional)

1. Heat the oil over medium heat in a large saucepan. Add the onion and sauté for 4 to 5 minutes or until slightly softened. Add the garlic, cumin, oregano, and cayenne pepper, and sauté for 1 minute.

2. Stir in the chicken broth, green chilies, beans, and chicken. Reduce heat to low and simmer for 15 minutes. Ladle into bowls and top with the cilantro and cheese, if desired.

NUTRITION INFORMATION PER SERVING (1 CUP): Calories 210 | Carbohydrate 17 g (Sugars 3 g) | Total Fat 6 g (Sat Fat 0 g) | Protein 1 g | Fiber 6 g | Sodium 80 mg | Food Exchanges: 3 Lean Meat, 1 Starch | Weight Watcher Smart Point Comparison: 1

Panera-Style Broccoli Cheddar Soup

IF YOU'RE A FAN OF PANERA BREAD'S BROCCOLI CHEDDAR SOUP, this recipe will make your day. I tested it many times over to nail the creamy texture, taste, and color of the original—and to make it quick and easy. NOTE: 1) Use a fresh carrot. Bagged shredded carrots do not impart the right color or sweetness. 2) Leftovers will be delicious, but not as thick. 3) More broccoli and half the fat of the original makes it taste even better!

MAKES 3 SERVINGS

1 teaspoon olive oil

⅓ cup finely chopped onions

1½ cups reduced-sodium chicken broth

1 cup shredded carrot (about 1 medium)

1¾ cups frozen broccoli florets

1 (10¾ ounce) can reduced-fat cream of celery soup

½ teaspoon garlic powder

⅜ teaspoon black pepper

6 tablespoons shredded reduced-fat cheddar cheese, divided

1. Heat the oil in a medium soup pot over medium-high heat. Add the onion and sauté for 3 to 4 minutes or until onion is soft (add a few tablespoons of the broth if needed to keep the onions moist). Add the carrot and cook for another 3 minutes or until well softened.

2. Cut any very large broccoli florets into spoon-sized pieces and add to pot. Add chicken broth, soup, garlic powder, and pepper, stir, bring to a simmer, and cook 8 to 10 minutes, or until vegetables are fully softened.

3. Remove from heat, add 3 tablespoons of cheddar cheese, and stir until melted. To serve, divide the soup between 3 bowls, and add 1 tablespoon of cheese into each bowl.

NUTRITION INFORMATION PER SERVING (1 CUP): Calories 135 | Carbohydrate 15 g (Sugars 5 g) | Total Fat 6 g (Sat Fat 2 g) | Protein 10 g | Fiber 4 g | Sodium 620 mg | Food Exchanges: ½ Starch, 1 Vegetable, 1 Nonfat Milk | Weight Watcher Smart Point Comparison: 3

Turkey Ranch Wrap

WHETHER EATING AT HOME, OR OUT, turkey is America's favorite sandwich meat. This wrap takes turkey and pairs it with a ranch-flavored spread, mimicking one of the most popular sandwich combinations at a local café. The café also includes Swiss cheese on their sandwich, but I don't find it necessary with the flavor punch of the spread. The thin slices of cucumber are my own addition; I love how their cool crunch mingles with the creamy spread and soft tortilla.

MAKES 1 SERVING

1 tablespoon reduced-fat mayonnaise

1 tablespoon nonfat plain Greek yogurt

⅛ teaspoon garlic powder

⅛ teaspoon onion powder

Slight pinch of salt

Slight pinch of black pepper

1 (8-inch) light high-fiber flour tortilla

3 to 4 thin slices of cucumber

2 ounces reduced-sodium deli-style turkey breast

¼ cup shredded romaine lettuce

3 tablespoons chopped tomato

1. In a small bowl, combine the first 6 ingredients (mayonnaise through pepper). Spread the ranch spread on half of one tortilla, and top with cucumber slices, then turkey, lettuce, and tomato.

2. Fold the empty part of the tortilla upward to cover the filling, and then fold in the sides and roll up. If you are not eating immediately, you can place a toothpick in the center of the wrap, if desired, to hold it shut.

> **DARE TO COMPARE:** A roast turkey and Swiss cheese sandwich with lettuce, tomato, and ranch dressing has 760 calories, 28 grams of fat, and 2,530 milligrams of sodium. Love cheese? Feel free to add a slice.

NUTRITION INFORMATION PER SERVING: Calories 200 | Carbohydrate 21 g (Sugars 3 g) | Total Fat 7 g (Sat Fat 1 g) | Protein 15 g | Fiber 7 g | Sodium 710 mg | Food Exchanges: 2 Lean Meat, 1 Starch, ½ Vegetable, 1 Fat | Weight Watcher Smart Point Comparison: 3

Tuna Tartine (aka My Favorite Toasted Tuna Sandwich)

"WHAT THE HECK IS A TARTINE?" I asked when a colleague took me to a Le Pain Quotidien, a tartine café and bakery. A tartine is basically a warm, open-faced, toasted-bread "sandwich," but there is nothing remotely basic about this one. I spread the toast with a lemony mayonnaise before topping it with flaky tuna, and the pièce de résistance, pickled red onions. While it requires little effort, this picturesque toasty tartine makes you feel like you're lunching at a fancy French café.

MAKES 2 SERVINGS

½ cup Fast-Fix Pickled Red Onions (see page 245)

1½ tablespoons plain nonfat Greek yogurt

1½ tablespoons light mayonnaise

¾ teaspoon lemon zest

2 slices dark rye or pumpernickel bread

1 (5-ounce) can water-packed albacore tuna, drained

1 teaspoon extra-virgin olive oil

1 teaspoon lemon juice

2 teaspoons capers, drained

1. Prepare pickled onions. In a small bowl, combine yogurt, mayonnaise, and lemon zest. Toast the bread, and spread each slice with 1½ tablespoons of lemon mayonnaise.

2. Using a fork, lightly flake tuna apart, placing half of the tuna across each slice of bread. Drizzle each with ½ teaspoon olive oil and lemon juice. Top with ¼ cup pickled onions and garnish with capers.

Marlene Says: *The pickled red onions really make this sandwich. The recipe will make more than you need, but once you taste them, you'll have no problem using them up!*

NUTRITION INFORMATION PER SERVING (1 TARTINE): Calories 205 | Carbohydrate 19 g (Sugars 3 g) | Total Fat 6 g (Sat Fat 0.5 g) | Protein 20 g | Fiber 2 g | Sodium 320 mg | Food Exchanges: 2½ Lean Meat, 1 Starch | Weight Watcher Smart Point Comparison: 4

Grown-Up Grilled Cheese

CHEESY GOODNESS INSIDE AND OUT! A little café near my home specializes in grilled cheese sandwiches and tomato soup. The soup is good, but the grilled cheese is outstanding. One of their crave-worthy tricks is to turn the outside of the bread into garlic bread. Yes, yum! This ooey, gooey three-cheese delight uses cheddar for flavor, Parmesan for crunch, and mozzarella for a great cheesy pull. Fresh slices of tomato embellish the center. Serve this with My La Madeleine Tomato Basil Soup on page 224 for the perfect lunch or dinner duo.

MAKES 1 SERVING

2 slices sourdough bread

2 teaspoons light mayonnaise

Pinch of garlic powder

1 tablespoon grated Parmesan cheese

2 tablespoons shredded reduced-fat sharp cheddar cheese

2 to 3 slices fresh tomato (¼-inch thick)

2 tablespoons shredded reduced-fat mozzarella cheese

1. Spread each slice of bread with 1 teaspoon mayonnaise, sprinkle with a pinch of garlic powder, and top with 1½ teaspoons Parmesan cheese, patting the cheese onto the mayonnaise.

2. Carefully turn one slice of bread (Parmesan-side down) onto a plate and top with cheddar. Add tomato slices and top tomatoes with mozzarella. Top with remaining slice of bread (Parmesan-side up).

3. Coat a small nonstick skillet with cooking spray and place over medium heat. Carefully place sandwich in pan and heat for 2 to 3 minutes, flip, and cook until golden brown and cheese is melted (flipping again if needed).

DARE TO COMPARE: The grilled cheese sandwich at my local café has 650 calories with 21 grams of saturated fat and 1,700 milligrams of sodium. Pair it with a cup of My La Madeleine Tomato Basil Soup on page 224 and save a whopping 640 calories and 63 grams of fat on the combo!

NUTRITION INFORMATION PER SERVING: Calories 250 | Carbohydrate 25 g (Sugars 1 g) | Total Fat 9 g (Sat Fat 4 g) | Protein 20 g | Fiber 1 g | Sodium 510 mg | Food Exchanges: 2 Starch, 2 Medium Fat Meat | Weight Watcher Smart Point Comparison: 7

Chocolate Chip Muffies

HERE IS ANOTHER RECIPE INSPIRED BY PANERA BREAD, the largest chain of café bakeries in the United States. With the crumb of a muffin and the shape of a cookie, their 50/50 muffin-cookie hybrids are 100% delicious! Thanks go out to Chef Kara, who helped get these just right. Tender, cakey, and lovingly dotted with chocolate chips, they look—and taste—just like the ones in the bakery case; only with half the carbs, calories, fat, and 75% less sugar, as compared to their café cousins.

MAKES 10 SERVINGS

1⅔ cup all-purpose flour

1½ teaspoons baking powder

½ teaspoon baking soda

¼ teaspoon salt

¼ cup mini semisweet chocolate chips

¼ cup margarine

3 tablespoons brown sugar

⅔ cup granulated no-calorie sweetener*

2 large eggs, divided

2 teaspoons vanilla

1 cup buttermilk

*See page 36 for sweetener options.

1. Preheat the oven to 425°F. Line a baking sheet with a silicone baking mat or parchment paper and spray with nonstick cooking spray. Set aside.

2. In a medium bowl, combine flour, baking powder, baking soda, and salt. Stir in chocolate chips and set aside.

3. In another medium bowl, with an electric mixer, beat margarine and brown sugar until light and creamy (about 3 to 4 minutes). Add sweetener and beat well to incorporate. Add 1 egg and vanilla and beat until smooth. Add half of the buttermilk, then half of the flour mixture, blend, and repeat, mixing just until smooth.

4. Using a small ice-cream scoop or a large spoon, spoon the batter by scant ¼ cupfuls onto the baking sheet, separated by 3 inches for spreading. In a small bowl, beat the remaining egg with 2 teaspoons of water and using your finger lightly coat, while smoothing and rounding each muffie, with egg. Bake for 13 to 15 minutes, or until golden brown.

Marlene Says: *The batter is slightly stiffer than muffin batter, and sticky. While I usually use a pastry brush for applying an egg wash, due to the stickiness, a clean finger works best here.*

NUTRITION INFORMATION PER SERVING: Calories 165 | Carbohydrate 24 g (Sugars 7 g) | Total Fat 7 g (Sat Fat 2 g) | Protein 4 g | Fiber 0 g | Sodium 270 mg | Food Exchanges: 1½ Carbohydrate, 1 Fat | Weight Watcher Smart Point Comparison: 4

Baker's Dozen Peanut Butter Scotchies

IF YOU HAVE A HANKERING FOR A WARM HOMEMADE COOKIE, but don't want to deal with the usual mess or fuss, you're in luck! Using my amazing peanut butter cookies for inspiration, this recipe also uses just a bowl and spoon (and takes mere minutes to make), only now you get a perfect baker's dozen with the added texture of oats and sweetness of butterscotch chips. My two boys adored these!! The combo reminds me of a butterscotch blondie. Pass me one please!

MAKES 13 SERVINGS

½ cup peanut butter

⅓ cup granulated sweetener*

2 tablespoons packed dark brown sugar

½ teaspoon baking soda

½ teaspoon almond extract

2 tablespoons egg substitute (or ½ large egg)

⅓ cup rolled oats

3 tablespoons chopped butterscotch chips

*See page 36 for sweetener options.

1. Preheat the oven to 350°F.

2. Combine first 5 ingredients (peanut butter through almond extract) in a medium bowl and stir until well mixed. Add the egg and stir until dough is formed. Gently stir in oats and butterscotch chips.

3. Shape the dough, by rounded tablespoons, into 1-inch balls. Place onto an ungreased baking sheet and flatten balls with a fork, forming a crisscross pattern on top of each cookie.

4. Bake for 9 to 11 minutes, or until the cookies are golden brown on the bottom but still slightly soft in the center. Remove from the oven and let cool on the baking sheet for 5 minutes. Remove to wire rack to finish cooling

Marlene Says: *Gluten-free, and with just 9 grams of carbohydrate each, these cookies can be enjoyed without worry by most everyone!*

NUTRITION INFORMATION PER SERVING (1 COOKIE): Calories 90 | Carbohydrate 7 g (Sugars 4 g) | Total Fat 6 g (Sat Fat 2 g) | Protein 3 g | Fiber 1 g | Sodium 50 mg | Food Exchanges: ½ Carbohydrate, 1 Fat | Weight Watcher Smart Point Comparison: 2

James' Lemon Blueberry Bars

NO WELL-REGARDED CAFÉ BAKERY WOULD BE WITHOUT A LEMON BAR in their bakery case, at least that's the way my son James sees it. As someone who loves, and as such knows a good lemon bar when he tastes it, I solicited James to be my official taste tester for these bars. With a traditional shortbread crust and just the right of amount of tart and sweet, he gave them two thumbs-up. The best feedback, however, was when he needed to ask, "Are these healthy?"

MAKES 12 SERVINGS

CRUST

1 cup all-purpose flour

¼ cup granulated sweetener*

¼ teaspoon salt

4 tablespoons cold margarine or butter

2 tablespoons buttermilk

TOPPING

2 large eggs plus 1 large egg white

3 tablespoons all-purpose flour

½ cup granulated sweetener*

½ cup granulated sugar

⅔ cup lemon juice

⅓ cup buttermilk

1 tablespoon lemon zest

¾ cup fresh blueberries

2 teaspoons powdered sugar

See page 36 for sweetener options.

1. Preheat the oven to 375°F. Spray an 8-inch square pan with non-stick baking spray.

2. For the crust, in a medium bowl, mix together the flour, sweetener, and salt. Cut in margarine until mixture resembles coarse crumbs, sprinkle with buttermilk, toss lightly, then press it onto the bottom of prepared pan. Chill for 15 minutes and then bake for 15 to 20 minutes, or until lightly browned.

3. While the crust is baking, in a large bowl, whisk eggs and egg white with flour, sweetener, and sugar. Whisk in lemon juice and zest and pour over hot crust (you can do so while it is still on the oven rack). Sprinkle the blueberries into the lemon topping, and use your fingers to adjust them for even coverage.

4. Reduce oven to 350°F and bake bars for 18 to 20 minutes, or until top is barely set. Cool completely, then place in the refrigerator. Dust with powdered sugar just prior to serving.

DARE TO COMPARE: A single Lemon Bar from the Corner Bakery Cafe is packed with the equivalent of 15 teaspoons of sugar. You would need to walk for almost three hours to burn off the 660 calories.

NUTRITION INFORMATION PER SERVING: Calories 125 | Carbohydrate 19 g (Sugars 6 g) | Total Fat 4 g (Sat Fat 1 g) | Protein 3 g | Fiber 1 g | Sodium 105 mg | Food Exchanges: 1 Carbohydrate, 1 Fat | Weight Watcher Smart Point Comparison: 4

Fresh Orange Scones

WARM SCONES FOR BREAKFAST, OR ANY TIME FOR THAT MATTER, are a real treat. Sadly, however, most scones are not a treat when it comes to calories (or carbs). When I tell people just how many calories are in a typical bakery scone (more than 500) they never fail to be surprised. Bursting with sweet biscuit-y goodness and a triple dose of orange flavor, these scones satisfy the urge to splurge with no "splurging" required. How fun is that?

MAKES 8 SERVINGS

1¾ cups all-purpose flour

6 tablespoons granulated sweetener*

2 teaspoons baking powder

½ teaspoons baking soda

¼ teaspoon salt

¼ cup cold margarine or butter

1 medium orange

½ cup plain nonfat Greek yogurt

1 large egg

½ teaspoon orange extract (optional)

8 teaspoons reduced-sugar orange marmalade

2 teaspoons powdered sugar

See page 36 for sweetener options.

1. Preheat the oven to 400°F. Lightly spray a cookie sheet with cooking spray.

2. In a large bowl, combine the first 5 ingredient (flour through salt). With your fingers or a fork, cut the margarine into flour mixture until crumbly. Grate 1 tablespoon zest from the orange and then juice it, measuring out ¼ cup. Add them to a small bowl and whisk in yogurt, egg, and extract, if desired. Pour over dry ingredients and stir just until moistened.

3. Coat your hands with flour and place dough onto a lightly floured surface. Knead dough gently once or twice just to bring it together, and pat into an 8-inch-diameter round. Using a sharp knife, cut into 8 wedges and transfer to cookie sheet.

4. Bake for 12 to 14 minutes or until the tops are lightly browned. Remove from the oven and brush each scone with 1 teaspoon marmalade. Just before serving, dust scones with powdered sugar.

DARE TO COMPARE: A typical orange scone, like those at Panera Bread, averages 540 calories, with 80 grams of carbohydrate and 37 grams of sugar. That's three times the calories and carbs (and four times the fat) you'll find here.

NUTRITION INFORMATION PER SERVING (1 SCONE): Calories 170 | Carbohydrate 25 g (Sugars 4 g) | Total Fat 5 g (Sat Fat 1 g) | Protein 5 g | Fiber 1 g | Sodium 315 mg | Food Exchanges: 1 Starch, 1 Fat, ½ Carbohydrate | Weight Watcher Smart Point Comparison: 4

RECIPE BUILDERS

RECIPE BUILDERS

All-Purpose Biscuits

Quick 'N' Easy Breakfast & Italian Sausage

Pico de Gallo

Blue Cheese Dressing

Fast-Fix Pickled Red Onions

Ranch Dressing Four Ways

Homemade Marinara (aka Martha's Marinara)

1-Minute Hollandaise or Béarnaise Sauce

Chocolate Sauce Three Ways

All-Purpose Raspberry Sauce

All-Purpose Biscuits

THE TRICK TO CREATING the layers in these versatile, wholesome all-purpose biscuits lies in folding the dough. While you will not find these biscuits referenced in another chapter, I find there are innumerable uses for them. Pair one with a Breakfast Sausage Patty (page 242) to create a bodacious sausage biscuit, add one to a plate of Crispy Chicken Strips (page 67) and Easy Southern Slaw (page 101) for a KFC-style meal, or simply serve them with any of the entrées in the Southern Kitchen chapter.

MAKES 9 SERVINGS

1 cup all-purpose flour

1 cup white whole wheat flour

1 tablespoon baking powder

½ teaspoon baking soda

2 teaspoons granulated sugar

Scant ¼ teaspoon salt

4 tablespoons shortening

1 cup plus 2 tablespoons buttermilk

1. Preheat the oven to 425°F. In a large bowl, stir together the first 6 ingredients (flour through salt). Use your fingertips or a pastry blender to cut the shortening into the flour mixture until it resembles rough crumbs. Create a well in the center, pour in the buttermilk, and mix lightly with a fork until dough forms a rough ball.

2. Turn the dough onto a lightly floured work surface and pat into a ½-inch-thick rectangle. Fold it in half, gently pat it down again, and repeat.

3. Using a floured round cookie cutter or glass (about 3 inches in diameter) cut out 8 biscuits, taking care to cut straight down without turning. Assemble scraps to make last biscuit. Transfer biscuits to 8-inch round cake pan with biscuits touching, and bake on the middle rack for 14 to 16 minutes, or until golden brown.

DARE TO COMPARE: A plain biscuit at McDonald's has 260 calories, 6 grams of saturated fat, and 760 milligrams of sodium. Add a sausage patty and you're looking at over a half a day's worth of saturated fat and sodium. This biscuit with a 2-ounce sausage patty (page 242) has just 2 grams of saturated fat and half the sodium.

NUTRITION INFORMATION PER SERVING (1 BISCUIT): Calories 140 | Carbohydrate 23 g (Sugars 2 g) | Total Fat 5 g (Sat Fat 1 g) | Protein 4 g | Fiber 2 g | Sodium 290 mg | Food Exchanges: 1½ | Weight Watcher Smart Point Comparison: 4

Quick 'N' Easy Breakfast & Italian Sausage

MAKING PORK SAUSAGE THAT'S BOTH HEALTHY AND TASTY IS EASY! Buy lean ground pork, add a few seasonings, and voilà, you've got flavorful pork sausage with 75% less fat and far less sodium than any you can buy. You'll find uses for both types of sausage in the book, including in the Sausage 'N' Egg Burrito on page 56, and rib-sticking Stovetop Rigatoni with Sausage and Peppers on page 185. To make both recipes—or 8 ounces of each Breakfast and Italian Sausage—follow Step 1, divide the mixture, and use half the spices listed for each recipe.

MAKES 8 SERVINGS

16-ounces lean ground pork

½ teaspoon salt

½ teaspoon black pepper

½ teaspoon dried sage

BREAKFAST SAUSAGE SEASONINGS

¼ teaspoon onion powder

½ teaspoon poultry seasoning

1 tablespoon light pancake syrup

ITALIAN SAUSAGE SEASONINGS

1 teaspoon fennel seeds, crushed

½ teaspoon onion powder

½ teaspoon Italian seasoning

½ teaspoon garlic powder

1 tablespoon water

1. **FOR BREAKFAST AND ITALIAN SAUSAGE:** In a large bowl combine pork, salt, pepper, and sage.

2. **FOR BREAKFAST SAUSAGE:** Add the breakfast sausage seasonings and mix well.

3. **FOR ITALIAN SAUSAGE:** Add the Italian sausage seasonings and mix well.

> **DARE TO COMPARE:** According to the USDA, two ounces of regular pork sausage averages 175 calories, with 15 grams of fat and 380 milligrams of sodium.

NUTRITION INFORMATION PER SERVING (2-OUNCE SAUSAGE): Calories 75 | Carbohydrate 0 g (Sugars 0 g) | Total Fat 2.5 g (Sat Fat 1 g) | Protein 14 g | Fiber 0 g | Sodium 195 mg | Food Exchanges: 2 Very Lean Meat | Weight Watcher Smart Point Comparison: 1

Pico de Gallo

EVERY MEXICAN RESTAURANT KNOWS THAT SALSA IS A MUST, and when it comes to salsa, pico de gallo is the freshest of them all. Bursting with ripe tomatoes, tangy onion, spicy jalapeño, fragrant cilantro, and a squeeze of lime, "pico" is less saucy than other salsas, and more versatile too. Beyond Mexican fare, it's a tremendous topper for omelettes, salads, and simple grilled entrées like chicken, steak, or fish. Expensive to buy, it's inexpensive and easy to make, and with just 10 calories per one-quarter cup, there's no reason not to go loco for pico.

MAKES 8 SERVINGS

2 cups diced Roma tomatoes

½ cup diced red onion

¼ cup minced cilantro

1 medium seeded jalapeño pepper, finely chopped (about 2 tablespoons)

1 tablespoon fresh lime juice

½ teaspoon salt, or to taste

1. Combine all of the ingredients in a medium bowl and stir. Let sit for 30 minutes to allow flavors to meld. Or cover and refrigerate for up to 2 days.

Marlene Says: *Feel free to adjust this to your own taste. Many recipes use a clove of garlic, but that is not my personal preference. Others add a small splash of oil, which I find nice, but not necessary. Be careful when removing the hot seeds from the pepper. I scrape them out with a knife, but wearing gloves is good too.*

NUTRITION INFORMATION PER SERVING (¼ CUP): Calories 10 | Carbohydrate 3 g (Sugars 2 g) | Total Fat 0 g (Sat Fat 0 g) | Protein 0 g | Fiber 1 g | Sodium 140 mg | Food Exchanges: Free | Weight Watcher Smart Point Comparison: 0

Blue Cheese Dressing

IF THERE'S ONE DRESSING THAT SCREAMS SPLURGE, it's blue cheese. It's the not-so-secret sauce for crafting everything from cravable Cobb salads to spectacular steakhouse wedges (like the ones on pages 82 and 194 respectively). It's probably no surprise that creamy blue cheese dressing is not waistline-friendly. The good news for blue cheese lovers is that with its dominant flavor, a little blue cheese goes a long way, allowing me to create a slim yet still splurge-worthy dressing. So go ahead, splurge!

MAKES 4 SERVINGS

¼ cup low-fat buttermilk

2 tablespoons light mayonnaise

2 tablespoons plain nonfat Greek yogurt

1½ teaspoons white wine vinegar

¼ teaspoon black pepper

¼ cup crumbled blue cheese

1. In a small bowl, whisk together the first 5 ingredients (buttermilk through pepper). Stir in the blue cheese. Cover and refrigerate until ready to use.

NUTRITION INFORMATION PER SERVING (2 TABLESPOONS): Calories 50 | Carbohydrate 2 g (Sugars 2 g) | Total Fat 3 g (Sat Fat 1 g) | Protein 3 g | Fiber 0 g | Sodium 150 mg | Food Exchanges: 1 Fat | Weight Watcher Smart Point Comparison: 2

Fast-Fix Pickled Red Onions

ADDING PICKLED RED ONIONS IS ONE OF THE EASIEST WAYS I know to take a dish from ordinary to extraordinary. At first glance, they may not seem that special, but every time I make them I am reminded of how very versatile, and most of all tasty, pickled onions are. I use them as a topper for my toasty Tuna Tartine (page 229), but also highly recommend using them to embellish tacos and shredded pork carnitas. You'll be amazed at the difference they make. While they continue to soften, they will keep another day or two in the refrigerator.

MAKES 6 SERVINGS

⅓ cup cider or rice vinegar

1 tablespoon granulated sugar

¼ teaspoon salt

1 medium red onion, cut in half, and very thinly sliced (about 2 cups)

1. In a medium bowl, combine the first 3 ingredients (vinegar through salt) and 3 tablespoons of water, and stir to dissolve sugar and salt. Add the onion and toss with liquid. For super-quick and tangy onions, let stand 20 minutes, turning the onions in the liquid two or three times. Just before using, drain off the liquid.

2. For onions with less bite, first heat the vinegar mixture in a microwave-safe bowl for 30 seconds before adding the onions and let sit longer.

Marlene Says: *The nutrition information reflects that less than half of sugar and salt are actually absorbed into the onions.*

NUTRITION INFORMATION PER SERVING (ABOUT ¼ CUP): Calories 20 | Carbohydrate 4 g (Sugars 3 g) | Total Fat 0 g (Sat Fat 0 g) | Protein 0 g | Fiber 1 g | Sodium 60 mg | Food Exchanges: 0 | Weight Watcher Smart Point Comparison: 0

Ranch Dressing Four Ways

WHEN SCOURING RESTAURANTS FOR THIS BOOK, I could hardly believe how many different ways ranch-style dressing is dressed up. To offer you some of the same options, I took to the kitchen. While my Homemade Ranch is as good—and slim—as ever, Dilly Ranch is nice served with veggies or fish, while Parmesan Ranch is delectable as a dipper or drizzle for fries or pizza. Spicy Ranch is a new favorite. With just a bit of warm heat, it adds the perfect creamy kick to burgers, quesadillas, crispy tortillas, and more.

MAKES 8 SERVINGS

⅓ to ½ cup low-fat milk

⅓ cup light mayonnaise

⅓ cup plain nonfat Greek yogurt

½ teaspoon dried parsley

½ teaspoon garlic powder

½ teaspoon onion powder

¼ teaspoon salt

¼ teaspoon black pepper

1. **FOR HOMESTYLE RANCH:** In a medium bowl, add all of the ingredients and whisk to combine, using ⅓ cup of milk for dip, and ½ cup for a drizzle or dressing. Thin additionally with water, if desired.

2. **FOR DILLY RANCH:** Follow the directions for Homestyle Ranch omitting the parsley and adding ¾ teaspoon dried dill weed or 1 tablespoon of finely minced fresh dill before whisking.

3. **FOR PARMESAN RANCH:** Follow the directions for Homestyle Ranch using water instead of milk. Add 3 tablespoons of finely grated Parmesan cheese before whisking. (Adds 40 milligrams of sodium.)

4. **FOR SPICY RANCH:** Follow the directions for Homestyle Ranch adding 1 to 1 ½ teaspoons hot sauce (I prefer 1 ½ teaspoons of Sriracha) before whisking.

DARE TO COMPARE: A modest serving of ranch dressing at a restaurant is three tablespoons. It averages 210 calories with 22 grams of fat and 360 milligrams of sodium. Some restaurants serve double that amount.

NUTRITION INFORMATION PER SERVING (2 TABLESPOONS): Calories 35 | Carbohydrate 2 g (Sugars 1 g) | Total Fat 3 g (Sat Fat 0 g) | Protein 1 g | Fiber 0 g | Sodium 140 mg | Food Exchanges: ½ Fat | Weight Watcher Smart Point Comparison: 1

Homemade Marinara (aka Martha's Marinara)

MARINARA, OR RED SAUCE, AS MY ITALIAN MOTHER calls it, is a core ingredient for many Italian-American dishes. I often buy it ready-made (which I then doctor up) for last-minute dinners, but when I have the time, this is my go-to sauce. The recipe was handed down from my mother who was, and still is, famous for her red sauce. When I am with her, I cook it as she did, letting the sauce take its time while it slowly simmers in the oven. At home, I cook it on my stovetop; the wafting aroma of tomatoes and garlic always makes me think of her. This recipe yields about six cups, or two 28-ounce jars.

MAKES 12 SERVINGS

1 tablespoon olive oil

1 medium onion, chopped (about 1¼ cups)

3 garlic cloves, minced, or 1 tablespoon jarred

½ cup dry red wine or reduced-sodium beef broth

1 (28-ounce) can crushed tomatoes

1 (8-ounce) can tomato sauce

1 (6-ounce) can tomato paste

2 teaspoons granulated sugar

1½ teaspoons dried basil leaves

1½ teaspoons dried oregano leaves

Salt, to taste

1. In a large saucepot, heat the oil over medium-high heat. Add onions and cook for 6 to 8 minutes, or until softened. Stir in garlic and cook for 2 minutes. Pour in the wine (or broth) and cook for 4 to 5 minutes, or until most of the liquid is evaporated.

2. Stir in the remaining ingredients, crushing the basil and oregano with your fingers as you add them to the pot. Stir in 1 cup of water. Reduce the heat to medium-low, cover, and cook for 20 to 30 minutes, stirring occasionally. Remove from heat and let cool completely before refrigerating.

Marlene Says: The amount of sodium in the finished sauce can vary significantly, depending on the tomato products you use. I use regular tomato sauce and crushed tomatoes. With them, I find I need to add very little salt (just ¼ teaspoon or so). Adjust the salt according to the products you use and your taste.

NUTRITION INFORMATION PER SERVING (½ CUP): Calories 60 | Carbohydrate 11 g (Sugars 3 g) | Total Fat 1.5 g (Sat Fat 0 g) | Protein 2 g | Fiber 2 g | Sodium 250 mg | Food Exchanges: 1½ Vegetable | Weight Watcher Smart Point Comparison: 1

1-Minute Hollandaise or Béarnaise Sauce

HOLLANDAISE SAUCE AND ITS COUSIN BÉARNAISE are two of the most common sauces used in restaurants—especially in fine dining. For my book Eat More of What You Love, *a classically trained chef helped create a rich-tasting, yet lighter Hollandaise sauce using the traditional method. When aiming to create a healthier Béarnaise, I wanted it to taste just as good, but also be easier to make. This recipe offers up a rich-tasting Béarnaise sauce—and now Hollandaise, too—with just one third of the usual calories, in just one minute!*

MAKES 4 SERVINGS

¼ cup egg substitute

¼ cup light mayonnaise

¼ cup light sour cream

⅛ teaspoon salt

HOLLANDAISE

1 tablespoon fresh lemon juice

¼ teaspoon Dijon mustard

BÉARNAISE

1½ teaspoons white wine vinegar

½ teaspoon dried tarragon

1. **FOR HOLLANDAISE SAUCE:** Place the first 4 ingredients (egg substitute through salt) in a very small saucepan. Whisk in the lemon juice and mustard and heat over low heat. Continue whisking constantly for 1 minute, or until mixture is smooth and coats a spoon. Serve immediately. Do not reheat.

2. **FOR BÉARNAISE SAUCE:** Place the first 4 ingredients (egg substitute through salt) in a very small saucepan. Whisk in the vinegar and tarragon and heat over low heat. Continue whisking constantly for 1 minutes, or until mixture is smooth and coats a spoon. Serve immediately. Do not reheat.

NUTRITION INFORMATION PER SERVING (3 TABLESPOONS): Calories 55 | Carbohydrate 1 g (Sugars 1 g) | Total Fat 5 g (Sat Fat 1 g) | Protein 2 g | Fiber 0 g | Sodium 220 mg | Food Exchanges: 1 Fat | Weight Watcher Smart Point Comparison: 2

Chocolate Sauce Three Ways

IF YOU'RE LOOKING FOR A DARK, RICH, DELICIOUS CHOCOLATE SAUCE that's also low in added sugar, calories, and carbs, you found it! I know how hard it is to find such things, so I "borrowed" this favorite recipe from Eat What You Love: Quick & Easy, *but I couldn't leave it at that. My son James and I tested the original sauce with various flavorings to create additional options. Drizzle any of the three over a Warm Chocolate Brownie Sundae (page 94), a slice of New York Cheesecake (page 213), or atop your own dazzling restaurant-worthy desserts.*

MAKES 7 SERVINGS

¼ teaspoon cornstarch

¼ cup Dutch-process cocoa powder

⅓ cup granulated no-calorie sweetener*

⅓ cup nonfat half-and-half

1 tablespoon light corn syrup (or granulated sugar)

⅓ cup dark or semisweet chocolate chips

1 teaspoon vanilla extract

Pinch of salt (optional)

*See page 36 for sweetener options.

1. **FOR DARK CHOCOLATE SAUCE:** In a small saucepan, whisk together the cornstarch, cocoa powder, and sweetener. Add the half-and-half, corn syrup, and ¼ cup water. Whisk over low heat until mixture barely simmers and thickens slightly. Remove from heat, add chocolate chips and vanilla, and whisk until chocolate melts and sauce is smooth.

2. **FOR CHOCOLATE ORANGE SAUCE:** Follow directions for Dark Chocolate Sauce omitting vanilla extract and adding ¼ teaspoon orange extract and ¼ teaspoon zest.

3. **FOR CHOCOLATE NUTELLA SAUCE:** Follow directions for Dark Chocolate Sauce, omitting vanilla and adding ½ teaspoon hazelnut extract.

> **DARE TO COMPARE:** Two tablespoons of restaurant-style dark chocolate sauce has 110 calories with 24 grams (or 6 tablespoons) of sugar.

NUTRITION INFORMATION PER SERVING (2 TABLESPOONS): Calories 60 | Carbohydrate 9 g (Sugars 5 g) | Total Fat 2 g (Sat Fat 1.5 g) | Protein 1 g | Fiber 1 g | Sodium 45 mg | Food Exchanges: ½ Starch | Weight Watcher Smart Point Comparison: 2

All-Purpose Raspberry Sauce

MADE WITH FROZEN RASPBERRIES—WHICH BREAK DOWN INTO A SAUCE more quickly and easily than fresh—this sweet sauce takes just minutes to make. Spoon it over a slice of New York Cheesecake (page 213), on top of an Individual Black Bottom Cheesecake (page 214), alongside a slice of Luscious Lemon Cream Cake (page 186), or over your favorite ice cream, yogurt, or oatmeal.

MAKES 7 SERVINGS

1 (12-ounce) bag frozen raspberries

⅓ cup granulated no-calorie sweetener*

2 teaspoons lemon juice

2 teaspoons cornstarch

1 tablespoon granulated sugar

Slight pinch of salt (optional)

See page 36 for sweetener options.

1. Place the berries in a medium saucepan with ½ cup of water, the sweetener, and lemon juice, and cook for 3 to 4 minutes or until berries break down.

2. Mix cornstarch with 2 tablespoons cold water and add to saucepan. Bring to a low simmer, stir in sugar, and salt, if desired, and cook until sauce thickens and clears. Remove from heat, let cool, then refrigerate.

Marlene Says: *With one-third of the calories and sugar and twice the fiber of jam, a mere 2 tablespoons of this amazing sauce provides 20% of your daily requirement for vitamin C.*

NUTRITION INFORMATION PER SERVING (2 TABLESPOONS): Calories 30 | Carbohydrate 8 g (Sugars 6 g) | Total Fat 0 g (Sat Fat 0 g) | Protein 0 g | Fiber 3 g | Sodium 30 mg | Food Exchanges: ½ Fruit | Weight Watcher Smart Point Comparison: 1

EAT *what you* LOVE
RESTAURANT
FAVORITES
MENUS

Fast-Food Fix—Classic Burger Meal

Asian Inspiration—Better-Than-Takeout Asian Dinner

Italian Classics—Lazy Day Sunday Supper

Mix-and-Match Menu—Steak or Seafood Dinner for Two

Café Bakeries—Easy Breakfast or Brunch Buffet

Fast-Food Fix

SERVES 2 TO 4

CLASSIC BURGER MEAL

Whether you order it from a drive-through or at a sit-down burger joint, nothing satisfies a burger craving quite like a classic burger with all the fixins served with hot crispy fries and a cold creamy milkshake. Unfortunately, this tempting trio is as famous for its unhealthy nutrition stats as its taste. With a fraction of the calories, saturated fat, sodium, and sugar this tasty menu delivers nothing but great taste.

To make this a meal for two, simply divide the burger ingredients in half and double the milkshake recipe. To create a meal for four, make the onion rings or double the seasoned fries recipe (to cook a double batch add one minute to the microwave and four minutes to the air-fryer cook time). By using a large blender with an entire four-serving box of pudding, you can easily make the four milkshakes at once. For the full burger meal experience, don't forget to add ketchup, straws, and plenty of napkins!

✦ Green Salad Served with Homestyle Ranch Dressing *(page 247)*

✦ Classic Quarter-Pound Burger with Special Sauce *(page 61)*

✦ Air-Fried Seasoned Fries *(page 70)* OR
Extra Crispy Onion Rings *(page 69)*

✦ Better-Than-Ever Thick & Creamy Milkshakes *(page 72)*

DARE TO COMPARE: A typical quarter-pound cheeseburger, fries, and a shake serves up 1,700 calories (or more) including a whopping 25 teaspoons of sugar, a day's worth of sodium, and two days' worth of saturated fat! With 100 percent of belly-filing protein and great taste satisfaction, this menu has half the sodium, 80 percent less saturated fat, 90 percent less added sugar—and 1,000 fewer calories!

Asian Inspiration

SERVES 2 TO 4

BETTER-THAN-TAKEOUT ASIAN DINNER

One of the things I love about Asian stir-fry dishes is that the typical combination of veggies and protein makes them an easy weeknight single-skillet (or wok) dinner. When I have a bit more time, I enjoy adding another dish to the meal. The lettuce wraps are a favorite. Because they require a bit of chopping and dicing, I usually pair them with a dish that requires no chopping and little preparation.

To make the meal, either prepare the filling for the chicken lettuce wraps ahead of time or prep and measure all the ingredients for both dishes at the same time and set aside. Get the rice started, make the filling for the lettuce wraps, and then make your chosen entrée. (The shrimp and snow peas cook in just five minutes, the beef and broccoli in just ten.) Plate everything family-style and don't forget to add the chopsticks!

✦ P.F. Chang's–Style Chicken Lettuce Wraps *(page 148)*

✦ Stir-Fried Shrimp with Snow Peas *(page 155)* OR
Better Beef & Broccoli *(page 156)*

✦ Quick-Cooking Brown Rice

✦ Fortune or Chinese Almond Cookies *(page 165)*

✦ Green Tea

DARE TO COMPARE: When served with one-half cup of rice and a fortune cookie, this waistline and diabetes-friendly menu has 525 calories, with just one serving of starch and three servings of vegetables! It also clocks in with less than one-half the calories and one-third of the sodium of takeout.

Italian Classics

LAZY DAY SUNDAY SUPPER

When I was growing up, Sunday suppers were synonymous with spaghetti and meatballs—made with my mother's famous marinara (see page 248). This menu offers two entrée choices (with appetizers, if desired) to allow you to relax and enjoy the day and still serve up a delicious Sunday supper. My "lazy" trick is to use a slow cooker. If you don't have one, no worries, the beef ragu can also be "slow-cooked" in the oven.

To make the meal, prepare the cake a day ahead of time, cover it, and place it in the refrigerator. Come Sunday, just load your slow cooker with the ragu in the morning or the lasagna in the afternoon. Make the dressing, set your table with red, white, and/or green linens, and then relax. When it's time to eat simply throw together either the fifteen-minute mussels or several fast-fix pizzas to start the meal, if desired. The rest of the menu will be ready for the table in a snap.

✦ 15-Minute Bruschetta Mussels *(page 171)* OR
Fast-Fix Pizza Margherita for One *(page 172)*

✦ Romaine Salad Served with Parmesan Ranch Dressing *(page 247)*

✦ Slow-Cooker Braised Beef Ragu Served with Pasta *(page 177)* OR
Lazy Day Lasagna *(page 178)*

✦ Whole-Grain Rolls or Garlic Bread

✦ Luscious Lemon Cream Cake *(page 186)*

✦ Chianti

Marlene Says: *While red-and-white-checkered linens scream "trattoria," I love the subtle combination of a plain red tablecloth and white napkins (or vica versa). Add a pretty bowl of fresh lemons to the middle of the table, along with a bottle of wine and a chunk of Parmesan set on a plate with a grater, and you're all set.*

Mix-and-Match Menu

SERVES 2

STEAK OR SEAFOOD DINNER FOR TWO

With the recipes categorized by cuisine in this book it's now easier than ever to create cuisine-specific menus from appetizers to dessert! You can also mix and match the recipes you love from various chapters. This particular restaurant-worthy menu for two—which I've made several times—uses recipes from three different chapters.

To make the meal, make the batter for the Warm Chocolate Brownie Sundaes, if desired, and set the ramekins aside (you can also make the brownie part of the sundaes ahead of time). If making the salmon, place it in the marinade, then prep everything for the salad and the broccoli. As soon as you start cooking the entrée, pop the potato in the microwave or start the rice on the stovetop. By the time you finish cooking the fish or steak, the sides will also be done. If you haven't baked the brownies yet, pop them in the oven while you clear the table. Add toppings and enjoy—no one will be bringing the bill.

✦ In-a-Flash Caesar Salad for Two *(page 168)*

✦ Scampied Sirloin and Shrimp *(page 201)* OR
Bourbon–Brown Sugar Salmon *(page 200)*

✦ Microwaved Baked Potato or Quick-Cooking Brown Rice

✦ Simply Steamed Lemon Butter Broccoli *(page 205)*

✦ Warm Chocolate Brownie Sundaes *(page 94)* OR
Scoop of Ice Cream with Chocolate Sauce *(page 250)*

DARE TO COMPARE: In comparison to ordering a similar menu at a mid-tier steakhouse, not only will you save over 1,000 calories; you'll slash 60% of the saturated fat and sodium—and a whopping 75% of the cost!

Café Bakeries

SERVES 4 TO 8*

BREAKFAST OR BRUNCH BUFFET

There's nothing I love better than creating memorable meals for family and friends, and that extends beyond hosting fabulous dinners. Truth be told, I love setting out a welcoming breakfast even more. The quiet of the morning allows me alone time in the kitchen to get things ready before everyone gets up, and when they do, smiles always ensue!

To make the meal, prepare the scones and while they are baking, make the filling for the breakfast bakes. Place the filling in the ramekins and set aside.* Place berries, nuts, and jam in pretty bowls and arrange the scones on a tray and set them all on the table along with small bowls, plates, napkins, and spoons. Twenty minutes before you are ready to serve the bakes, place them in the oven and top them according to the recipe. Serve them warm.

✦ Fresh Orange Scones *(page 236)*

✦ Bowl of Plain Greek Yogurt (or Individual Cups)

✦ Fresh Berries and Toasted Nuts

✦ Spinach & Artichoke Breakfast Bakes *(page 218)*

✦ Reduced-Sugar Jam

✦ Coffee and/or Tea

***Marlene Says:** If you are not going to bake the breakfast bakes within one hour, keep the ramekins in the refrigerator and bring back to room temperature fifteen minutes before baking. The recipe for the breakfast bakes makes four, but you have will have enough leftover dough to double it. The yield of the Fresh Orange Scones recipe is eight.*

Acknowledgments

From concept to creation, writing a cookbook is no small feat—if only writing about food was as easy as eating the food you love! Fortunately, I have lots of fabulous friends, fans, and colleagues—along with family members—who generously offer their kind support and cheer me on! My heartfelt appreciation goes out to:

Chuck, Stephen, and James for your love and unending support. As exhibited throughout this book, it's clear, there's no one I'd rather cook (or bake) for.

Charisse Petruno, Elana Hunter, and Kara Ricciardi, from shopping and recipe collaboration to cooking and cleanup, this book would not have been possible without you. Thank you for your patience, flexibility and understanding, especially when testing a recipe over, and over . . .

Deanna Seagrave-Daly, your willingness to jump in and contribute your delicious way with words and Chef Judy LaCara for your willingness to jump in, to translate the recipes from kitchen scrawl to editable pages, again, despite your busy schedules, meant the world to me.

Food and prop stylist Erin McDowell and kitchen assistant Theresa Katan, for your incredible energy, talent, and professionalism. To photographer Steve Legato for your keen eye and steady hand, thank you for so calmly and skillfully turning the recipes into a visual feast.

Kristin Kiser, Jennifer Kasius, and Jessica Schmidt at Running Press for your generous and unwavering support. Frances Soo Ping Chow for designing another crave-worthy creation and to Sharon Huerta and the sales team at Hachette Book Group for your sales assistance.

The wonderful team at QVC. Christina, I can't thank you enough for your many years of support. To all of the stellar hosts, you're amazing. Carole, your talent and tireless dedication are surpassed only by your remarkable heart. And to the ultimate foodie (and gentleman) Mr. David Venable, I thank you once again for your extraordinary kindness, enthusiasm, and support.

PJ for being by my side both personally and professionally since day one. Perla, for taking such good care of "my best friend." To my bestie Nancie, life would not be the same without you.

My marvelous "kochbook" fans. You inspire and motivate me to do what I do. Without you, this book would not exist. Thank you for your support. I sincerely hope you love this book.

INDEX

Also Available from Marlene's
EAT *what you* LOVE
COOKBOOK SERIES!

MARLENE KOCH

EAT *what you* LOVE

Great for WEIGHT LOSS & DIABETES DIETS

More Than **300 INCREDIBLE RECIPES**
Low in Sugar, Fat, and Calories

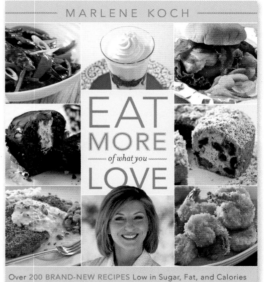

MARLENE KOCH

EAT MORE *of what you* LOVE

Over 200 **BRAND-NEW RECIPES** Low in Sugar, Fat, and Calories

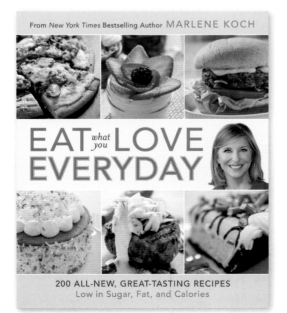

From *New York Times* Bestselling Author MARLENE KOCH

EAT *what you* LOVE EVERYDAY

200 ALL-NEW, GREAT-TASTING RECIPES
Low in Sugar, Fat, and Calories

EAT *what you* LOVE QUICK & EASY

GREAT RECIPES LOW IN SUGAR, FAT, AND CALORIES
From *New York Times* Bestselling Author MARLENE KOCH

UPDATED EDITION WITH NEW POINTS & AIR FRYER RECIPES!

Connect with Marlene:

QUESTIONS? COMMENTS?

"ASK" MARLENE AT
www.marlenekoch.com

E-MAIL:
marlene@marlenekoch.com

LIKE, SHARE, AND FOLLOW FACEBOOK:
www.facebook.com/kochmarlene

TWITTER:
@marlenekoch

VISIT www.marlenekoch.com FOR

✦ Personalized Nutrition Tools
✦ Marlene's Monthly Newsletter
✦ Seasonally Featured Recipes